Handbook *of* Illustration

Handbook *of* Illustration

JOHN ROWLAND WOOD

DESIGN PRESS

*Dedicated to my family
and to all illustration and
graphic design students.*

First Edition, First Printing

Copyright © 1991 by John Rowland Wood

Printed in Hong Kong

Designed by Patrice M. Rossi

Library of Congress Cataloging-in-Publication Data

Wood, John Rowland, 1937–
     Handbook of illustration / John Rowland Wood.
          p.   cm.
     Includes bibliographical references and index.
     ISBN 0-8306-3560-2
     1. Graphic arts—Technique. 2. Commercial art—Technique.
     NC1000.W66 1991
     741.6—dc20   90-20873
                                          CIP

Design Press offers posters and The Cropper, a device for cropping artwork, for sale. For information, contact Mail-order Department. Design Press books are available at special discounts for bulk purchases for sales promotions, fund raisers, or premiums. For details contact Special Sales Manager. Questions regarding the content of the book should be addressed to:

Design Press
11 West 19th Street
New York, NY 10011

Design Press books are published by Design Press, an imprint of TAB BOOKS. TAB BOOKS is a Division of McGraw-Hill, Inc. The Design Press logo is a trademark of TAB BOOKS.

Illustrations not otherwise credited are by the author.

Acknowledgments

I wish to express my deep appreciation and gratitude to the numerous people who have helped me bring this book to fruition.

My thanks first to the late William Firth, who was Dean of Visual Arts at Sheridan College, for instilling in me the idea that I should consider writing a book.

Thanks are also due to all the illustration and graphic design students with whom I have worked. Their ongoing enthusiasm has helped sustain me in my arduous task. I will not thank these artists by name here, since their names appear beside their fine artwork throughout this manual. I have made every reasonable effort to secure permission to reproduce the works used in this book and to correctly credit the artists. I sincerely apologize for any errors or omissions.

Special mention goes to my teachers at Dover and Folkestone Schools of Art, and particularly to Roy Chambers, my illustration and printmaking teacher at Canterbury College of Art. His work and on-the-spot sketching trips inspired me to become an illustrator.

I would like to express my gratitude to Sue Heinemann for her knowledgeable and sensitive job of editing, as well as to Nancy Green and Gina Webster at Design Press.

For their significant and unique contributions, I am indebted to Ivy Wharton, Wallace G. Wood, F. G. Thomas, Mr. Barratt, Len Rosen, John Clark, and Bill Hanna.

Most important, I am indebted to two generous individuals. Marta Dal Farra provided inspiration and support in the early stages of the book. She translated my hieroglyphic scrawl into an intelligible text and constantly offered her encouragement. Martha Staigys brought this project to its conclusion. Without her help, this book would not have been possible.

Contents

NOTE: ARTISTS' MATERIALS CAN BE HAZARDOUS

The hazards of artists' materials are well documented. Various toxic fumes and chemicals used in studios present serious health risks that are not always readily apparent.

Read the labels of products, handle them carefully, and be mindful of storage (keep out of reach of children!) and disposal considerations. A studio equipped with an exhaust system is ideal for the reduction of fumes, but failing that, try to always work in a well-ventilated room, keeping a window open. Use a fan to direct fumes out the window. However, spray fixatives for pastel and graphite renderings and spray can rubber cement must be used outdoors.

Printmaking studios contain some of the most deadly toxins available in the form of acids, inks, and cleaning solvents. The fumes are deadly enough to melt soft contact lenses!

Water must be available to bathe eyes and hands in the event of any spills. Wash your hands frequently. Also, it is not a good idea to eat or smoke while working with toxic or flammable materials.

Treat all products and equipment with care and respect and do not hesitate to consult a professional for advice.

Introduction

The need for this book was first drawn to my attention several years ago by my students, who had been unable to find an all-inclusive manual pertaining to the philosophy and career training of a contemporary illustrator. Most art books related to illustration feature either the works of the old masters (historical illustrators) or the work of highly specialized practicing professionals. Although inspirational, these books do not focus on the basic training necessary for a student to become a professional artist. With this book, I have attempted to fill the void and simultaneously to encourage a greater appreciation and respect for illustration as a profession and an applied art form.

The information in this book is presented simply and concisely, using a series of sequential step-by-step exercises covering all areas of illustration. Because this handbook is also a working reference manual, the terminology and work methods used by current freelancing illustrators and studio artists are emphasized.

What makes this book unique is that most aspects of the learning process are illustrated with student work. This is purposely done to encourage readers to see that they too can achieve results displaying the same freshness, vitality, and creativity evident in the samples shown.

This book is designed for the self-learner, for the practicing artist who wants to know more about illustration, and for the art teacher who may wish to set similar assignments in the classroom. Completing many of the exercises outlined in this book will also enable the student to build up a strong working portfolio.

Illustration is a disciplined art form, and throughout history it has made significant contributions in conjunction with the written and printed word. It continues to be a most stimulating and powerful vehicle of visual communication, especially with the advent of electronic media that help it reach an even greater audience.

This book is designed to help aspiring artists improve their creative capabilities. Their success will fulfill its prime objective.

Handbook *of*
Illustration

Ink drawing by Paula Watson. India ink, brush, and pen.

Composition and Design

"But I want to be an illustrator, not a graphic designer!"

at first glance the statement at left seems reasonable. However, too many students of illustration mistakenly rate drawing and painting techniques ahead of design in importance. In the work of such diverse illustrators as Aubrey Beardsley, Alphonse Mucha, Milton Glaser, and Alan E. Cober, there is just one common ingredient: good, strong design. Their illustrations would be effective in any technique, regardless of the subject matter or treatment. It is the strength of the underlying design that makes these works successful.

Composition and design are concerned with the arrangement of different elements—lines, shapes, values, textures, and so on—into an organized whole. Simplicity is key to effective composition. Begin by eliminating all nonessential elements. You can then reduce the remaining subject matter to basic geometric shapes and arrange these harmoniously.

One way to gain an appreciation for good design and composition is to study Japanese art. Many Western artists and illustrators, including Beardsley and Toulouse-Lautrec, have been greatly influenced by Japanese woodcuts. These prints exemplify the principles and elements of strong two-dimensional design; the artists captured the essence of a subject by rendering it to its most simple form. To further this objective, they used maximum contrast of bold, flat shapes, values, and colors. Decorative, repetitive patterns delight the eye by creating illusions of movement and rhythm. However, unadorned areas (empty shapes and spaces) are the most powerful elements of any artwork and are used to accentuate and asymmetrically balance positive forms, reflecting nature's own asymmetry (see Fig. 1–1).

In his book *Bonsai*, Norio Kobayashi states, "The canons of aesthetic taste [in Japan] dictate a beauty that comes from a studied violation of symmetry." The ideal of *shibui*, or restrained elegance, also contributes to Japanese art and design.

In creating a picture, every artist goes through a selection process, organizing a lot of visual information to communicate most effectively what the artist or client wants to say. An awareness of four basic principles: balance, emphasis, rhythm, and proportion—can help you choose the best way to express the subject of an illustration. Ask yourself how you want to balance the visual elements. Do you want a symmetrical, centered design or an asymmetrical, off-center arrangement? How will you emphasize different elements—by their placement, by the use of contrast, or by showing action? To create a sense of rhythm, you may decide to repeat fixed elements or to show these elements changing or moving. You may also choose to portray a subject in correct proportion or to distort it for a particular impact. As you read through these pages, the importance of these principles will become clearer.

1-1. Japanese wood block print by Kunisada Gogotei (1786–1864). Kabuki actor, Kikugoro Ono-ue. From the kabuki series.

Variables in Composition

Balance, emphasis, rhythm, and proportion help you organize visual information, but many other variables must also be considered. The perspective you choose, for example, can have a dramatic effect on the illustration, as can the use of light against dark. The following definitions pinpoint some of the variables you can play with. The more you understand how these different picture-making elements work, the better you will get at producing the visual effects you want.

The *surface space* is the actual size of the paper being used. It is the first geometric shape to consider.

Negative space, also called *counterform*, refers to all the shapes and spaces other than the positive form of an image (Fig. 1–2).

The *picture plane* is an imaginary flat plane onto which three-dimensional reality is projected. In actual practice it is the drawing surface (Fig. 1–3).

The artist's *eye level* determines the horizon, which moves up or down depending on the artist's position relative to the subject. The eye level also determines how much of the subject is shown (Figs. 1–4 and 1–5).

Viewpoint refers to the artist's position and distance in relation to the subject. It determines the angle from which the subject is viewed (Fig. 1–6).

Vanishing points are points on the horizon at which parallel lines converge (Fig. 1–7).

The *eye path* leads the viewer's eye through the composition to the *focal point*—the center of interest (Fig. 1–8). Sometimes, however, an artwork generates interest as a whole, without using a focal point.

The *field of vision* is a 180-degree area that viewers can see without moving their head or eyes. Within this area they can see objects clearly only in a 45- to 60-degree cone. Everything outside this cone appears distorted and out of focus (Fig. 1–9).

Open composition describes any arrangement of elements that does not use the paper edges to reinforce the design (Fig. 1–10).

Closed compositions use the paper edges as a strong compositional device, often by echoing the borders with shapes or elements within the composition (Fig. 1–11).

Cropping means moving and repositioning borders. You can crop into a subject tightly or angle or expand the subject's size within the surface (Fig. 1–12).

Curvilinear refers to curved lines or to shapes with curved edges (Fig. 1–13), while *rectilinear* refers to straight lines or to shapes with straight edges (Fig. 1–14).

A *contour* or outline drawing describes the outer edges of a subject (Fig. 1–15).

1–2. Variety and contrast of shape through the use of negative spaces or counterforms is key to good design.

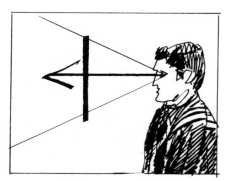

1–3. Picture plane.

1–4. High eye level.

1–5. Low eye level.

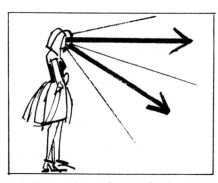

1–6. Viewpoint and artist's station point.

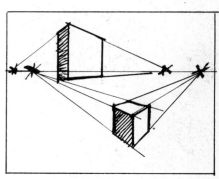

1–7. Vanishing points.

1–8. Focal point from water's edge to sun. Planes advancing toward (or receding from) the viewer.

1–9. Field of vision and cone of vision.

1–10. Open composition.

Proportion refers to the size of one object or part of an object relative to another (Fig. 1–16).

Scale is a broader term, often used to describe the proportion between the actual object and the drawn object. In a scale model, for example, the original object is reduced by specific dimensions.

Distortion occurs when proportion and scale are ignored. Artists may purposely use distortion to give a subject greater excitement and impact (Fig. 1–17).

There are many ways of indicating space in an artwork. *Planes*, for example, are flat surfaces that may be parallel to the viewer or may advance toward or recede from the viewer (Fig. 1–18).

Foreshortening occurs when surfaces that are not parallel to the picture plane recede or advance in perspective. As a result, their proportions and dimensions change (Fig. 1–19).

Convergence — when parallel lines appear to meet at a vanishing point — can create a dramatic feeling of going back in space (Fig. 1–20).

Overlapping shapes and objects can also give the impression of spatial depth (Fig. 1–21).

Diminution involves objects becoming smaller the farther away they are from the viewer. This is another way of suggesting space (Fig. 1–22).

Interval describes the amount of space between lines or shapes. By varying intervals, you can make subjects interesting and simulate space (Fig. 1–23).

Clarity is often achieved by contrast, with objects in the distance becoming less distinct and moving out of focus. Similarly, if action gradually becomes less defined from the foreground to the middle ground and background, a sense of depth results (Fig. 1–24).

Atmospheric or *aerial perspective* is the effect of atmosphere on distance. In such perspective the details, textures, tones, and colors di-

1–11. Closed composition.

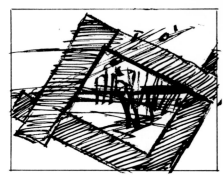
1–12. Cropping.

1–13. Curvilinear lines and shapes.

1–14. Rectilinear lines and shapes.

1–15. Contour or outline drawing with minimal shading.

1–16. Proportion and relative scale.

minish in size, sharpness, and intensity (Fig. 1–25).

Linear perspective is a system used in the Western world to project forms in space onto a flat two-dimensional surface. It assumes that viewers are standing in one fixed position and viewing with one eye only (Fig. 1–26).

Light and *shade* are important in describing form. The *light source* may be the sun (whose rays have direction and angle), or an artificial light. Strong directional lighting creates *cast shadows*, which help to establish and define form when they fall across another object (Fig. 1–27).

1–17. Distortion.

1–18. Planes.

1–19. Foreshortening.

1–20. Convergence of parallel lines to a vanishing point.

1–21. Transparency using overlapping shapes and objects.

1–22. Diminution—the appearance of objects and shapes getting smaller with increasing distance.

1–23. Interval—spaces between lines or forms.

1–24. Contrast and action—using rhythm and movement of repetitive curvilinear lines and dots.

1–25. Atmospheric or aerial perspective.

Value, the lightness or darkness of an area, is very important in depicting distance (Fig. 1–28). Objects appear to recede when their value or tone is close to that of the background. To make them come forward, simply increase the value contrast with the background. A background in a middle tone sug-gests less space. The greater the contrast, the greater the sense of distance.

High key means a profuse amount of light unmodulated by darks or strong tones (Fig. 1–29).

Low key means the opposite. No light tones are present, and all contrast is subdued. Dark tones prevail (Fig. 1–30).

With *high contrast* there are no middle tones, so the opposition of light and dark is accentuated (Fig. 1–31). *Notan,* a Japanese term for light and dark, refers to the principle of emphasis through strongly contrasting darks and lights.

1-26. Linear perspective.

1-27. Shadows indicating directional lighting.

1-28. Value—the gray scale in sequence.

1-29. High-key lighting.

1-30. Low-key lighting.

1-31. High-contrast lighting.

Achieving Unity

The separate components of an illustration must all work together to create a satisfying whole. How can you bring unity to the diverse elements in a composition?

One way is through *repetition*. An obvious form of repetition involves repeating the same object, such as a series of shoes or different hats (Figs. 1–32 and 1–33).

A variation of repetition involves echoing certain shapes, lines, colors, or textures within a composition. You might, for example, emphasize the rectangular shapes in an interior or the triangles in a seascape (Figs. 1–34 and 1–35). Although the objects are different, they have *similar characteristics*, and these help to unify the composition.

Another way to achieve unity is by *proximity*—placing elements close together in a way that interrelates them. This kind of clustering can be used to organize such scenes as still lifes or landscapes (Figs. 1–36 and 1–37).

Finally, *sequence* can be employed. Here you design the composition so that the viewer's eye moves easily from one element or point to another. In other words, a clear eye path exists to lead the viewer's eye through the composition (Figs. 1–38 and 1–39).

If your composition lacks unity, check to see whether you have failed to use any of these principles.

Exploring Compositional Possibilities

Now it is time to apply the principles we have been discussing. Where do you begin? Two important elements of a composition are generally decided by the art director or client: the size and shape of the illustration. Usually you will be working in a vertical or horizontal rectangle. The specific size and shape selected influence all of your remaining design decisions, since the other elements of your composition must work within these.

Selection, emphasis, and balance

Once you know the size and shape of your illustration, you can begin thinking about your subject matter. You may be given a complicated subject with many different aspects. At this stage you must decide what you want to say and how you want to emphasize it.

In determining emphasis, make decisions about the subject's placement, its relative size and scale, and the position of the center of interest.

1–32. Repetition of shapes.

1–33. Repetition of shapes.

1–34. Variety of shapes. Angles add tension to a composition.

1–35. Variety of shapes. Triangles create rhythm, tension, and action in a unified manner.

1–36. Proximity of shapes.

1–37. Proximity of shapes.

1–38. Sequence. A fixed arrangement of shapes and elements lead the eye into the composition.

1–39. Sequence of similar shapes.

How much contrast should you use? Is it more effective to depict the subject in strong contrast or in soft, high-key pastels? And what about action? Will tranquillity, motion, or rhythmic action best express what you are trying to say?

Now decide which type of balance is most appropriate: symmetrical or asymmetrical. A symmetrical composition has an axis at its center, with the design on one side and a mirror image on the other (Fig. 1–40); alternatively, the design may radiate from a central point (called *radial symmetry*). Symmetry is considered to be quiet and formal.

In contrast, an asymmetrical illustration is off-centered and thus more dynamic and informal. Although it is a more interesting type of balance, asymmetry is subtler and far more difficult to work with (Fig. 1–41).

Eye level

To have a horizon in the illustration, you must first position the eye level. Placing it either high or low creates interesting divisions of space. Specifically, dividing the surface into thirds creates a harmonious, eye-pleasing proportion (Fig. 1–42). In contrast, placing the eye level halfway down cuts the surface shape in two and is rather uninteresting (Fig. 1–43). It is similarly unimaginative to place the subject in the exact center (Fig. 1–44).

Negative spaces

People without visual training are often too interested in detail to be aware of total impact. It is easy to concentrate overmuch on the positive form, without regard for the negative spaces. While working on small roughs, think of the subject in a positive way but remain aware of the negative spaces. The sky, for example, is not just an empty area; it should have a definite shape (Figs. 1–45 and 1–46).

1–41. Asymmetry.

1–40. Symmetry is based on a central axis. Both sides mirror each other.

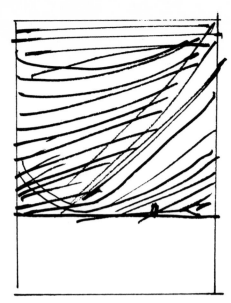

1–42. Low eye-level view of a surface, dividing it into thirds. This creates an asymmetrical balance of space.

1–44. Equal division of space horizontally and vertically with a centrally positioned subject creates a weak composition.

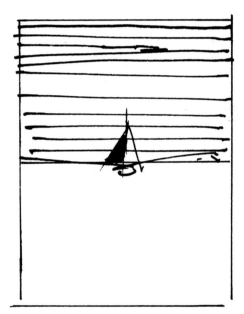

1–43. Middle eye-level view of a surface, dividing it into halves. This is compositionally weak.

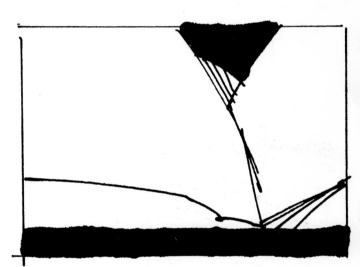

1–45. Development of negative spaces.

1–46. Further development of negative spaces.

Line

Line is another important element to consider. By playing vertical lines against horizontals, for example, you can enhance the sense of balance in a composition. Or consider the difference between static, repeating lines and a more active arrangement, with different intervals between the lines (Figs. 1–47 and 1–48). You can vary the thickness of the lines to create depth, since heavy lines come forward and light lines recede (Fig. 1–49).

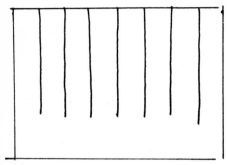

1–47. Static, repeating lines or shapes stress the principle of rhythm.

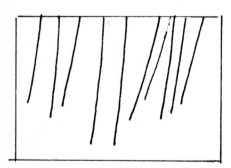

1–48. Varying line intervals suggest action.

1–49. Lines of different weight or thickness create depth.

Repetition

You can increase linear activity through rhythm and repetition. Pure repetition involves the regular reappearance of elements having the same shape, interval, and value (Fig. 1–50). A different effect is produced by randomly repeating value, while keeping shape and interval constant (Fig. 1–51). Compare this with the random repetition of value and interval while shape is kept constant (Fig. 1–52). And finally, notice what happens when value, interval, and shape are all repeated at random (Fig. 1–53).

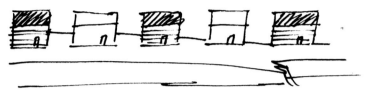

1–50. Pure repetition, with value, interval, and shape all kept constant.

1–51. Repetition with random value, but with interval and shape kept constant.

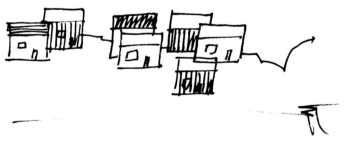

1–52. Progressive repetition of shape using value and interval at random.

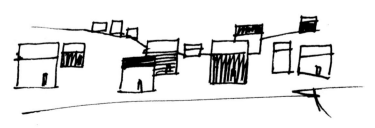

1–53. Random repetition of shape, interval, and value.

Depth

So far we have treated our compositions two-dimensionally, accentuating the flatness of the surface by working parallel to the edges of the picture plane. Now, let's create an illusion of depth by leading the eye *into* the picture rather than across its surface. Using an eye path, you can direct the viewer's eye to the picture's focal point, creating a feeling of depth and space at the same time. A good example is a highway that leads the eye farther and farther into the distance (Fig. 1–54). By breaking this straight path to suggest an up-and-down movement of the road, you can set up a distinctive rhythm while still leading the eye back in space (Fig. 1–55).

As we have already discussed, two other ways to show depth are by convergence (Fig. 1–56) and by diminution (Fig. 1–57). Remember, too, that small objects close up appear larger than large objects far away. Grass in the foreground, for example, might appear larger than boats in the distance.

Other choices

Practice on your own using the different variables discussed thus far. In addition to the choices offered here, explore different possibilities for the light source. Should the light be strong or soft? How much contrast either in value (the gray scale) or in color should you use? How much detail and texture do you want?

Look at the finished illustration in Figure 1–58. Can you identify the artist's decisions regarding balance, repetition, positive/negative, and so on?

Playing with Shapes

Even the most free-flowing composition usually has an underlying geometry. As we have seen, repeating or echoing a particular geometric shape can help you achieve unity. Let's look at some more examples.

The sun, the moon, balls, trees, and heads are just a few possibilities for *circles*. Emphasized throughout a composition, the circle has a harmonious effect (Figs. 1–59 and 1–60).

Paintings, illustrations, graphic designs, and photographs all make extensive use of the *triangle* in their compositions. In thinking about shape, don't focus entirely on objects; also consider cast shadows and reflections. In some cases these create more exciting shapes than the objects themselves. Practice using cast shadows or reflections to strengthen a triangular emphasis (Figs. 1–61 and 1–62).

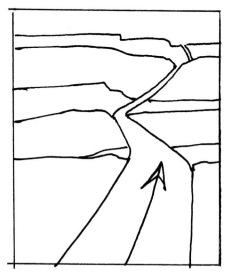

1–54. Depth suggested by a continuous eye path.

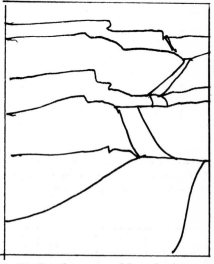

1–55. Depth suggested by a broken eye path.

1–56. Depth suggested by convergence.

1–57. Depth suggested by diminution.

1–58. Compositional decisions
reflected in a finished illustration.

1-59. Circles emphasized throughout a composition: beach balls.

1-60. Circles emphasized throughout a composition: heads.

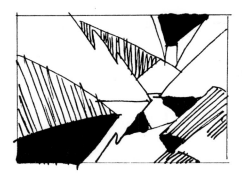

1-61. Triangles emphasized throughout a composition: landscape elements.

1-62. Triangles emphasized throughout a composition: sailboats.

The most basic shapes in design are the *square* and the *rectangle,* which echo the shape of the working surface. When used to reinforce the edges of the picture plane, they create a strong two-dimensional effect (Fig. 1–63). When placed in opposition to the edges, they can produce a dynamic tension (Fig. 1–64).

The rectangle is a difficult element to use well in composition—especially when many rectangles of different sizes and shapes must be organized in a planned and balanced order. A grid composed of vertical and horizontal lines spaced equally far apart is useful in organizing rectangles. Shade in some of the smaller squares to find a balance of shapes (Fig. 1–65). Try overlapping rectangles of different gray values in a page layout (Fig. 1–66).

One element should generally predominate in a composition. If different elements are given equal importance, they will fight each other for attention. Thus, if the circle is important, other geometric shapes should be deemphasized or used to strengthen the impact of the circle (Figs. 1–67 and 1–68).

Experienced illustrators intuitively see every subject as a basic geometric shape. In addition, they try to select visually exciting shapes to work with. In sailboat composition, experiment with different possibilities for the underlying triangle (Fig. 1–69). Or imagine that you have chosen pine trees as the main element in a piece because of their triangular shape. What are the different possibilities? Remember that, even though trees conform to certain basic proportions, they have definite individual characteristics. Symmetrically shaped trees, like figures in boring poses, are not very interesting to draw or to look at.

The triangle can also be extremely important in figure compositions (Fig. 1–70). In working with it, don't just think about the shape of the figure; also draw the counterform or negative space.

1–63. Rectangles used to create a strong two-dimensional effect.

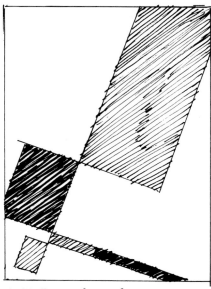

1–64. Rectangles used to create dynamic tension.

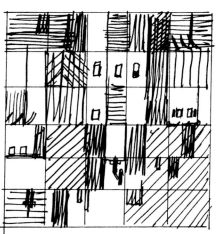

1–65. Achieving a balance of rectangular shapes through shading.

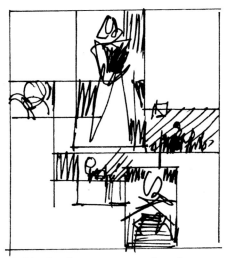

1–66. Overlapping rectangles of different gray values.

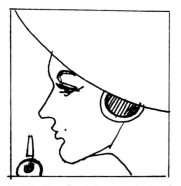

1–67. Emphasizing semi-circular shapes in a design.

1–68. Using rectangular forms that contrast with and accentuate spherical forms.

1-69. Experimenting with triangular shapes.

1-70. Using the triangle in figure compositions.

If you are having trouble working within a predetermined border, do a loose drawing first and then define the borders by cropping. Cut two right-angle pieces of white or dark gray matboard and move them around on your design to establish the most interesting background shapes or counterforms. Cropping can give you a new perspective on the shapes within your composition, as well as adding impact to an existing design.

Your Sketchbook

A sketchbook is probably an illustrator's most important educational tool. Its contents will demonstrate your thinking and drawing ability more than anything else you do. Accurate drawing done quickly is a great accomplishment.

Purchase a strong hardcover book, 8½ × 11 inches (22 × 28 cm) or 11 × 14 inches (28 × 36 cm). Use your sketchbook as an observational tool and as a way of satisfying your curiosity about a subject by unraveling, reconstructing, and drawing it. It is not a place for meaningless doodles; rather, it should be a creative visual diary.

A sketchbook should contain a variety of subjects drawn at different speeds, from super-quick sketches to slower, more serious study drawings.

Here is a list of suggested studies for your sketchbook:

- Natural and man-made forms, and combinations of the two

- Lines and dots in the man-made environment and in nature (Figs. 1–71 and 1–72)

- Rhythm and repetition of shape and line

- Geometry in nature

- Negative space studies (Fig. 1–73)

- Pattern and texture

- Silhouettes of interesting objects

- Circular and semicircular shapes

- Triangular shapes and conic forms

- Square shapes and cubic forms

- Rectangular shapes and prismatic forms

- Silhouettes of figure poses

1–71. Investigating rhythmic linear interval and pattern in nature and manmade objects.

1-72. Curvilinear line and dot studies.

SPIRALS, SEASHELLS, WHIRLPOOLS

GALAXIES

DOT AND 6 LINES

BIRDS ON TELEPHONE - HYDRO WIRES

ZIA PUEBLO INDIAN SYMBOL

'BIG WHEEL' MONTANA

PLANETARY FORCES.

END OF LOGS - STONEHENGE

HOPI PETROGLYPH - SYMBOL, ARIZONA

TAMARACK CONES, FIELDS, MESA LANDSCAPE, SHEET MUSIC ETC...

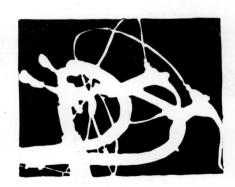

1-73. Negative space studies by Margo Stahl. India ink, brush, and pen.

Mistakes to Avoid

Figure 1-74 shows some common mistakes in compositions. These include the following:

- Centering the horizon line (a)

- Cutting the composition in half with shapes (b)

- Letting the main subject float on the surface (c)

- Randomly scattering many shapes all over the surface (d)

- Cutting the corners off with shapes (e)

- Framing the side edges with shapes (f)

- Centering the subject by using shapes of lines that come from the corners (g)

- Placing background objects so that they appear to be growing out of people's heads (h)

- Overusing textures (i)

- Overusing diagonals (j)

- Placing shapes so that they just touch each other and create an uncomfortable visual effect (k)

- Creating an overall gray and boring tone (l)

1-74. Common mistakes in compositions.

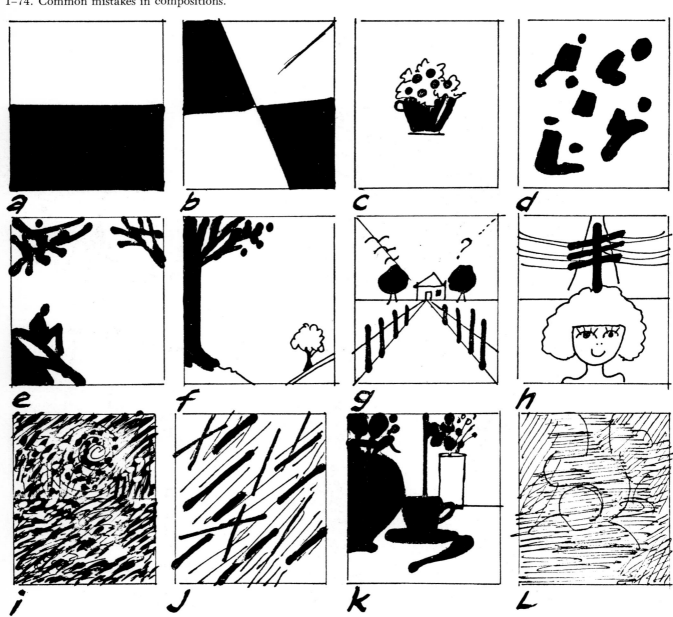

Keys to Good Composition

Here are some ways to enliven your compositions:

- Using asymmetry

- Simplifying shapes, and arranging them effectively

- Eliminating all unnecessary elements, shapes, and details

- Being aware of negative shapes

- Using strong contrasts in value, color, and shapes

- Using action, motion, rhythm, and repetition

- Using exciting and unusual viewpoints

- Changing the scale of subjects and their proportions

- Using tight and interesting cropping

A good way of improving your skills in composition is to analyze famous artists' illustrations and paintings. Sit down at your drawing board and, using a layout pad and a black pen, do small sketches that analyze why a particular composition is effective (Figs. 1–75a and b). You may be surprised at the insights you gain from this simple exercise.

1–75a. *Judith 1, 1901* by Gustav Klimt. Oils. Printed by permission of Österreichische Galerie, Vienna.

1–75b. Linear analysis of Klimt's painting investigating the principles and elements of art used in his composition.

Basic Drawing Skills

anyone considering a profession in the visual arts needs good basic drawing skills. For illustrators and animators, drawing is of paramount importance, but fine artists, graphic designers, architects, fashion and interior designers, and craftspeople must all be able to put their visual ideas down on paper. Drawing skills are so important that having them can make the difference between getting a job and not getting one.

Sound drawing is a combination of seeing, analyzing, comparing, and putting the results down on paper. As the master Leonardo da Vinci stated, "To see is to know — to know is to see." Most of the student drawings in this chapter represent the first time their makers really *saw* their environment and related to it through freehand drawing.

The process, which is not at all complicated, resembles the way da Vinci learned about the landscape around his home as a boy. Moved by his intense curiosity, as he wandered outside, he tried to understand the things he saw around him — the structure of seed pods, plants, trees, rocks, water, clouds, and birds. To draw well you must understand the subject you are drawing — why it has a certain shape, how it grows, and how it is built. Seeing is not the same as looking; it involves applying logic, analysis, and reason to close observation.

In drawing, everything has to be broken down into basic shapes and forms. And form is usually dictated by function. If you know an object's function, you will have insight into its structure, which in turn helps you draw it more accurately. Eye, brain, and hand all work together in re-creating the surrounding world on paper.

Guidelines for Freehand Drawing

Figure 2–1 reviews some of the basic elements in drawing, which we discussed in Chapter 1. Here are some other points to keep in mind:

1. Do not use an eraser; if you do, you will negate what you are learning about drawing. If you make a mistake, just redraw the correct line a bit more heavily. Mistakes are part of the learning process. Use a black felt-tip pen so that you cannot erase.

Ink drawing by Gary Alphonso. India
ink and pen.

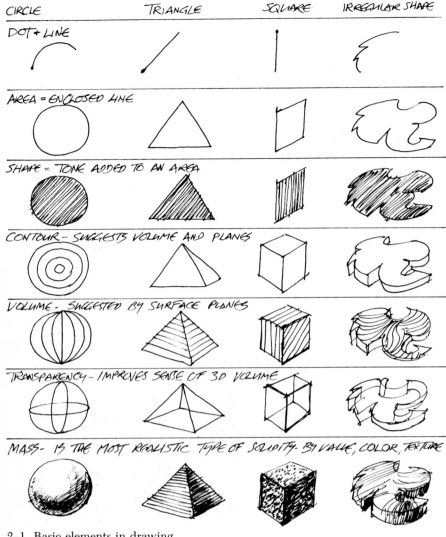

CIRCLE   TRIANGLE   SQUARE   IRREGULAR SHAPE

DOT + LINE

AREA = ENCLOSED LINE

SHAPE = TONE ADDED TO AN AREA

CONTOUR - SUGGESTS VOLUME AND PLANES

VOLUME - SUGGESTED BY SURFACE PLANES

TRANSPARENCY - IMPROVES SENSE OF 3D VOLUME

MASS- IS THE MOST REALISTIC TYPE OF SOLIDITY- BY VALUE, COLOR, TEXTURE

2–1. Basic elements in drawing. Two-dimensional shapes become three-dimensional forms.

2. Do not use mechanical equipment in freehand drawing. You are trying to perfect your eye/brain/hand coordination; using rulers, compasses, and so on will not help in this. Keep your mechanical equipment for technical drawing.

3. Try to develop some empathy for your subject. The quality of your drawing often depends on your feeling for the subject. It is easy to get worked up about exciting subjects, but try to become equally involved in everything you draw.

4. Don't make the mistake of thinking that technique is all-important. Flashy or slick technique can never save an inaccurate, insensitive drawing. Your subject should suggest to you which techniques are best for rendering it.

5. Let tools or drawing equipment perform for you. In your hand, each pencil, pen, brush, Conté crayon, pastel, or marker has its own unique characteristics. Learn to use these in conjunction with your own feelings toward the subject.

6. Experiment as much as possible with all media. Vary the pressure of your hand, roll or twist at the wrist, and hold your pencil or pen in different ways to achieve interesting results.

7. Make your own tools. It is possible to use *anything* to make a mark on paper, so try to be innovative.

8. Avoid weak, monotonous drawings with a flat overall gray tone and balanced, same-size areas. Likewise, avoid too much overall texture, which yields a busy and confusing drawing. In other words, remember that contrast is very important.

Understanding Perspective

There are three keys to successful freehand perspective drawing:

1. See comparative angles and their relationships, especially at the base corners of objects.

2. Sense and draw the correct degree of convergence between top edge angles and bottom edge angles. This convergence factor is the clue to where the vanishing points should be and consequently where the eye level should be. Comparing the bottom angles to the top ones also indicates the object's size and its distance from the viewer and therefore the viewer's station point.

3. Compare the length of the side surfaces to the length of the nearest vertical edge. This is important when you are trying to determine the correct side surfaces on a cube or prism.

Figure 2–2 illustrates these principles. It is done freehand and totally intuitively. It shows a square surface turning in space, much as the pages of a book turn. Notice the square's change in angles and shape as it moves toward the center vertical. Compare the upper and lower angles in each square. Imagine that each square is the side of a cube, and envision what its opposite side would look like.

Knowing these principles enables you to draw more difficult subjects. Cars, for example, should be broken down into their simplest geometric shapes in perspective (Fig. 2–3). Then the details can be added.

Observe how many objects around you are based on the square, the cube, and the prism—for example, desks, chairs, cabinets, modular ceiling and floor coverings, and light fixtures. Think of these familiar objects as simple blocks, and practice drawing them. Then work on drawing from memory. Look at an object—for example, a chair—analyze it, and then turn away from it and draw it (Fig. 2–4). Compare your drawing with the real chair to see if your mental image was accurate. Do this with several objects of varying complexity.

Everything we see around us is in scale relative to us. Because most forms—natural or manmade—grow out of, touch, or rest on the ground, you should draw them from the ground up. This makes it much easier to work out correct proportions and the scale of elements to one another.

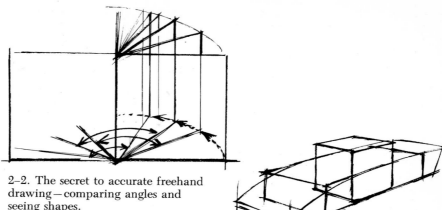

2–2. The secret to accurate freehand drawing—comparing angles and seeing shapes.

2–3. Draw complex subjects accurately by using basic geometric forms.

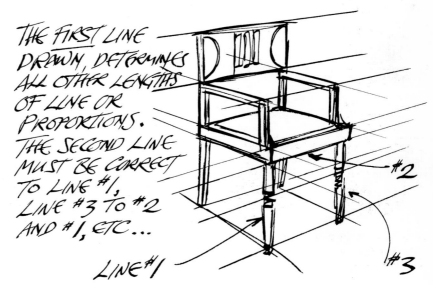

THE FIRST LINE DRAWN, DETERMINES ALL OTHER LENGTHS OF LINE OR PROPORTIONS. THE SECOND LINE MUST BE CORRECT TO LINE #1, LINE #3 TO #2 AND #1, ETC...

LINE #1

#2

#3

2–4. Freehand drawing of a chair from memory.

A must-do exercise

DIRECTIONS: From where you are sitting now, with both arms extended in front of you, hold up a piece of letter paper. Using the top edge as a horizontal guide, raise or lower the paper until the edge lines up with the closest bottom corner of a cubic or prismatic object.

Compare the bottom angles on both sides, relative to the horizontal edge of the paper sheet, and draw what you have observed.

Now repeat the process, but this time compare the top surface angles to the bottom ones.

Note where the vertical edges fall. Look at the length of the vertical edge, and judge how it compares to the length of the object.

Draw many objects in the room, using this same seeing and thinking process; but instead of using the sheet of paper as a guide, draw a series of horizontal dotted lines across your sketchpad as a guide.

Distortion and other common mistakes

Many students identify the object in Figure 2–5(a) as a cigarette pack. When the cab and wheels are added, as in 2–5(b), you can see that it is actually the bed of a logging truck. The fact that it shows a large-scale object should be apparent from the convergence factor. By way of comparison, hold a cigarette pack in front of you and see how little its edges converge.

One of the most common drawing errors made by beginners involves this type of distortion. This may be due in part to the influence of the wide-angle photography and comic-book imagery seen in many advertisements. Look at the drawing of a car in Figure 2–6. Does it appear accurate to you? The reason it is not accurate is that the vanishing points are too close together. Because the object itself possesses a 90-degree angle, it must be drawn with angles greater than 90 degrees. Figure 2–7 shows how the car should have been drawn. Although a slightly exaggerated perspective can sometimes have a very desirable impact, knowing when to employ it takes considerable training.

Figures 2–8 through 2–10 illustrate some other common errors in freehand perspective drawing.

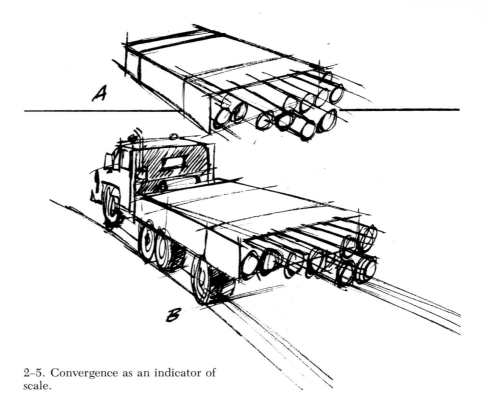

2–5. Convergence as an indicator of scale.

Keys to accuracy

The importance of understanding and drawing the cube cannot be overstated. It is essential to understanding all structural solids. The basic principles of perspective — proportion, scale, eye level, diminution, convergence, foreshortening, and so on — can all be acquired through a complete mastery of the cube.

To draw a freehand cube in any size or any view, you need only draw nine lines in correct and accurate relationship to one another. The length of the first line establishes all the other dimensions of the object.

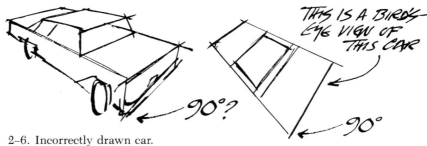

2–6. Incorrectly drawn car. Horizontal surface planes should always be greater than 90 degrees. Only when viewed directly from above will there be any 90-degree angles.

Therefore, it is important to visualize the entire drawing before starting.

In order to achieve accuracy, you must get the second, then the third, and then the remaining lines in exact relationship to the first. For example, to draw a television set, begin by drawing the vertical edge closest to you (Fig. 2–11). Since this is the longest vertical line in the object, it is the best one to use to establish the overall proportions of the cube and the lengths of the other eight lines or edges.

The second line you draw, which starts at the bottom of the first line, determines the rest of the corresponding angles and indicates your viewpoint with respect to the object.

2–7. Correctly drawn car. The correct degree of convergence is based on accurately seeing angles relative to each other.

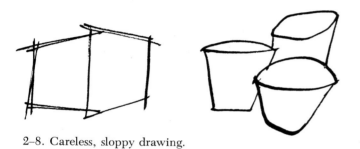

2–8. Careless, sloppy drawing.

2–9. These three-dimensional forms are overlapping. This happens when you concentrate on drawing the fronts only.

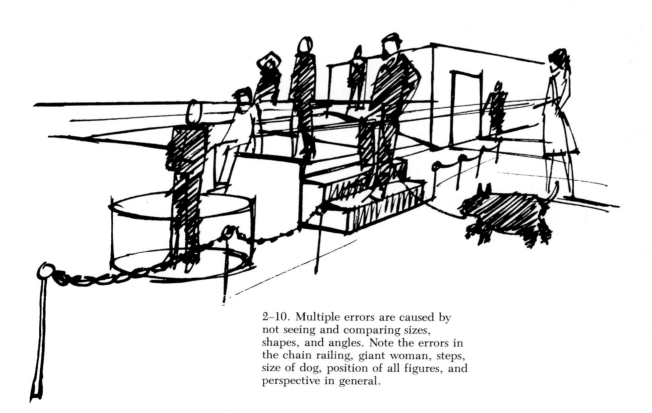

2–10. Multiple errors are caused by not seeing and comparing sizes, shapes, and angles. Note the errors in the chain railing, giant woman, steps, size of dog, position of all figures, and perspective in general.

The third line, which goes at the top, and its angle in relation to the second line determine the eye level, the point at which the lines would converge, and the size and scale of the object.

The fourth line, representing the rear edge, can be drawn using the first line as a measuring unit. This line is *always* shorter than the first line. Having drawn one surface accurately, you should find it comparatively easy to work out the other side and the top.

Do you now understand the importance of seeing, thinking, and comparing? The degree of accuracy you attain in your drawing is entirely up to you. But unless you concentrate on every line you draw, the finished composition may not work.

Basic perspective definitions

The ultimate goal of freehand drawing is to draw objects in perspective without any guides — by eye. If you can really see in perspective, you will only need to refer to mechanical perspective when you are in doubt about a drawing you have done.

There are four different kinds of mechanical perspective. *One-point perspective* uses only one vanishing point on the horizon line (eye level). Horizontal lines or shapes remain parallel to the eye level and to the top and bottom of the drawing sheet (Fig. 2–12). This kind of perspective is rarely used in illustration because it is too simplistic.

Two-point perspective is much more common in illustration. Here all surface planes converge to two vanishing points on the horizon, and vertical lines and edges remain parallel (Fig. 2–13). All object shapes that appear at right angles and parallel to each other use common vanishing points. This kind of perspective is based on seeing objects on the same ground or level as that of the artist/viewer. The ground is assumed to be flat, and the artist is

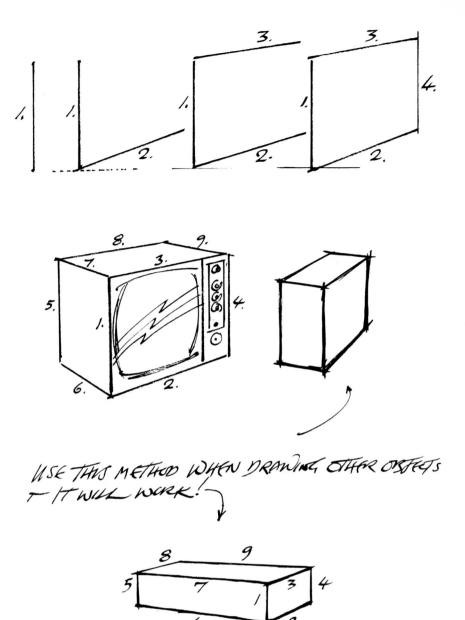

2–11. Accurate freehand drawing requires seeing and comparing relative angles (convergence) and lengths of edges (shapes).

assumed to be looking straight ahead — not up or down.

Three-point perspective is used for scenes below or above the viewer, and the third vanishing point is located directly below (Fig. 2–14) or above (Fig. 2–15) the viewer/artist. No sides are parallel, because all ver-

tical edges converge to the third vanishing point.

Four-point perspective adds a fourth vanishing point directly below the third (Fig. 2–16). It is only used when large objects overlap the horizon or when reflections of an object are being depicted.

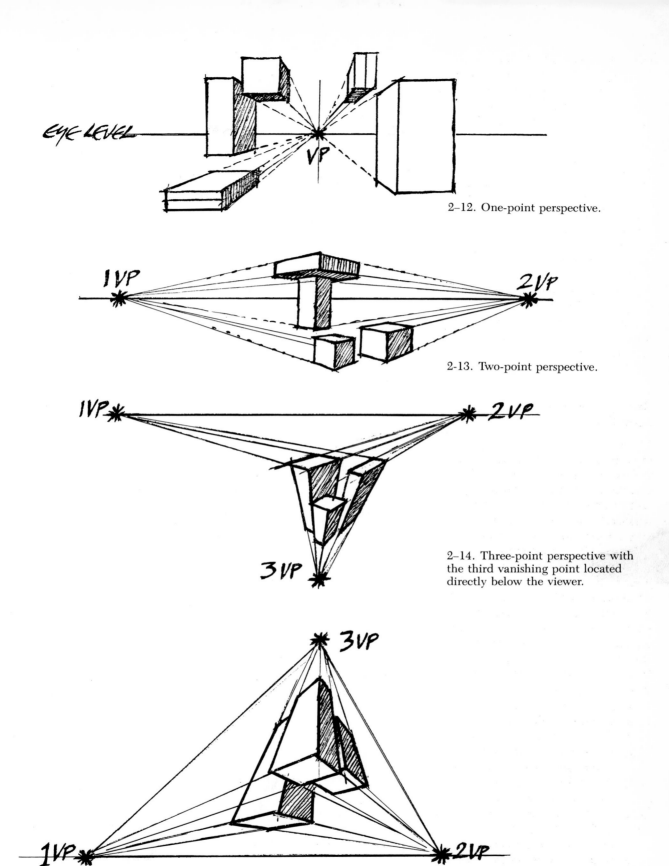

EYE LEVEL

VP

2–12. One-point perspective.

1VP   2VP

2-13. Two-point perspective.

1VP   2VP

3VP

2–14. Three-point perspective with the third vanishing point located directly below the viewer.

3VP

1VP   2VP

2–15. Three-point perspective with the third vanishing point located directly above the viewer.

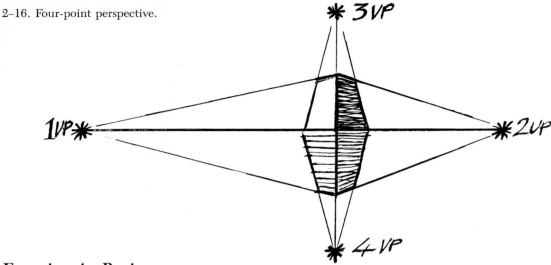

Exercises in Basic Drawing

The following instructions apply to all of the exercises that follow:

1. Use 19- x 24-inch (48 x 61 cm) bond layout paper, a semitransparent paper.

2. Do all drawings with a black felt-tip pen, unless otherwise indicated. This forces you to think before drawing.

3. Do not use rulers, T-squares, or other mechanical equipment, unless specified.

4. Do not copy the examples that follow each exercise; instead, use them as guides.

5. Feel free to choose your own subject matter within the framework of each exercise.

6. Always do a preliminary, full-size drawing to plan each exercise. Then lay a new sheet of paper on top of it and do the final drawing.

7. Draw all guidelines in very fine lines and the actual objects in a heavier lines.

8. Use the measurements in Figure 2–17 as a guide to set up your assignment sheet.

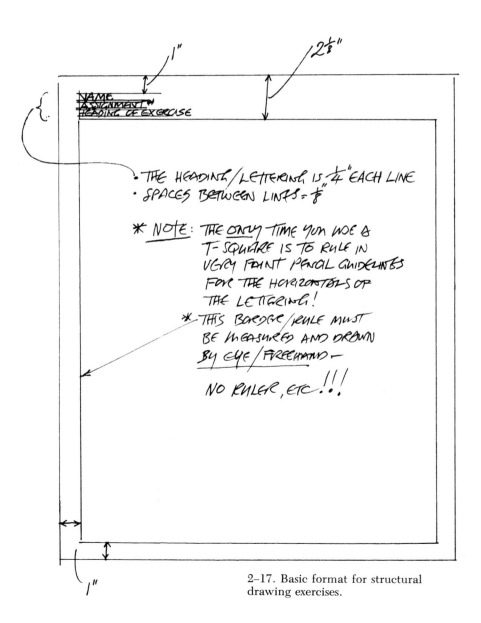

2–17. Basic format for structural drawing exercises.

The grid

This exercise helps develop your eye-hand coordination and dexterity. Repeat it as many times as you feel you need to. Work slowly and concentrate on each step.

STEP 1: Using a single continuous freehand stroke, draw a border 1 inch (2.5 cm) in from the edge of the paper. Then, beginning 1 inch (2.5 cm) in from the left-hand border, draw a perfectly straight vertical line from the top of the sheet two-thirds of the way down. Continue drawing very precise parallel lines exactly 1 inch (2.5 cm) apart, measured by eye, until the whole sheet is covered.

STEP 2: Without turning the pad, start 1 inch (2.5 cm) down from the top and draw perfect horizontal lines in the same manner, 1 inch (2.5 cm) apart. You now have a checkerboard grid.

STEP 3: Look over your grid and find perfect squares. Within these, draw perfect circles of different sizes in a nonstop motion. Make sure that each circle touches all four edges of the square smoothly and does not come to a point. You can check the quality of your draftsmanship by placing a large coin on top of a finished circle and comparing the curves of the two perimeters.

STEP 4: Add triangles, cubes, and prisms of various sizes.

STEP 5: Create combined geometric shapes or forms such as cylinders, pyramids, and cones.

2–18. Finished grid and objects exercise (Exercise 2). Black marker and felt-tip pen.

STEP 6: Hand-letter your name in capital or lowercase letters. Add your telephone number and initials.

STEP 7: Reverse or mirror-image the elements in Step 6, as in Figure 2–18.

STEP 8: Draw a potted plant, a simple building, a sailboat, paper cup,

a telephone, or anything that you can from memory, in the bottom third of the sheet.

STEP 9: Now start over on a fresh sheet with the checkerboard grid. This time choose different subjects. Try to draw slowly and concentrate fully as you work. This exercise may seem difficult at first, but it is of great value.

Squares, cubes, and horizontal ellipses

This exercise is extremely important. It will give you an understanding of basic intuitive perspective drawing. To get the most out of it, you must work slowly and accurately.

DIRECTIONS: Set up the paper vertically, and draw with a black felt-tip pen. Follow the steps given in Figure 2–19. The lines are numbered in working sequence.

STEP 1: Draw freehand lines 1 inch (2.5 cm) from the side and bottom edges of the paper and 2⅛ inch (5.5 cm) from the top edge. Now draw a small square in the upper left-hand corner of the box. By eye, swing an arc corner to corner, using a dotted line to indicate a 90-degree angle.

STEP 2: Next to the square, draw a cube, as seen slightly from above, with both sides of equal width. The top should be a shallow diamond shape.

STEP 3: Beside this cube, draw another cube, this time with the two top edges converging to a center point beyond it. Give the top only a shallow depth, and remember that it is actually a square in perspective.

STEP 4: Below the original square, draw a cube with sides of slightly different sizes and all edges converging at angles to two vanishing points. This cube is in two-point perspective. Notice that, because the side faces are not equal, the rear corner is not directly over the front corner as in

the first cube you drew. This is the key to drawing a cube without perspective guidelines.

STEP 5: Beside the three drawings at the top of the sheet, letter the following in small capital letters: "A square is a quadrilateral figure with four equal sides bounded by four straight lines. A cube is a figure with six equal faces, all square and all with 90-degree angles."

STEP 6: A little less than halfway down the sheet, draw a straight horizontal line across the sheet from border to border. This represents the horizon line or eye level—a line that extends 360 degrees around us. The eye level is determined by the viewer's position on or above the ground. If the viewer is lying on the ground and looking up at objects, a low eye level results. If he or she is standing on a hill and looking down, a high eye level results. The eye level or horizon is always a straight line parallel to the drawing surface. The only time it would curve is if the artist were viewing the earth from a satellite, so that the curvature of the earth's surface was apparent.

STEP 7: At each end of the eye-level line, place an asterisk to represent the left and right vanishing points. Label them LVP and RVP. This is the only exercise in which vanishing points will be placed on the sheet. In most intuitive perspective drawing, the vanishing points are well off the sheet.

STEP 8: Draw a circle with an 8-inch (20 cm) diameter centered on the eye-level line. This represents your cone of vision. Now draw a vertical line through it from top to bottom, and extend it above and below. Mark the exact center with a dot.

The easiest way to envision the picture plane and the cone of vision is to imagine that you are looking through a camera's viewfinder. The picture plane is parallel and at right angles to your line of sight, as is the viewfinder. In the center of the rectangular viewfinder glass is a circle with a dot at its center. This dot is the center of the cone of vision—a point on the object you are focusing on. Around this point you can see the object itself within a cone of about 60 degrees (Fig. 2–20). The eyes only take in this much when looking at anything. Everything outside the cone is out of focus. Test this yourself by looking at an object that is about 10 feet (3 m) away, without moving your eyes. Notice that objects a few feet away from the object you're looking at are out of focus.

STEP 9: Locate the viewpoint and the station point. The viewpoint is the direction from which the artist is looking at an object. The station point is the artist's position, raised or lowered, in relation to the object. Thus, the station point is located on the eye level and on the ground where the artist is standing. The station point/viewpoint combination is assumed to be in the center of the page, but it can be moved to either side. In this exercise the vertical line through the center of the cone-of-vision circle represents your station point and viewpoint. The asterisk at the base of the line is where you are standing and represents your line of sight.

STEP 10: Now you are going to draw cubes. Most of them will be the same size, but they will appear larger or smaller, depending on their placement. Use very fine lines for the construction guidelines. Then draw the objects in heavier lines, and tone them if necessary for clarification. Because

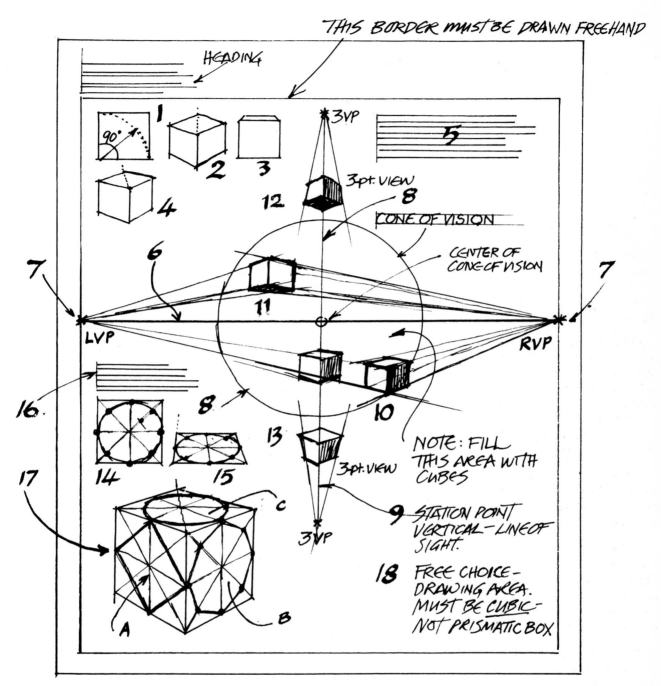

THIS BORDER MUST BE DRAWN FREEHAND

HEADING

90°
1
2
3
4

3VP
12
3pt. VIEW
8
5
CONE OF VISION
CENTER OF CONE OF VISION

6
7
11
7

LVP
RVP

16
8
10

14
13
15

NOTE: FILL THIS AREA WITH CUBES

17
C
A
B

3pt. VIEW

9 STATION POINT VERTICAL—LINE OF SIGHT.

3VP

18 FREE CHOICE— DRAWING AREA. MUST BE CUBIC— NOT PRISMATIC BOX

NOTE: 3 pt. VIEW CUBES ARE OUTSIDE THE CONE OF VISION. THAT'S WHY THE SIDES TAPER IN

2–19. Steps in Exercise 3 using squares, cubes, and horizontal ellipses. The completed drawing contains all the principles of two-point linear perspective, using simple forms and drawing in an intuitive manner.

this exercise is in two-point perspective, all cubes should have perpendicular vertical edges that are parallel to each other and to the edge of the sheet.

First, from the left vanishing point, draw a fine line across the sheet below the eye level at about a 20-degree angle. From the right vanishing point, draw a fine line at a slightly greater angle to intersect the first line. Where they meet, draw a vertical line. This represents the vertical edge of a cube. Mark off the required depth. From the left vanishing point, draw another line to meet that point on the vertical. Do the same from the right vanishing point. Now you have two sides of a cube that converge. It is imperative that you draw all of these lines very straight.

Using the vertical edge as a measuring unit, calculate by eye the length of the two sides that face you. They have to be shorter than the length of the vertical edge. As always, the closest vertical edge is the longest line in a cubic object. Moreover, the base length cannot exceed the length of the nearest vertical edge. If it does, you are drawing a rectangular prism, not a cube.

Now draw in the two vertical side edges. Connect the left vanishing point to the side, and structure the back surface edge. From the right vanishing point, bring another line through to the left edge, so you can structure the entire cube. It is that easy.

STEP 11: Using the same methods, draw other cubes within and just outside the cone of vision, above and below eye level. All lines must be drawn *from* the vanishing points, not to the vanishing points; otherwise, you'll only be guessing about the lines' accuracy.

Notice that, if the diagonal guidelines intersect on the vertical line of the cone of vision, the cube lies exactly between the two vanishing points; conse-

quently, both its sides should be of equal width. This is the same view as for the second cube at the top of the sheet. If the lines intersect to the left of the center of vision, the right surface will be larger. And conversely, if the lines intersect to the right of the center, the left surface will be larger.

STEP 12: On the vertical center of the vision line, 3 inches (7.6 cm) above the circle, draw a three-point perspective view of a cube. You can see the underside of this cube. Its sides converge into the third vanishing point, which is above the cube on the station-point vertical. Since this cube is outside your cone of vision, it is not in two-point perspective. Label it 3-pt. view.

STEP 13: Now draw a three-point perspective view of a cube positioned 3 inches (8 cm) below the circle. Its sides taper in at the bottom to the third vanishing point. Label it 3-pt. view.

STEP 14: Beneath the drawings of cubes in the cone of vision, draw a 2-inch (5 cm) square. On it, draw diagonal lines from corner to corner to establish the center point. Using this center point, accurately draw the vertical and horizontal mid-lines. On each half-diagonal, one-third of the way in from the corner to the center, mark a dot. Put

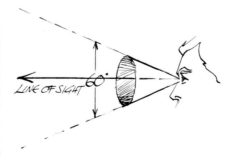

2-20. Diagram indicating the cone of vision.

additional dots on the outside of the square where the vertical and horizontal edges meet the perimeter. Finally, connect all the dots in a smoothly rounded circle. You have now plotted a circle in a square.

STEP 15: Now draw a 2-inch-deep square in perspective so that it is lying on the ground. As you did in the previous step, draw in diagonals to establish the center point, add the horizontal and vertical mid-lines, and mark dots one-third of the way in from the corner to the center. Draw a curve connecting all the dots to the outside vertical and horizontal edges. You will have drawn an accurate ellipse freehand (Fig. 2–21).

STEP 16: Letter the following caption above these diagrams: "Use the relationship of the circle to the square to construct ellipses."

STEP 17: In the bottom left-hand portion of the sheet, draw a 4-inch (10 cm) cube in two-point perspective showing a slight top view. Then draw diagonal lines from corner to corner to establish the center of each surface. Now construct an ellipse in three stages: (a) draw a diamond on the surface: (b) plot and draw in an octagon: and (c) draw in the ellipse freehand. You should have a three-step progression from diamond to octagon to ellipse (Fig. 2–22).

STEP 18: In the bottom right-hand portion of the sheet, draw a cubic object of your choice. Apply the principles used in this exercise to draw accurately.

Figure 2–23 is included to show you one method for drawing in perspective mechanically. You can use this method to check the accuracy of a freehand drawing.

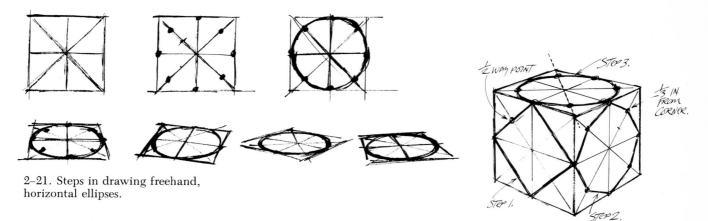

2-21. Steps in drawing freehand, horizontal ellipses.

2-22. Progressing in three steps from a perspective square, to a perspective octagon, to an ellipse.

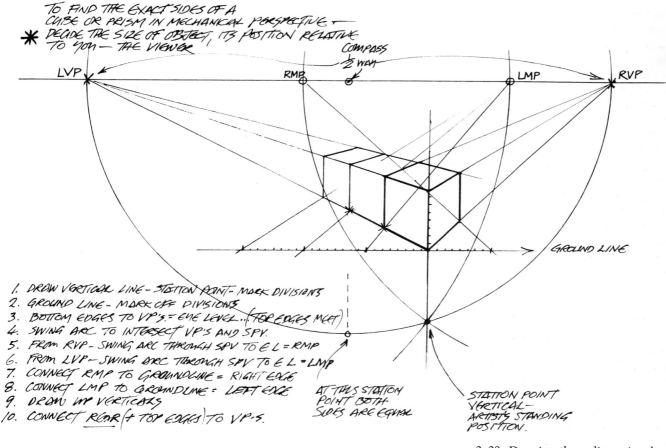

TO FIND THE EXACT SIDES OF A CUBE OR PRISM IN MECHANICAL PERSPECTIVE —
★ DECIDE THE SIZE OF OBJECT, ITS POSITION RELATIVE TO YOU — THE VIEWER

LVP   RMP   COMPASS ½ WAY   LMP   RVP

GROUND LINE

1. DRAW VERTICAL LINE - STATION POINT - MARK DIVISIONS
2. GROUND LINE - MARK OFF DIVISIONS
3. BOTTOM EDGES TO VP's = EYE LEVEL...(TOP EDGES MEET)
4. SWING ARC TO INTERSECT VP'S AND SPV.
5. FROM RVP - SWING ARC THROUGH SPV TO E L = RMP
6. FROM LVP — SWING ARC THROUGH SPV TO E L = LMP
7. CONNECT RMP TO GROUNDLINE = RIGHT EDGE
8. CONNECT LMP TO GROUNDLINE = LEFT EDGE
9. DRAW UP VERTICALS
10. CONNECT REAR (+ TOP EDGES) TO VP·S

AT THIS STATION POINT BOTH SIDES ARE EQUAL

STATION POINT VERTICAL— ARTIST'S STANDING POSITION.

2-23. Drawing three-dimensional forms using the measuring-point system is a mechanical, not intuitive, method of drawing.

Rectangles and prisms

Now that you have a good understanding of the cube, you can begin exploring its variations. We will first consider the 2 × 1 rectangle and the 2 × 1 rectangular prism—the most commonly used forms in our environment. Then we will investigate various rectangles and prisms in the man-made environment.

DIRECTIONS: Draw with a black felt-tip pen on a vertically oriented sheet. Use fine lines for the construction guidelines and heavy lines for the forms. Follow the steps given in Figure 2–24.

STEP 1: Draw the border, again freehand, with the same dimensions as in Exercise 3.

STEP 2: In the upper left-hand corner, draw two small equal-sized squares that share a vertical side. This is a 2 × 1 rectangle. Draw a diagonal across the left square, and then draw a diagonal across both squares.

STEP 3: Draw another rectangle of the same size beside the first one. Add the top edges of the sides, making them converge slightly, and then complete the rear horizontal edge. This is a 2 × 1 rectangular prism in one-point perspective.

STEP 4: To the right of this prism, draw a 2 × 1 rectangular prism in two-point perspective. Use diagonal parallel lines on the surfaces to ensure accurate convergence.

STEP 5: Next to the first three figures, draw a 2 × 1 rectangular prism standing on its small end. It should be oriented vertically with the viewer looking down on it. Because the prism is rendered in three-point perspective, its sides taper in at the bottom.

STEP 6: In the upper right-hand corner, draw a phi or golden-section rectangle. To construct it, first draw a freehand square. Then position an imaginary compass point at the midpoint of the square's base, and draw in a dotted semicircle, touching both top corners of the square and striking a point level with the square's base. Then draw a vertical line from where the arc touches the baseline outside the square (either left or right), and complete the rectangle. If the square's base is 1 unit, the length of the small rectangle's base is .618 unit, so phi is 1.618 units. This rectangle is a particularly pleasing and harmonious one.

STEP 7: Underneath the phi rectangle, letter the following in capitals: "A rectangle is a parallelogram with all angles 90 degrees. In a prism the end faces are equal and parallel; the side faces are parallelograms."

STEP 8: Draw a 3- × 4-inch (8 × 10 cm) rectangle in the upper left-hand corner. This will serve as a ground plan for an arrangement of office furniture including a filing cabinet, a desk, a chair, two small coffee tables with hexagonal and octagonal tops, and a rectangular box.

The cabinet, desk, and chair are all arranged parallel to each other, at right angles to a straight line on the floor, which is represented as a heavy line (8A in Fig. 2–24). This line will be the first one in your perspective view, and the whole arrangement will use the same two vanishing points on the horizon line (eye level).

The coffee tables, however, are not parallel or at right angles to the other furniture or to each other. Each will have its own two vanishing points, located at the same eye level but in different positions from those used in the first arrangement. The vanishing points will be the same distance apart as in the first case; they will simply slide along the eye-level line one way or the other.

STEP 9: To interpret the ground plan and put it into two-point perspective, first draw a horizontal line across the sheet, border to border, approximately halfway down from the top of the sheet. Place both the left and the right vanishing points *well off* the sheet. For the LVP, mark a dot on your desktop 12 inches (30.5 cm) to the left of the paper edge. Then, for the RVP, mark a dot 18 inches (45.7 cm) to the right of the paper edge. Both should line up horizontally on your eye-level line.

STEP 10: For this exercise, the cone of vision and viewpoint are located away from center to make the drawing more interesting. That the LVP and RVP are not equally placed on either side of the sheet is a clue. This time, rather than drawing the circle for the cone of vision, you will only sense it.

First, imagine a line from the LVP, coming onto your sheet at a 15-degree angle. Draw it as it crosses the sheet (10A).

From the RVP, draw a line at the same angle (10B). It will intersect with line A at a distance approximately one-third of the way from the right border.

At the intersection point, draw a vertical line (10C). Notice that line A, drawn from the LVP, is the baseline for the desk, chair, and cabinet. Line B, drawn from the RVP, represents the base of the other side of the filing cabinet. The third line, C, represents the

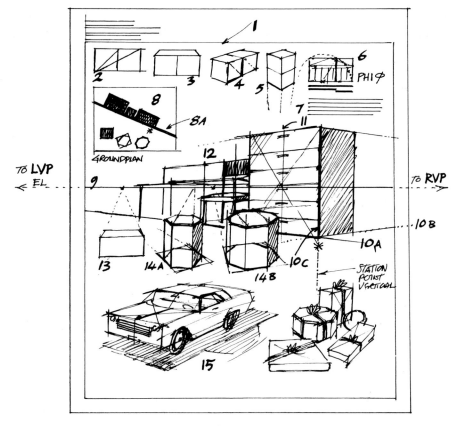

2–24. Steps in Exercise 4 using rectangles and prisms.

nearest and closest edge of this object to you. Do you see how easy it is to translate a two-dimensional ground plan into a three-dimensional perspective view? It is as simple as drawing the comparative angles of one cube.

STEP 11: Assume that the filing cabinet is 6 feet high, 4 feet wide, and 2 feet deep (or 6 × 4 × 2 in whatever units you choose). Draw six equally spaced dots on the vertical line. Then, from the LVP, draw a straight line at an angle above eye level to meet the top dot. This represents the top front edge. Next, from the RVP, draw a straight line to meet the same dot. This represents the top side edge.

Noting that the depth of this cabinet is one-third its height, drop a vertical line. Don't forget that it is really less than one-third because of convergence.

Noting that the width of the cabinet is two-thirds its height, draw the last vertical. Now make the lines heavier, to distinguish the cabinet from the guidelines.

Finally, draw diagonals from corner to corner to find the center of the front surface. Drop a vertical line to intersect with this point, and on this line draw in six handles.

STEP 12: Arrange the remainder of the furniture to the left of the filing cabinet. Make sure that all of the pieces rest on the same baseline. Follow the same steps as in drawing the filing cabinet. Don't expect that everything will come out perfectly the first time you try it. You must practice.

STEP 13: In the foreground draw a box parallel to you—that is, in one-point perspective.

STEP 14: Now draw the hexagonal and octagonal tables in the foreground. First see how they look from the top (Fig. 2–25), and then put them into perspective.

For the hexagon (A), start with a square base in perspective and draw the six-pointed shape within it much as you would an ellipse. Notice that there are three sets of parallel sides and that this hexagon has three vanishing points—each meeting the eye level—as determined by the viewpoint of the original square.

For the octagon, again draw a square in perspective. Draw in the diagonals, and mark off points one-third of the way in from corner to center. Position all four vanishing points on the eye level. The square will help to guide you.

STEP 15: On the bottom third of the sheet, draw rectangular objects of your choice in perspective. If you choose to draw a car, think of it as a cube within a prism.

ADDITIONAL PRACTICE: To apply what you have learned so far, sit at a window and draw the street scene you see. Include a road, houses, cars, trucks, and so on.

Next do an interior view. Study the many different square, rectangular, cubic, and prismatic objects in any room. Do a ground plan, and then draw what you see in perspective.

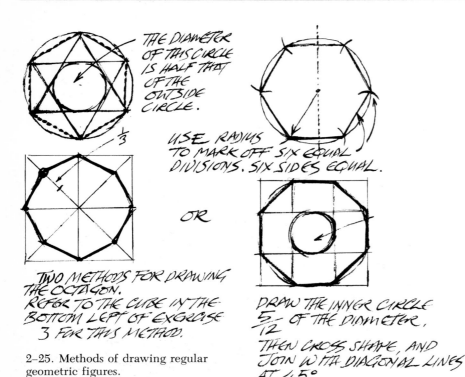

THE DIAMETER OF THIS CIRCLE IS HALF THAT OF THE OUTSIDE CIRCLE.

USE RADIUS TO MARK OFF SIX EQUAL DIVISIONS. SIX SIDES EQUAL.

OR

TWO METHODS FOR DRAWING THE OCTAGON. REFER TO THE CUBE IN THE BOTTOM LEFT OF EXERCISE 3 FOR THIS METHOD.

DRAW THE INNER CIRCLE 5/12 OF THE DIAMETER. THEN CROSS SHAPE, AND JOIN WITH DIAGONAL LINES AT 45°.

2–25. Methods of drawing regular geometric figures.

Finally, design a large building in outline only. You will have to bring points in close, so there will be considerable convergence. Use diagonals to subdivide the surface and to position doorways, pillars, steps, and windows. Let your imagination go.

Figure 2–26 serves as a guide, but don't copy it. Keep dividing the surface into smaller square and rectangular shapes, and then use the method for constructing circles in perspective within a square shape. For most conventional arches, windows, and doorways you need only the top half of the circle.

Now look at Figure 2–27, which shows you how to space lines or areas that are equal yet become smaller and converge in perspective. First you draw parallel diagonal lines from the top of one vertical to the bottom of the next, as shown (A). From this you can go on to plot the cast shadows (B), or you can divide the surface into equal units by using a diagonal line (C).

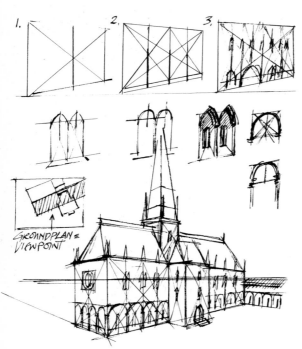

2–26. Intersecting diagonal lines subdivide rectilinear surface shapes accurately in perspective.

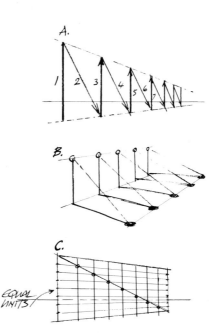

2–27. Methods for subdividing shapes in perspective and for drawing equal spacing.

Other geometric forms

In addition to cubes and prisms, illustrators need to know how to draw spheres, hemispheres, cylinders, arches, triangles, cones, truncated cones, pyramids, truncated pyramids, oblique cones, and oblique prisms. This exercise teaches you about these geometric forms and encourages you to put them to imaginative use in creating a building of your own design with a related abstract sculpture in front.

DIRECTIONS: Set up the sheet vertically, and draw with black felt-tip pen, following the layout in Figure 2–28. Do as many preliminary drawings as you require.

STEP 1: Subdivide the top of the sheet into five equal areas by eye, and mark these with dots. Then draw four vertical lines approximately 5 inches (12.7 cm) deep, using these marks.

STEP 2: In the upper left-hand corner, draw a small square with an accurate circle inside it. This represents a sphere. Draw in and tone a semicircular shape from its axis.

Now draw a second sphere of the same size. Using diagonal lines, tone in a shadow underneath it. This sphere is side-lit.

Next draw a small cylinder with parallel sides, as viewed from above. From its center, draw a rectangle in perspective at an angle to touch the top and bottom edges.

As you can see, a sphere is created by rotating a semicircle about its axis, while a cylinder is formed by rotating a rectangle about its axis.

STEP 3: In the adjoining area, draw a freehand semicircle in the cen-

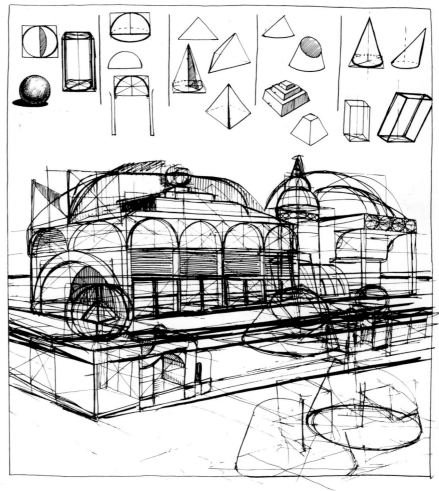

2–28. Preliminary underlay layout for Exercise 5 by Paul McCusker. Black marker felt-tip pen.

ter. Above this, draw two squares side by side; and within this rectangular shape draw another semicircle. Now draw an ellipse onto the bottom, and you have created a hemispherical shape in perspective. Notice the position of the center axis.

Next draw a vertical rectangle, and within the upper part draw a horizontal line. Add two diagonals to find the center, and draw a vertical line to it. Now create an arched window shape, using

a semicircular line. If you like, include a small drawing of a true arch, pointed at the top.

STEP 4: In the third top area, draw an equilateral triangle. Then draw a cone with a curved base in perspective. To do this, first draw a square on the ground in two-point perspective; then draw in diagonals to find the center; then from the center draw a vertical; and then complete the sides. Add the ellipse for the base.

Now try a tetrahedron—a pyramidic shape with four sides. Draw another small square in two-point perspective, with the sides converging slightly. Add diagonals, and from the center draw a vertical. Using three lines, connect all three corners of the square base to a point on the vertical line. This is an accurate method for plotting the apex of a four-sided pyramid.

Creating a truncated pyramid involves a similar process, but you must decide where to cut off or flatten the pyramid. Then you simply take this surface to your imaginary vanishing points (shown in the fourth column in Fig. 2–28).

STEP 5: Arrange and draw a truncated cone and a truncated stepped pyramid. For the cone, begin by drawing a horizontal ellipse to serve as the base. Then cut off the peak of the cone by drawing a small angled ellipse. This bottom portion is called the *frustum*. Now draw the small top part of the cone, known as the *gnomon* (Fig. 2–29).

For a truncated pyramid, there are two ways to draw the step arrangements. You can line up either the top edges of the steps or the bottom corner edges. Use the same drawing procedures as for the four-sided pyramid. Decide how many steps you want. Make sure that the horizontal planes of all the tiered steps converge; use the same two vanishing points as for the base. Remember that the tops of each tiered step go completely around each level, and allow for this in the drawing.

STEP 6: In the last area at the top, draw a regular cone, an oblique cone, a regular prism, and an oblique prism. Draw the oblique cone with its base parallel and horizontal but its center axis tilted to one side.

The principle is much the same for the oblique prism. After drawing a regular, vertically positioned prism in two-point perspective, draw the same base for the oblique prism. This time, however, tilt the center axis, and draw the side surface edges parallel to this tilted center line. Notice that the top is flat and parallel to the base; only the sides are drawn at a tilt.

STEP 7: In the bottom portion of your sheet, create a building that incorporates these geometric forms. Give free rein to your imagination. If you like, add a sculpture made up of the same forms in front (Fig. 2–30).

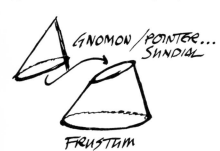

2–29. The construction of gnomon and frustum.

2–30. Finished drawing for Exercise 5 by Paul McCusker. Black marker felt-tip pen. The completed drawing of complex geometric three-dimensional forms demonstrates a disciplined yet intuitive use of freehand perspective drawing.

Perspective tips— symmetrical objects

Symmetrical forms have identical sides to the left and to the right of a center axis (which may or may not be visible). Although symmetrical objects look easy to draw, they are not. If you are preparing to draw a vase like the one in Figure 2–31, ask yourself the following questions:

1. Where is the axis or center line?

2. What is the proportion of the width to the height?

3. What is the basic shape?

4. What is the relationship of the ellipses to the eye level, and how shallow or deep are they?

5. What are the other characteristic shapes or configurations?

When you are drawing symmetrical objects by eye, it is difficult to monitor the accuracy of the left and right sides. The best way to check this is to flip the sheet over and hold it up to the light. Any discrepancies in the drawing will be much more noticeable this way. Another way to find mistakes is to hold your artwork up to a mirror.

Now consider one of the most difficult subjects to draw: a cup and saucer. Because the saucer is concave, the cup must be lowered into the top rim of the saucer ellipse (Fig. 2–32).

Perspective tips— foreshortening

What about the diminution of a cylinder through foreshortening, as seen in pipes, rods, and poles? Although the actual diameter of the object does not change, it appears to do so as the object recedes in space. This creates a feeling of depth.

Figure 2–33 explains foreshortening in several views of a pipe. The diameter is constant but appears to

2–31. The visualizing process required for accurate freehand drawing of a symmetrical object.

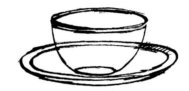

2–32. This process helps one to draw a cup and saucer.

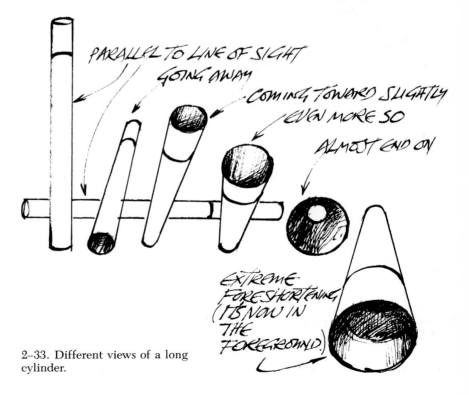

2–33. Different views of a long cylinder.

change with shifts in perspective and viewpoint. Any object with parallel sides must converge and foreshorten, unless it is at right angles to your line of sight and to the picture plane.

It is important to be aware of the centerline and axis of all three-dimensional forms. Never draw an object's outer edges and details without first seeing and understanding its basic inner form. Remember that a centerline or spine is present in trees, plants, humans, and animals, as well as in man-made objects such as automobiles and boats.

Vertical ellipses

Drawing circles that become ellipses on vertical surfaces requires a knowledge of major and minor axes. Look at Figure 2–34. On top is a two-dimensional circle inscribed in a square. Below this is a rectangular box whose sides converge slightly. Diagonals are drawn in order to find the centers of the surfaces. Then a dotted line is drawn from the center point to meet the edge lines at the vanishing points. This dotted line, called the *minor axis*, defines the width of the ellipse. The length of the ellipse is defined by a line perpendicular to the minor axis—the major axis.

DIRECTIONS: Use a black felt-tip pen or pen and ink on a vertical or horizontal sheet.

STEP 1: On a box like the one shown in Figure 2–34, draw the minor axis to one of the vanishing points, using a dotted line. At right angles to this dotted line, draw another line to represent the major axis. With or without a plotted square in perspective on the surface, draw an ellipse—faintly at first, and then heavily when it is accurate. Practice as much as you need to in order to perfect this.

If you look closely at the ellipses you have drawn, you will notice that they seem to tilt or lean at a slight angle; they are not vertical. In addition, the center (where the major and minor axes intersect) is off a bit so that one side is fuller than the other (Fig. 2–35).

STEP 2: Now draw the ellipse on the other side of the box (Fig. 2–36).

STEP 3: Finally, use what you have learned to draw a car (Fig. 2–36). Think of the tires as continuous cylinders going right through the underside of the car, but just draw the end faces and thickness of the tires. If the front wheel turns, change the minor and major axes. Only the front-wheel tires change in minor axis, however the rear ones always remain parallel to the side surface of the car.

For further practice, draw other objects with vertical ellipses, such as a locomotive, a projector, or a rack of drying dishes, pots, and pans.

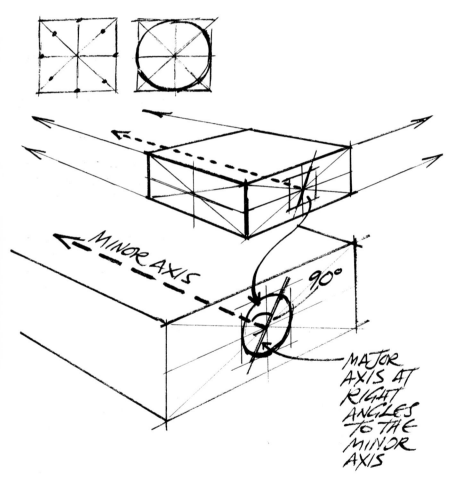

2–34. Drawing vertical ellipses.

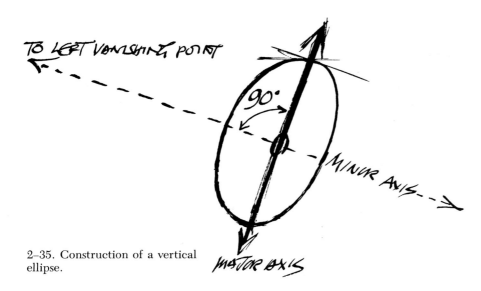

2–35. Construction of a vertical ellipse.

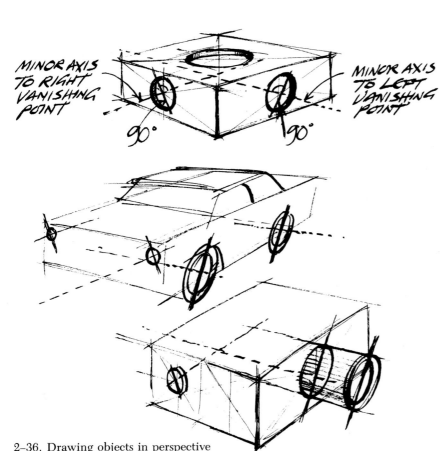

2–36. Drawing objects in perspective and indicating ellipses on each surface.

Spirals

Geometry is everywhere. It exists in nature, in man-made objects, and even in the forms of entire galaxies. The spiral is a curve that recedes or advances from a fixed center or pole by some continuous factor. By exploring the spiral, you will become more aware of curvilinear lines and shapes.

DIRECTIONS: Set up the sheet vertically, and draw with a black felt-tip pen. Following the layout in Figure 2–37, draw four vertical lines, 6 inches (15 cm) deep, at the top of your paper, creating five equal panels. Arrange and draw four spirals within the first four panels, in accordance with Steps 1 through 4.

STEP 1: In the leftmost panel, construct a scroll spiral. First draw a horizontal line halfway down the panel and put a dot in the middle. Above the line and radiating from the center dot, draw a series of semicircular arcs an equal distance (about 1/2 inch or 1.3 cm) apart.

Now, between the first dot and the first semicircular line, mark another dot on the horizontal line. Using this dot as an imaginary compass point, draw semicircular lines below the horizontal line, connecting the first dot to the first semicircle. Continue to draw accurate freehand arcs meeting those above the horizontal line.

STEP 2: In the next panel, construct an Archimedean spiral. First draw a cross in the center of the area. Then add diagonal crosses to it so that eight lines radiate from the center point.

On any one of the lines, mark a dot 1/4 inch (0.6 cm) from the center. On the next line, either to the right or left, mark

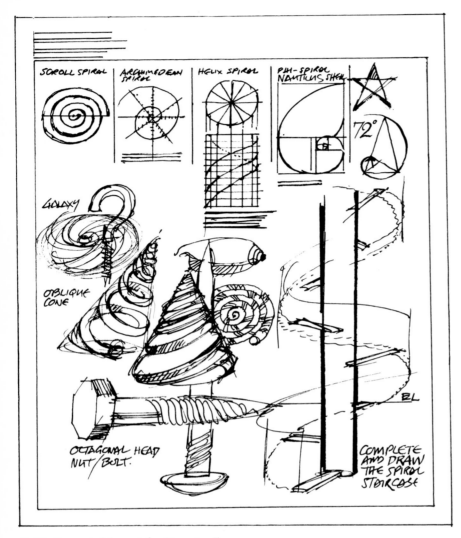

Labels within figure: SCROLL SPIRAL | ARCHIMEDEAN SPIRAL | HELIX SPIRAL | PHI-SPIRAL NAUTILUS SHELL; GALAXY; OBLIQUE CONE; OCTAGONAL HEAD NUT/BOLT.; 72°; COMPLETE AND DRAW THE SPIRAL STAIRCASE

2–37. Suggested layout for Exercise 7.

another dot, this time ½ inch (1.3 cm) from the center. In the same direction, on the third line, mark another dot, this time ¾ inch (1.9 cm) from the center. On the fourth line, add a dot at 1 inch (2.5 cm); and on the fifth line, add one at 1¼ inch (3.2 cm).

Continue placing dots on each line in a similar fashion. This progression of dots expands in equal divisions on every line with each turn, and the spiral advances one point or division every one-eighth turn.

To complete the drawing, simply connect all the dots with a curving line, starting at the center.

STEP 3: In the third panel, construct a helix spiral, which derives from a point moving on the surface of a cylinder or cone. First draw a perfect circle at the top of the area. Subdivide this circle into twelve equal divisions (like a watch face) with diagonal lines. Leave a 1-inch (2.5 cm) space below this circle.

Now draw a rectangular shape with a width equal to the diameter of the circle, about 4 inches (10 cm) deep. The circle represents the top of a cylinder, and the rectangle represents a side view of the cylinder.

Drop vertical lines from the division points on the circle down to the rectangular shape. The divisions on the rectangle give the effect of a fluted column in perspective.

Now draw a series of equally spaced horizontal lines across the rectangle. Place a dot at the bottom corner of the right-hand edge. Put another dot one horizontal line up and one vertical line in from this corner. Then put another dot at the second horizontal line up and vertical line in. Continue this sequence across the rectangle.

Next, starting from the bottom corner, join all the dots (the points where the lines intersect) with a smooth, curved upward line. Make this line heavier than the vertical and horizontal lines. It represents the curved thread on a bolt or screw.

Move one or two spaces above this line and, working parallel to it, draw another curved line through the intersecting verticals and horizontals. You can plot the curve at the back of the rectangle by using the same intersecting lines. Draw this line in dots so that it is not confused with the line on front.

NOTE: If the horizontal division lines are very close together, the pitch of the curved line will be shallow. Conversely, if the lines are far apart, the pitch will be steep. Try it both ways.

STEP 4: Construct a phi equiangular spiral. In the center of the fourth panel, draw a very small golden-section rectangle (see page 46). On top of this shape, add a perfect square of the same width as the original rectangle. Now add a square to the right of this total shape, equal in depth to its combined depth. Finally, add a square below this shape equal in width to the combined width of the other parts, and another on the left, equal in depth to the combined depth of the other parts.

This arrangement will give you a clockwise spiral. (For a counterclockwise spiral, you must arrange the squares first on the top and then to the left, bottom, and right.) Notice that, although the squares get progressively larger as they expand outward, each new composite shape remains a phi rectangle. These are called *whirling squares.*

Within the first small rectangle, starting at a point one-third of the way in from the right side, draw a curved line outward that ends in the upper left-hand corner. Continue to draw a curving diagonal line from one corner to the opposite corner of each expanding square. You are drawing the spiral of the chambered nautilus—the most beautiful spiral of all.

STEP 5: Use the fifth panel for hand-lettered information or for drawing any other spiral.

STEP 6: On the remainder of the sheet, draw studies of objects such as nuts and bolts, screws, screw-eye hooks, drill bits, springs, and seashells, using the diagrams at the top as reference guides (Fig. 2–38).

STEP 7: Plot and draw a spiral staircase, using the knowledge you have gained. Make this drawing large on the sheet. Do not copy a photograph; instead plot and design your own staircase. The helix spiral may help you here (Figure 2–39).

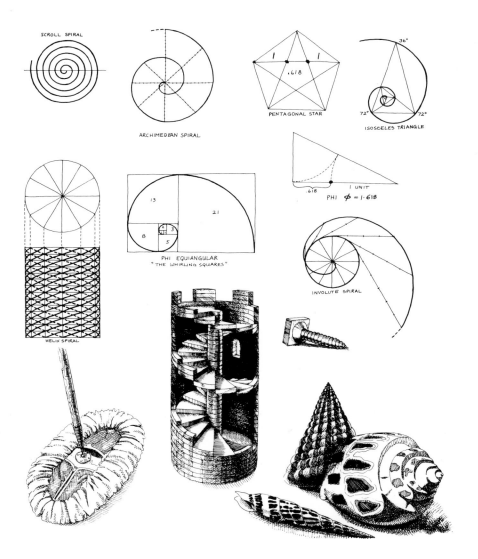

2–38. Finished drawing for Exercise 7 by Amanda Northfield. Black marker felt-tip pen. An appreciation of geometry in nature and in manmade forms is gained through drawing.

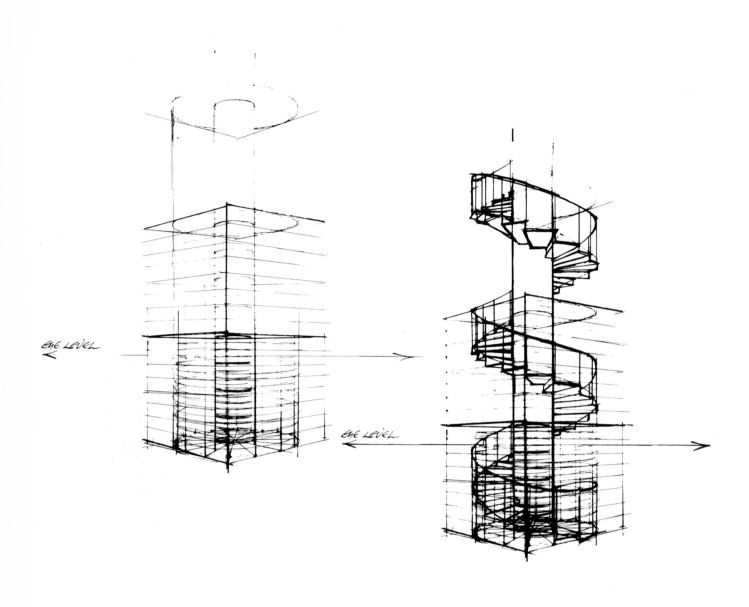

EYE LEVEL

EYE LEVEL

2–39a. Plotting a spiral staircase using the principles of the helix spiral.

2–39b. Freehand preliminary drawing of the spiral staircase with an awareness of three-dimensional form. This drawing should be examined *after* you have attempted your own solution.

Phi, the divine proportion

Earlier in this chapter you became acquainted with the pleasing proportion of the phi or golden-section rectangle. Knowing this proportion will make your structural drawing of many subjects much easier. It is a constant proportion found in seashells, plants, our own bodies, and the intervals between the planets. The Parthenon in Athens is based on the golden section, as is the Great Pyramid of Giza.

Specifically, phi is the division of a line or geometric figure such that the ratio of the smaller section to the larger equals that of the larger section to the whole. For example, on a line AB with point C in between, the phi proportion is such that AB:AC = AC:CB (Fig. 2–40).

DIRECTIONS: On vertical or horizontal paper, using a black felt-tip pen, conduct your own exploration into phi, the divine proportion. Take any subject in nature and do a series of investigative drawings, searching for this constant proportion (Fig. 2–41). Also look at man-made objects to see if they conform to the phi rectangle.

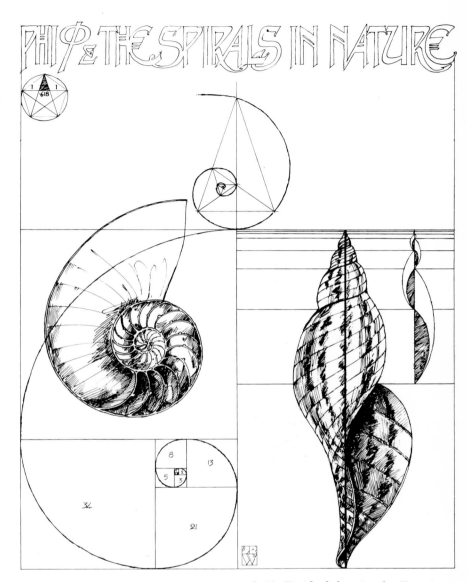

2–41. Finished drawing for Exercise 8. The golden section is a harmonious ratio underlying natural growth.

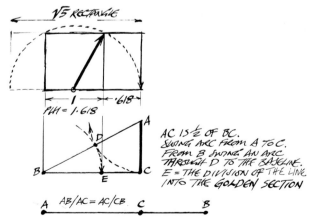

AC IS ½ OF BC. SWING ARC FROM A TO C. FROM B SWING AN ARC THROUGH D TO THE BASELINE. E = THE DIVISION OF THE LINE INTO THE GOLDEN SECTION

2–40. Phi golden section.

Drawing natural forms

Now that you understand the basic geometric forms and the centerline axis, let's investigate how these combine in subjects found in nature. Many natural subjects have a linear quality — for example, leaf veins, twigs, stalks, branches, and trunks. But geometric forms also play a significant role — for example, in flower-petal arrangements. And observe how natural things grow, decreasing in diameter as they rise farther up from the ground.

Fibonacci numbers

In 1202, a young man named Leonardo Fibonacci wrote a book called *Liber Abaci* (The Book of the Abacus). In it he explained the Hindu-Arabic method of numeration and mathematics. This system,

Drawing with the plant

This drawing combines creativity, emotion, and perspective. It is primarily done for a change of pace. Set up the sheet vertically, and work in black ink. Figures 2–42 and 2–43 present finished examples of this exercise.

STEP 1: Go outdoors and collect the most interesting dead plant you can find.

STEP 2: Back in the studio, break a small piece off the plant. Use this to draw with. Do not sharpen the end. Dip it in the bottle of ink; and experiment to see what textures you can produce. Use different pressures of your hand; roll your wrist; experiment.

Many line drawings are stiff, dull, and tight-looking as a result of being made with pointed mechanical tools. Metal pen nibs, ballpoint nibs, and

2–42. Finished drawing for Exercise 9 by Amanda Northfield. India ink. The unique character of a plant can be expressed by using a piece of it as a drawing tool.

which he had learned from Muslim mathematicians in North Africa, quickly replaced the Roman numeration system that was in use in Europe at the time.

In addition, Fibonacci worked out a sequence of numbers that related to the golden section. The Fibonacci sequence is 0, 1, 1, 2, 3, 5, 8, 13, 21, 34, 55, 89, 144, 233, 377, . . . Each number in the series is the sum of the two numbers immediately preceding it.

Dividing any Fibonacci number by the number preceding it gives a value of phi. For example, 89/55 = 1.6181818. The higher the number in the Fibonacci sequence, the closer it is to the phi proportion of 1.618034. These numbers are found in many natural proportions (Fig. 2–44). An excellent example is the sunflower, whose seeds are arranged in 55 equiangular phi spirals in a

2–43. Finished drawing for Exercise 9 by Mark Hughes. India ink and plant stalk.

hard graphite pencils tend to produce a uniform, characterless line. By using a natural drawing implement, such as a plant stalk, you may discover a more interesting line.

STEP 3: Start with a fresh sheet of paper. Draw the border around the sheet with the plant stalk.

STEP 4: Select an interesting section of the plant and draw it within a 3- × 4-inch (8 × 10 cm) rectangle in the upper corner. Leave the plant section white, and fill in the background shapes with black ink. These black shapes are the counterforms or negative spaces. The plant is the form. Both should display variety.

STEP 5: Using this small rectangle as a design guide, draw the whole plant with the stalk. Arrange it interestingly on the sheet. The placement should be off-center and not strictly vertical. Be sure to show the tapering and foreshortening of the stalks.

STEP 6: In a small section of the sheet, do a geometric study of the plant and its forms.

clockwise direction, as well as in 34 or 89 counterclockwise spirals—a total of 89 or 144 spirals.

It is evident that nature possesses geometry and order. Scientists have even discovered order in what appears to be chaos. Being aware of this will help you make your drawing more meaningful.

Leaf and petal arrangements

The previous plant drawing was done expressively and graphically. This exercise combines emotional drawing with accurate perspective. The emphasis here is on structure, with geometry as the key. Specifically, you will investigate leaf arrangements on stems and petal arrangements in flowers as sequences of numbers.

DIRECTIONS: Set up the sheet vertically and draw with a plant stalk, pen and ink, or black felt-tip pen. Look at the layout in Figure 2–45 for guidance.

STEP 1: At the top of the sheet, draw and arrange the following geometric shapes: triangle (3 sides), square (4), pentagon (5), hexagon (6), octagon (8), and decagon (10). Within each shape, draw the number of petals suggested by the shape. For a pentagon, for example, choose a flower with five petals.

STEP 2: Arrange and draw the following leaf arrangements: opposite, alternate, and whorled. Make the drawings dimensional, as in Figure 2–45.

STEP 3: Having done the petal and leaf studies separately, combine them in a drawing of an actual flowering plant. Investigate the plant by rendering it in different ways: line and dot, silhouette, counterform or negative space, and closeup of texture and pattern or study of seed pods (if any).

STEP 4: Do a large two-point perspective drawing of a house with a flower garden. Either use a photo reference or draw on the spot. The perspective must be accurate.

2–45. Finished drawing for Exercise 10 by Amanda Northfield. Black marker felt-tip pen. Geometry is evident in petal and leaf arrangements.

2–44. The Fibonacci numbers and golden section in natural growth.

Line and interval in trees

exercise 11

DIRECTIONS: Set up the sheet vertically, and draw with a twig and ink or with a felt-tip pen. Refer to Figure 2–46 as a guide, but make your own arrangement. Like smaller plants, trees have a definite structure, as well as expressive characteristics such as shape and age. In this exercise we will investigate negative space again, this time as the intervals between tree trunks. Recognizing this space is a key to arranging trees effectively in an illustration.

STEP 1: Draw a row of trees in full foliage across the top of the sheet. Sim-

plify them to their most basic geometric shapes.

STEP 2: Now draw different types of trees as skeletal silhouettes arranged together as a group. Note that trees taper gradually from the base of the trunk at the ground up to the delicate outermost branches. Try to draw this accurately.

STEP 3: Add three drawings of one tree: a closeup study of a tree trunk with its bark texture; a counterform drawing of tree branches; and a closeup study of its seed (for example, a pine cone) or of a bud and a leaf (Fig. 2–47).

STEP 4: Finally, draw a series of diagrams pertaining to line and interval. The tree trunks are lines of varying weight, and the spaces between the tree trunks are intervals or counterforms. Draw at least five diagrams: repetition with constant intervals; progressive repetition; intervals showing depth; rhythmic repetition with constant intervals; and random repetition with random intervals.

STEP 5: Find a photograph of an interesting house surrounded by trees, and use this as your reference. Make this house the featured part of the exercise. The perspective in both the building and the trees should be accurate.

BASIC TREE SHAPES

STATIC   RANDOM

PROGRESSIVE

c. LINEAR INTERVALS

NEG. SPACE

CLOSE UP OF BUD, LEAF
AND BRANCH

CLOSE UP OF TREE BARK

2–46. Finished drawing for Exercise
11 by Margo Stahl. Black marker
felt-tip pen. The quality of a drawing
relies heavily on the empathy that the
artist feels for the subject.

2–47. Closeup study of a budding
stem by Henry Van Der Linde. Black
marker and felt-tip pen.

Line and interval in landscape

Line and interval in landforms and rocks

DIRECTIONS: Set up the sheet either horizontally or vertically to do a drawing of a rural scene (Fig. 2–48). Choose from among these ideas: tractor or plow furrows; fences of any type; closeups of wood grain; old barns and other buildings; grass, trees, and clouds. Accentuate the linear aspects of your subject. If you want texture or tone, create it with line only. Do not use any washes.

DIRECTIONS: Set up the sheet either horizontally or vertically, with the same criteria as in the previous exercise. Find photo references and investigate the linear aspects of rocks and mountains—including gorges, canyons, and unusual formations such as pinnacles. Many types of rock are formed in distinct layers called *strata*. Often they are eroded by wind and water. All have a linear quality.

Arrange five or more interesting rock formations in a composition (Fig. 2–49). You may want to include sky and clouds to help hold the background shape.

2–48. Final high-contrast drawing for Exercise 12 by Douglas Donald. Black marker felt-tip pen.

Within the illustration, the following labels appear:

LIMESTONE CLIFFS
- QUEBEC

ICE BERG

TASMAN
ARCH
-TASMANIA

SAND DUNES
-WESTERN
AUSTRALIA

BRIDALVEIL FALLS

SANDSTONE +
CONGLOMERATES
- AYERS ROCK
AUSTRALIA

GRAND
CANYON
- COLORADO
RIVER

MARBLE

SAND-SMOOTHED
ARCH
- AUSTRALIA

DRIPSTONE FORMATIONS
- LIMESTONE

2–49. Finished drawings for Exercise
13 by Margo Stahl. Black marker
felt-tip pen. These study drawings
investigate the pattern and linear
intervals of rock formations.

Line, pattern, and interval in water

DIRECTIONS: With the sheet set up horizontally or vertically, use a felt-tip pen to investigate the linear aspects of water, including its direction and motion as it flows (Fig. 2–50). Use photo references for this exercise.

Pay particular attention to the pattern in cresting waves, froth, and bubbles. Look for a rhythmic repetition, a progression of curvilinear, asymmetrical white shapes. Watch for the effects of wind. And do not forget that relationships underneath the surface are responsible for how water acts at the surface.

Using contrasting sizes, shapes, and tones (in line only), arrange several different studies of water into a composition. Choose from waterfalls,

2–50. Finished drawing for Exercise 14 by Henry Van Der Linde. Black marker felt-tip pen. Pattern, texture, and movement are investigated in this study.

whirlpools, ice and icebergs, oceans and seashores, rocks and rapids, gorges and weirs, rivers, ponds and lakes, and waterwheels and sluices.

Use a theme if you wish. For example, imagine a leaf falling into a mountain stream, down waterfalls and rapids, into a river, through a weir, and finally into the ocean. Keep in mind how water can be used to create moods of tranquillity, excitement, romance, and so on.

Line, interval, and shape in land and sky

DIRECTIONS: Using the same procedure as in the previous three exercises, create and design several small landscapes from your imagination (Fig. 2–51). Base the composition on information developed in the previous studies, but do not refer to them.

Draw mountains, rocks, valleys, fields, or cultivated land. Add water where appropriate, as in a waterfall, mountain gorge, or river. Include clouds, making sure that they become smaller as they recede in space. If de-

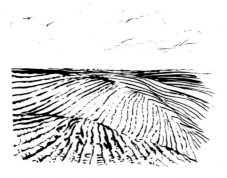

sired, place farmhouses and figures in the foreground.

NOTE: Do a preliminary drawing or two to work out the composition, tonal contrast, and details. Accentuate negative space, rhythm, action, and pattern. Lead the viewer's eye into the scene by creating a directional path to the center of interest.

2–51. Final drawing for Exercise 15 by Henry Van Der Linde. Black marker felt-tip pen. Line, interval, pattern, and texture show the principle of rhythm through repetition.

Clouds

As illustrators we must look at everything around us. We cannot afford to ignore what is above us—beautiful cloud shapes and formations. Clouds can be used to make backgrounds more interesting and to indicate space through atmospheric or aerial perspective. Different types of clouds have definite shapes and conform to various perspective principles.

To learn about clouds, draw a series of black-and-white studies using soft graphite pencil, black Conté crayon, or a water-soluble black felt-tip pen (wetting the line to create grays). Alternatively, you can use black and white hard wax pencils or square hard pastel sticks on a sheet of mid-gray paper. If you use pastels, fix the drawing to prevent it from smudging.

Memory drawing and other experiments

The next exercises involve using memory, the opposite hand to your normal drawing hand, and the visualizing process. In all cases, these exercises are designed to help you improve your drawing ability.

You can learn to draw in basically two ways: by drawing objects as you look at them or at photos of them; or by drawing from the mind's eye. Drawing from the mind's eye requires good memory recall, coordination, and the ability to visualize. You look at a subject, record what you see in your mind, and then draw. It is as if you are photographing what you see with your mind. Memory drawing also increases your powers of observation.

Opposite-hand drawing helps your coordination and forces you out of your usual habits. You may find that you like the line quality you get with this type of drawing and may choose to use it on purpose when the drawing calls for it.

Still-life memory drawing

DIRECTIONS: Set up a still life, indoors or outdoors, and view it from about 15 feet (4.5 m) away. On a table, arrange cylindrical, cubic, conic, and prismatic man-made objects. The greater the variety of objects the better. Now mark your viewing point on the ground with tape, and look at the still life for *60 seconds only.*

Compare sizes, shapes, proportions, and the relative positions of objects, one to the other. Observe and note the eye level. Imagine the still life from a bird's-eye view, too, to clarify the placement and position of objects relative to the tabletop.

Now go into another room and draw what you saw from memory. The drawing should fill the sheet, and it's important to draw the tabletop in correct perspective (Fig. 2–52). After drawing for an hour and a half, go back to the same spot with your drawing and compare it to the still life. How accurate is your drawing?

Now try it again, from a different viewpoint. Keep practicing. Assemble different still-life arrangements; but each time you draw, cut back on the viewing time—to 30 seconds, 20 seconds, and finally 10 seconds.

This exercise should strengthen your powers of observation, thinking, and memory. It forces you to concentrate, continually evaluating and *comparing* object forms and their perspective, one to the other, as a whole. It also helps you to sense and use perspective intuitively.

2–52. Finished drawing for Exercise 16 by Henry Van Der Linde. Black marker felt-tip pen. Drawing from memory demands acute observation and strong memory recall.

Rotating a box in space

This is a memory, logic, and visualizing exercise, similar to the situation of a client giving job instructions over the phone. The artist must translate the instructions correctly. In the classroom the information is given to students verbally only. No diagrams are used to explain the required drawing. The time limit is an hour and a half. The assignment: to draw a freely tumbling, rotating 2 × 1 box in space. Do approximately twenty views, as shown in Figure 2–53, with the box moving in a figure-eight above the ground, receding and advancing, and finally settling on the ground where you started the drawing sequence. Identify the different surfaces of your box with marks such as the dots on dice to help the viewer sense the motion as the object freely rotates.

DIRECTIONS: Setting the sheet up horizontally, draw the eye level or horizon line one-third of the way up from the bottom. Now draw a 2 × 1 box in two-point perspective so that it appears to be sitting on the ground approximately 40 feet away from you. Start to lift and rotate the next box, making it smaller than the first. Mark its surfaces.

Repeat this process, making the box smaller and turning it more as it goes farther back, freely tumbling and rotating. To make it advance, simply draw it bigger than the original box on the ground.

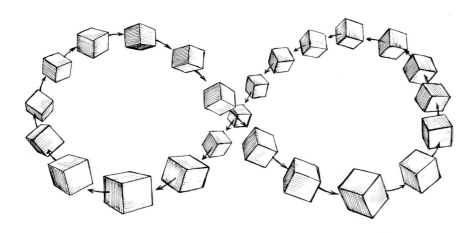

2–53. Final drawing for Exercise 17 by Henry Van Der Linde. Black marker felt-tip pen. A cube freely rotating in space tests an artist's ability to visualize and use an intuitive sense of perspective.

Opposite-hand drawing

Drawing with your opposite hand will improve your coordination from eye and brain to hand. Drawing nonstop means observing and recording simultaneously.

DRAWING 1: Set up the sheet in either direction, and draw with the opposite hand to the one you normally draw with. Work with a nonstop continuous line, and do not take the pen off the sheet of paper until you are finished. The time limit is two hours. Choose from among the following subjects:

• A basement containing an assortment of articles and including a window or door as the light source.

• The interior of an artist's studio, containing a drafting board and a variety of equipment and including a window or door as the light source.

• The interior of a room, studio, or hall area in a building, concentrating on the ceiling and including a window or door as the light source.

DRAWING 2: Do another drawing with your opposite hand, but this time accentuate the counterforms or negative spaces within the subject. Draw in a nonstop, continuous line, and then fill in the counterforms solidly or with line, tone, or texture (Fig. 2–54). First find a subject that has interesting counterforms—for example, a bicycle, plants, or a still-life object.

2–54. Finished drawing for the second part of Exercise 18 by Paul McCusker. Black marker felt-tip pen. Line and negative space study drawn using the opposite hand.

Utilitarian objects

DIRECTIONS: Set up the sheet horizontally, and create your own layout (Fig. 2–55). Your objective in this exercise is to try to achieve total precision with freehand drawing.

STEP 1: Draw a table fork at three stages of construction. Draw it in a three-quarter view at about a 30-degree angle. The fork prongs and the intervals between them must be accurately drawn. Use an actual fork for the final stage.

STEP 2: Draw a table knife in three-quarter view. Then draw a three-quarter view of a tablespoon. Note the shape of the spoon's bowl.

STEP 3: Draw a cross-sectional view of a cup and saucer. Note that they are thinner near the edges and thicken toward the bottom and middle. Draw this accurately. Then draw a three-quarter top view of the cup and saucer together. Note that the saucer is concave, which makes it different from other ellipses you've drawn. The center of the lower ellipse of the saucer has to be drawn closer to the bottom front edge of the saucer to make the cup sink down into it (Fig. 2–56).

2–55. Finished drawing for Exercise 19 by Mark Hughes. Black marker felt-tip pen. Phi golden section analysis of hand relative to form and function.

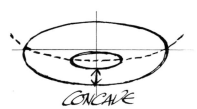

2–56. Placement of the inner ellipse in a concave saucer.

Composite view of a musical instrument

DIRECTIONS: Draw three views of a musical instrument: a top view, a side view, and a three-quarter view, arranged together in a composite, overlapped composition (Fig. 2–57). Find an interesting instrument, and draw from the instrument itself or a photo of it, *not* from a drawing. Draw it accurately freehand, accentuating the pattern, texture, and detail. Use light and dark contrast on the individual views to create a design. If you wish, letter in some information about the instrument. As in Exercise 19, the objective is to draw everything very precisely.

2–57. Finished drawing for Exercise 20 by Mark Grice. Black marker felt-tip pen. Drawing many views of a complex subject requires the use of all the skills learned so far regarding freehand perspective and design.

Opposite-hand and memory drawing

DRAWING 1: Do a drawing of any complicated object, still life, or indoor view, using the opposite hand to your normal drawing hand (Fig. 2–58). You should even draw the border for this exercise with your opposite hand. This process forces you to concentrate and improves control of your hand. Make sure that the basic perspective is accurate.

DRAWING 2: Now combine observation and concentration with memory recall. View a complicated still life for 30 seconds. Then, without looking at the arrangement, draw it as accurately as possible, using the hand with which you normally draw. Use an interesting line quality to make the drawing come alive.

2–58. Final drawing for Exercise 21 by Marie Sequens. Black marker felt-tip pen. It is possible to draw well with either hand if enough concentration is used.

Three views of one building

DIRECTIONS: Set up the sheet either horizontally or vertically. Working with a photographic reference, draw three views of one building, including a perspective view (Fig. 2–59). The building can be historical or contemporary, but it must be visually exciting. Use your sense of design in arranging the three views together. Vary the tonal values and quality of the drawings.

NOTE: Whether working from a photo or drawing from your mind's eye, you must understand the structure of the subject to draw it effectively. This applies especially to photographic references. Before the advent of the camera, artists had to draw from life, and the drawings they produced were very three-dimensional. An artist like da Vinci was able to use his eye to stop action much as a camera does and to analyze a complex subject like fast-moving water. Although photographs make drawing easier, they can result in flat and lifeless drawings. Understanding the subject makes all the difference.

Line and interval in the man-made environment

Line drawing is particularly suitable for illustration, since it reflects the linear quality of type and letterform characteristics. Vigorous, expressive linework also reproduces well in print media. It is particularly effective when rendered in black and white or when combined with flat colors.

DIRECTIONS: Set up the sheet either horizontally or vertically, and use a black marker or pen and ink. Working in black and white only (no grays), investigate variations in line weights and thicknesses in the man-made environment (Fig. 2–60). Contrast of line is evident, for example, in all architecture.

Choose several different subjects. Stress the asymmetric use of negative space or counterform in each composition, and crop your subject to promote excitement. Design the views to work together as a unified whole.

2–59. Final drawing for Exercise 22 by Gary Alphonso. Black marker felt-tip pen. Good line drawing and a strong sense of design are very important to aspiring illustrators.

Observation of the environment and letterforms

This exercise involves observation and awareness of your local environment, both indoors and outdoors. It encourages you to see things as you have never seen them before. Everything around you can be translated into a graphic illustration.

DIRECTIONS: Use a sheet of white illustration board, 20 × 30 inches (51 × 76 cm), and a sheet of Letraset (or similar brand) transfer type with the capital letters in 60-point size. Working with a ruling pen or technical pen and black India ink, draw grid rules for the alphabet letters, as shown in Figure 2–61. You will have twenty-eight equal areas (one for each letter, plus two left over).

Now search for shapes in the environment that form letters. Each subject you use should be the same way around as the letter itself. Don't twist or turn it to fit the actual letter because doing that would negate the searching and observation at the heart of this assignment.

You may choose and investigate one theme only if you wish, such as insects or mechanical tools. Whatever you choose, your studies should display unity of design, tone, and technique.

2–60. Final rendering for Exercise 23 by Mark Hughes. India ink, pen, and brush. Line and contrast as pattern.

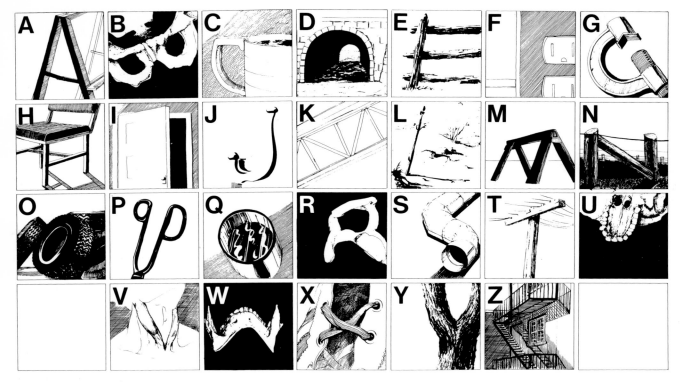

2–61. Final drawing for Exercise 24 by Paul McCusker. Black marker felt-tip pen.

Positive and negative cubic forms

Inner shape and form are always as important as outer shape and form. This exercise combines imagination, an intuitive sense of perspective, and an understanding of three-dimensional form. If the inner structure of a subject — whether mechanical or organic — is known, the subject itself will be drawn more convincingly.

STEP 1: In the middle of a sheet of paper, oriented either horizontally or vertically, use very fine pencil lines to draw a 10-inch (25.5 cm) cube in two- or three-point perspective, with more of the left or right side showing. Next, mark off eleven divisions on the vertical edge of the cube. Then do the same on the front top edges. Remember that the twelve spaces decrease as they recede.

Now draw fine lines from the marks on the vertical to the assumed vanishing points on both side surfaces. (Don't forget the correct convergence factor.) Do the same for the top surface of the cube, so that you produce a checkerboard grid of fine intersecting lines.

From the same marks on the top edge, drop vertical lines to the bottom edges. You have now drawn and subdivided the cube into smaller cubes — 1,728 cubes, to be precise.

Using a heavier pen line, create a three-dimensional sculptural form out of this subdivided master cube. Break some edges, retain others, and create inside sculptural forms as well. Just follow the directional guidelines you first established, using the same perspective. Make your drawing of the form as complex in design as you possibly can. The results are entirely up to you (Fig. 2–62). Now erase the original pencil drawing underneath.

STEP 2: Take out another sheet of paper, and tape it over the first. Using a heavier line, draw in the edges, forms, and shapes that you *did not* draw in on the first sheet. These are the negative shapes (Fig. 2–63). You have now created a three-dimensional form that should fit into the first one. In other words, the two drawings, when held one over the other, should show the complete cube — the one you started with.

Creative lettering and typography

Because as an illustrator you will be working with art directors and designers, you need to develop your awareness of type layout and design. This four-part exercise is an introduction to basic lettering and basic typography (Fig. 2–64). It will give you a sense of the tremendous potential of letterforms and typography for illustrators, as well as an appreciation of how illustration grew out of or evolved from calligraphy.

STEP 1: Make a *monogram.* Using a 1-inch (2.5 cm) acrylic chisel-point brush and India ink, create an abstract design based on your initials. When you are satisfied with the composition, cut it out, leaving a square background.

STEP 2: Make a *calligram* — a pictorial element that combines illustration and calligraphy. Choose a subject and define the basic shapes and tonal areas by using changing weights (light and heavy) of your own handwriting. Write in any direction within the areas of your subject. Create a border by using a quote or a poem.

STEP 3: Create a *typogram,* following the same instructions as in the previous step (Fig. 2–65) but in this case using *type* forms instead of handwriting. Work with transfer sheets of rub-down lettering in different sizes, with both capitals and small letters.

Use these type letterforms to define the subject, describing and holding its basic shapes.

STEP 4: Now work on *letter and word spacing.* Use transfer type, as in Step 3, with capital or lowercase letters. Choose a quote or a few words for this exercise. On one line, space the letters optically, rubbing down each letter as you go. If you are using capitals, leave a space the width of the capital letter *N* between words. If you are using lowercase letters, leave a space the width of the letter *e* between words.

NOTE: The trick to hand-lettering and typography is to create the optical effect of *even grayness* when you look at it. In other words, when you squint your eyes and look at any example, there should be no awkward black lumps or open white holes in the work.

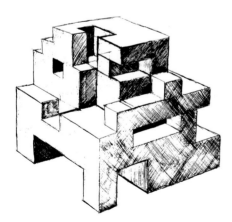

2–62. Drawing for Part 1 of Exercise 25 by Cindy Holmes. Black marker felt-tip pen. Creating an interesting cubic form from imagination requires one to think about structure.

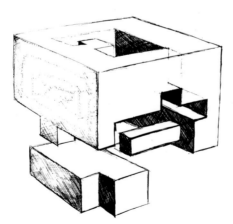

2–63. Drawing for Part 2 of Exercise 25 by Cindy Holmes. Black marker felt-tip pen. Knowledge of the inner structure of forms is helpful for drawing outer surfaces and shapes much more convincingly.

"BUT WHAT TYRANNY IS SO HIDEOUS AS THAT OF AN AUTOMATICALLY IDEAL HUMANITY?"
D.H. LAWRENCE

2–64. Final monogram, calligram, and typogram for Exercise 26 by Mark Hughes. Black marker felt-tip pen.

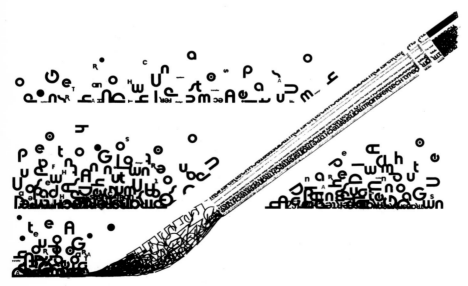

2–65. Final typogram for Exercise 26 by Amanda Northfield. Adhesive rub-down type. Pictorial images can be created by using type letterforms as pattern and texture.

Understanding light and shadow

Shadows anchor objects to the ground. Even the height and distance away of flying objects such as birds and aircraft can be indicated by the use of shadows. Using shadows is comparatively easy. You only have to know two factors: the direction of the light source, and the angle of the light.

The two types of light are natural and artificial. The sun's and moon's rays are considered to be parallel, while artificial light radiates.

Learning how to plot and make shadows work can best be done by first studying the sun as a light source, since it is the easiest to understand. The first step is to establish the direction the light is coming from: front, three-quarters front, side, three-quarters rear, or behind. Next, check to see if the sun is high or low in the sky; this determines the angle of the light and thus the length of the shadows. At noon there are short shadows, whereas in the morning and evening there are long shadows. Long shadows are the most graphically exciting.

Sidelighting

Sidelighting is the easiest form of lighting to execute and understand. Following the steps in Figure 2–66, draw a similar arrangement.

STEP 1: First draw the objects in perspective, with the vanishing points on the horizon.

STEP 2: Draw horizontal parallel lines from the bottom corners of the objects. The light is parallel to the horizon.

STEP 3: Add parallel angular lines that strike the top corners and the ground. Put dots where horizontal and angle lines meet.

STEP 4: Connect these dots, and draw a line back to the same vanishing points of the object. (A shadow's vanishing point is the same as the object's.) Then add tone to the objects and heavier tone for shadows, keeping in mind that shadows are transparent and get lighter with increasing distance (Fig. 2–67).

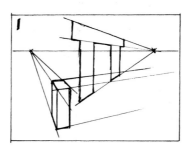
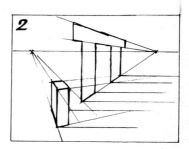
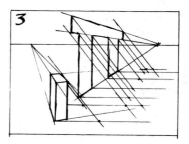
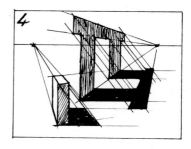

2–66. Steps in Exercise 27 (sidelighting), combining both two- and three-dimensional forms in perspective for drawing cast shadows.

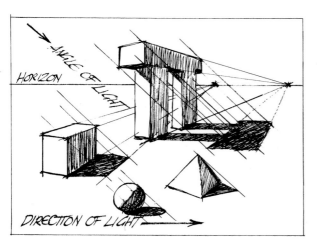

2–67. Adding tone to objects and cast shadows. Sidelighting is the easiest of all lighting to understand and draw.

Sun three-quarters front

Use Figure 2–68 as a guide in this exercise.

STEP 1: Draw several objects in three-quarters view, with their vanishing points on the horizon line.

STEP 2: After establishing where the sun is (in front of you and slightly to one side), draw a vertical line from the center of the sun to the horizon. From this point, draw lines through the bottom corners of the objects. This is the direction of the light. (The objects are being backlit.)

STEP 3: Now draw lines from the center of the sun that touch all the top corners of the objects and then hit the ground. This represents the angle of the light.

STEP 4: Mark where the top and bottom lines intersect. Connect these dots, and take them back to the object's vanishing point to outline the cast shadows. Then tone in the object and the shadows.

When the light is from the front, the shadows come forward but still converge toward the horizon. Don't forget that the lengths of the shadows vary according to the time of day.

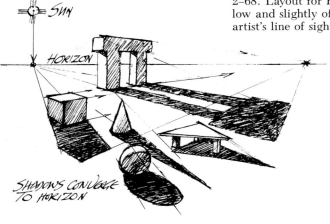

2-68. Layout for Exercise 28. Sun is low and slightly off-center from artist's line of sight.

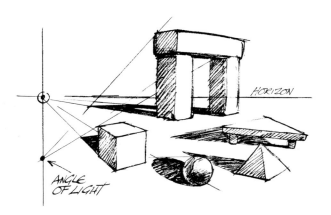

Sun three-quarters behind

Shadows recede and converge to the horizon when the light source is behind you. Follow Figure 2–69 in doing this exercise.

STEP 1: Draw the object in relation to the horizon. Determine the convergence point for the shadows (by deciding where the sun is positioned relative to you), and mark this point with a dot on the horizon. (NOTE: This convergence point can be to the right or to the left of objects anywhere on the horizon, depending on whether the shadows fall on the right side or on the left side.) Draw a long vertical line through this convergence point on the horizon.

STEP 2: Now mark another dot on the vertical line you just drew. This dot shows the angle of the light; its placement is determined by the time of day. (At midday shadows are short, so the dots are farther apart; early or late in the day, the shadows are longer and the dots are closer together.)

STEP 3: Draw in ground lines from the convergence point on the horizon to meet the bottom corners of the object. Then draw up from the lower dot on the vertical line to meet the top corners of the objects.

STEP 4: Mark the points where the angle lines intersect the ground lines, and connect these dots to complete the shadow shape. Then tone in the shadow.

2-69. Layout for Exercise 29. Sun is behind artist's right shoulder.

More complex situations

The same principles described in Exercises 27 through 29 apply to slightly more complicated forms. You simply plot the intersecting lines on the ground (Figs. 2–70 and 2–71). In Figure 2–70, the sun is directly in front of the artist, so the object (in this case, a building) is lit from above. Notice that the shadow converges to the point on the horizon directly below the sun. Figure 2–71 is a variation of Figure 2–69 (where the sun is behind and slightly to the right of the artist); here the sun is slightly behind and to the left of the artist's line of sight.

The shape of a shadow is always determined by two factors: the form of the object and the contours of the surface on which it is cast. The angle of the light determines the length or height of shadows cast on surfaces other than horizontal ones (Fig. 2–72). Such a shadow is drawn onto the surface upon which it falls by using the same vanishing points as the surface plane itself. If a surface contour is uneven, the resulting shadow may be foreshortened and distorted.

Artificial light

Artificial light radiates in a circular fashion. The shadows emanate from the center of a circle, directly under the light (Fig. 2–73). A lampshade controls this radiating effect, allowing the light to fall where desired (Fig. 2–74).

Indoor situations, however, almost always involve more than one light source. Every object, when lit, develops a cast shadow. The surfaces of the object which are opposite the light source are in shadow. Thus two or three lights together create overlapping shadows of different tones, depending on the different distances of the sources. Where they overlap, the shadows are always darkest. Shadow tones are also modified by the distance an object is from the light source, and the tone of the ground itself.

The more intense the light from the light source, the darker the shadow tone. Tone is also modified by the distance an object lies from the light source.

Adding realism

Reflections, shadows, and inclined planes all add to the realism of an illustration by giving the illusion of a third dimension. They can also be used as exciting compositional devices to create action, mood, and visual impact. The mechanics of perspective, however, are needed to make them work. Learning the rudiments now will enable you to do more complicated work later.

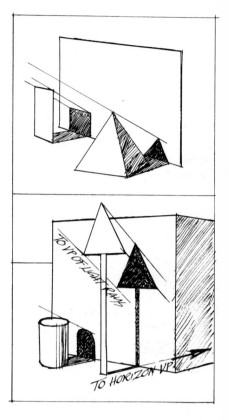

2–72. Shadows cast on non-horizontal surfaces.

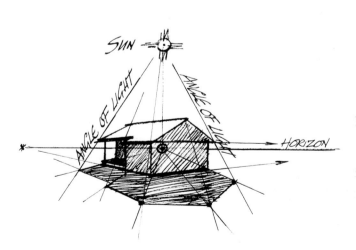

2–70. Shadows in a front-lit scene. Sun directly in front of artist.

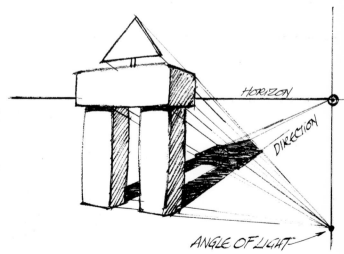

2–71. Shadows. Sun is behind artist's left shoulder.

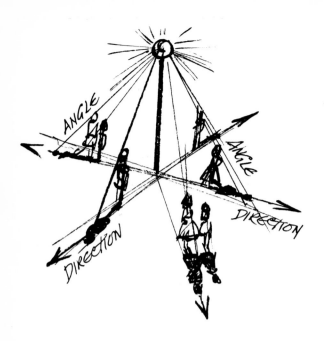

2-73. Shadows from unscreened artificial light cause cast shadows to emanate from the light source.

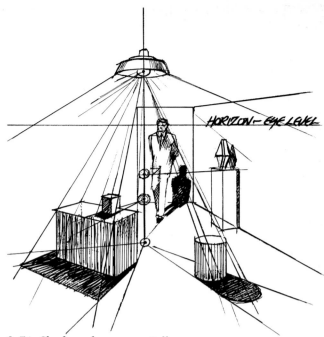

2-74. Shadows from a partially screened indoor light radiate from a point directly below the light source.

exercise 30

Outdoor and indoor light

DRAWING 1: Collect a few interesting photographs of different and strongly lit outdoor subjects with good cast shadows. On tracing-paper overlays, applying the principles discussed heretofore, analyze the shadows.

DRAWING 2: Go outdoors on a sunny day and draw the shadows you see. Buildings are a good subject to start with. Draw more complex subjects later.

DRAWING 3: Set up a simple still life on a large flat surface. Turn off all the lights except one. Working with this one spotlight, draw the objects and the shadows they cast (Fig. 2-75).

DRAWING 4: Using the same still life and light source, draw from a different position. Repeat this task at various angles.

2-75. Finished drawing for Exercise 30 by Douglas Donald. Black marker felt-tip pen. Cast shadows effectively anchor objects to the ground.

Reflections

In a composition involving reflections, the first thing to draw is the subject that is to be reflected. Its reflection is always directly below it (Fig. 2–76). The size and dimensions of the subject are generally the same in the reflection. To plot the reflection, however, you must take the reflecting surface into account. Usually it is in essence another ground surface parallel to the one that the object is standing on. If not, it reflects the subject at an angle and requires other vanishing points.

The length of a reflection is determined by two factors: the distance of the object from the reflecting surface and the angle of the light. (The angle of natural light and the resulting reflections of objects are determined by the time of day—the position of the sun in relation to the horizon and to the artist.) A high angle of light creates shorter reflections and a low angle creates longer reflections. The reflective surface may be dull or bright, as in the case of cloudy or sunlit water. If a gap exists between the subject and the place where it is being reflected, simply continue the reflection as if the gap weren't there. Then erase the drawing lines that are not in the reflection (Fig. 2–77).

The shape of the reflected image is also affected by the contours of the reflective surface. A boat on calm water, for example, has a reflection the same size as itself, while a boat on rougher water has a longer, distorted image.

DIRECTIONS: Experiment with actual objects and reflective surfaces. A room reflected in a mirror is a good subject. Try unusual reflective surfaces such as spoons, bowls, and cylinders. The distortion can sometimes be more exciting to work with than the actual subject itself.

2–76. Placement of a reflection beneath an object.

2–77. Drawing interrupted surface reflections.

Sit by a river or go to a harbor and draw the reflections. You know the principles now. On a sunny day, you will have to deal with shadows as well as reflections. If the shadows partly overlap the reflections, simply adjust the intensity of the tones accordingly.

Declined and inclined planes

Like shadows and reflections, declined and inclined planes can make an illustration more believable and dramatic. Such planes are surfaces that are not parallel to the ground (which is always assumed to be flat and horizontal). Their vanishing points are therefore not at the normal eye level. Anything attached to or standing on a declined or inclined plane will vanish

or converge to the same vanishing point as the plane itself, which we will call the *convergence vanishing point* or *CVP.*

Now look at Figures 2–78 through 2–80. Imagine that the rectangle represents a section of roadway, that the boxes are houses, and that their open lids are angled roofs. In Figure 2–78, the ground plane is flat and horizontal. The road-surface rectangle and the boxes converge and appear to meet at the same vanishing points at the horizon. The lids of the boxes converge to

their own vanishing points above the eye level. In Figure 2–79, however, the road-surface rectangle is tilted down or angled into the ground; it is a declined plane. In contrast, the road-surface rectangle in Figure 2–80 is tilted up or angled into the sky; it is an inclined plane. Notice that in both cases the lids stay the same, but the car's perspective is determined by the road's vanishing point.

Now take a closer look at the CVPs in Figures 2–79 and 2–80: they are directly *above* and *below* the boxes' vanishing point on the horizon. Notice, too, that the closer the CVP to the horizon—either above or below it—the smaller the angle of the declined or inclined plane.

Whether the road is going downhill or uphill, the windows, doorways, tops of houses, buildings, and roofs have a vanishing point on the eye level/horizon. This vanishing point is located vertically above or below the CVP. It is this that creates the illusion that the road is going downhill or uphill. In a sense, there are two vanishing points instead of one.

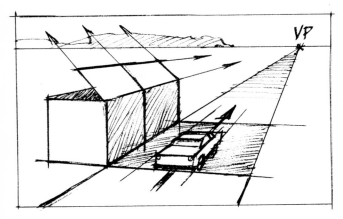

2–78. Objects sharing a common vanishing point.

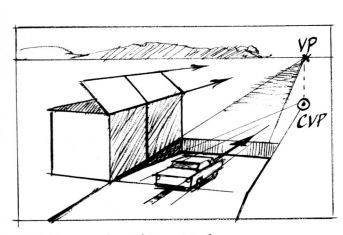

2–79. Downward vanishing point of a car on a declined plane.

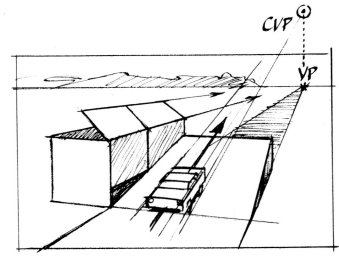

2–80. Upward vanishing point of a car on an inclined plane.

Up to now, we have dealt only with situations involving one CVP for a single declined or inclined plane. But as a road goes up and down, it also twists and turns to the left and right. This may sound like a problem, but it is not. You simply break the road into sections and move the CVP in relation to the horizon/eye level. Any houses or buildings in the scene follow this breakdown, with the vanishing point moving in relation to the CVP (Fig. 2–81).

If the road turns or curves a great deal and goes out of sight slightly, don't panic. You will not see the front surfaces of the houses and buildings, so don't try to draw them. You can pick up the road and the buildings again in the distance.

Look at the downhill view in Figure 2–82 and the uphill view in Figure 2–83. Pay careful attention to the CVP and VP for each section. Also notice the black wedge shapes at the bottom of the buildings. These wedges indicate the difference between the houses' horizontal floors and the declined or inclined plane of the road—a difference compensated for by steps.

Cars, people on the road, and the pavement all vanish toward the CVP, not the VP. The VP is for the buildings only, in both the downhill and uphill views.

DRAWINGS 1 AND 2: Use separate sheets of paper horizontally—

one for a downhill view, the other for an uphill view—or do both views on one sheet (Fig. 2–84). First draw a road going downhill through a village. The road should twist and turn slightly and its gradient should change. Intersperse houses on each side of the road and add cars, people, and trees.

2–81. Breaking a road into sections as it turns. Plot and use different vanishing points.

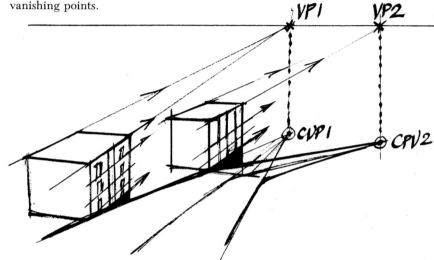

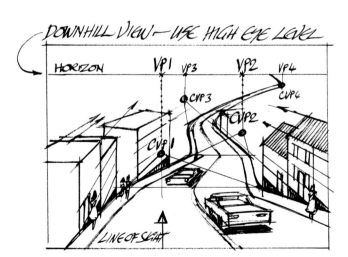

2–82. Downhill view of a street scene.

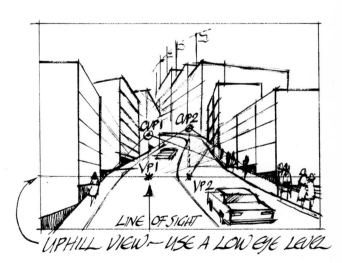

2–83. Uphill view of a street scene.

Draw flat or sloping roofs on some of the houses.

Now draw a road going uphill through a town. This road should also twist, turn, and change gradient. Draw office and apartment buildings on either side of the street, as well as people, cars, trees, and anything else you want.

Be sure to draw the door steps correctly in each view, and take care to draw the length of each house or building accurately.

DRAWINGS 3 AND 4: These drawings should be done as an advanced memory and visualization exercise with a three-hour limit. Using a sheet of paper for each view, draw an uphill and a downhill street scene from imagination. Start with a street going downhill through a small village. Let the road curve once or twice. Put a few houses on both sides and a small pond at the bottom where the street levels off. The street should be one lane wide, although it handles two-way traffic. Indicate a few cars, several people, and some trees planted near the curb. Use the information from the previous drawings but don't look at them. Draw and use a known constant unit of reference (such as a human figure) to proportion and scale all other drawn elements in the scene correctly.

For the uphill street scene, make the street four lanes wide and let it twist and turn at the top of the hill. As before, include people, cars, and other forms.

The objective is to make both of these drawings believable and realistic. Use accurate perspective, proportion, and relative scale. This exercise can be an illustration layout.

2–84. Finished drawing for Exercise 32 by Henry Van Der Linde. Black marker felt-tip pen. Uphill- and downhill-inclined planes are combined in this conceptual drawing.

Drawing the human body

You are now ready to begin an in-depth study of the human figure, which accounts for about 80 percent of most illustration work (except technical illustration). Here we are going to reverse the usual learning process and start with the most difficult aspects first: the head and the face. After examining the proportions of the head, we will discuss drawing the head in perspective and rotating it. We will then look at the proportions of the idealized adult figure, practice drawing hands and feet, and practice drawing the figure in perspective.

The place to begin is with the most familiar model—yourself. Before proceeding, however, study the information in Figure 2–85, which explains the fixed geometry of the head and face. Memorize this information so that you will be able to use it whenever you need it. Later you will draw the head in different perspective views, using this information in a very creative manner.

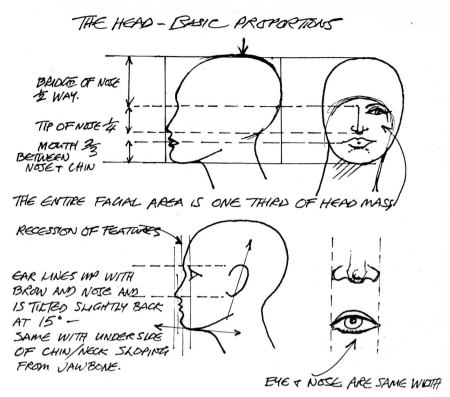

2–85. Geometry of the head and face.

Proportions of the human head

This exercise investigates the geometrical relationships found in the human head, both in proportions and in the placement of facial features. It also incorporates a study of the phi or golden-section proportion (see page 57).

STEP 1: After setting up the sheet horizontally, look into a mirror and draw an accurate front view of yourself, from the top of your head to just below your chest (Fig. 2–86). Pay careful at-

tention to correct placement and size of the eyes and to the relationship of iris to pupil. The drawing should occupy the full depth of the sheet, on either the left or the right side of the paper.

STEP 2: Using a T-square, draw parallel horizontal lines across the sheet and over the face so that they extend to the far side of the sheet. These lines will intersect the top of the head, all facial features, the chin, and the lower neck and chest.

STEP 3: Now, using the horizontal guidelines, draw your head in profile view, either left or right, depending on

which way you extended the lines from the front view. You will need a second small mirror in order to see yourself in the first mirror. Everything should fit into the guidelines. Take special note of the angles of your ear, jaw, and chin. It is also important to set the eye well back from the bridge of the nose.

STEP 4: This step examines the golden section in relation to the head—a constant proportion of 1 to .618, or approximately 60 percent of the original length. In Figures 2–86 and 2–87, thin lines have been drawn over the self-portrait and the front and profile views of the head. The divisions be-

tween these lines indicate the location of this phi golden section. Using a thick black marker and a T-square, draw in the vertical lines between the horizontal guidelines—first the longest line, and then the shortest one (see the right side of Fig. 2–86). On the profile drawing, use the T-square again to draw in thin vertical lines to establish the recession of features from the tip of the nose, eye, eyebrow, upper to lower lip, and so on to the back of the ear and head. Your head should roughly fit into a square.

Look at the sketch of da Vinci's skull in Figure 2–87. Notice how far the nose sticks out and how the eye is set back from the brow. This point is halfway between the top of the head and the chin. The mouth is positioned one-third to two-thirds of the way from the nose to the chin.

2–86. Finished drawing for Exercise 33 by Mark Hughes. Black marker felt-tip pen. Self-portrait using the phi golden section proportional ratio analysis.

2–87. Leonardo da Vinci's analysis of the phi golden section in a profile view of a head.

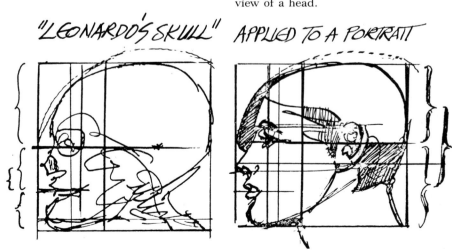

"LEONARDO'S SKULL"   APPLIED TO A PORTRAIT

Drawing the head in perspective

The nose can express a person's whole character and can represent other proportions. A thin, hooked nose, for example, may be found on a thin, tall, hawkish person who has a long skull. The nose is a good place to start in any case, because the closest vertical edge of the head is the centerline down the bridge of the nose. The trick to drawing the nose accurately is to use the centerline to help position the tip of the nose. The centerline also divides the facial features into two halves, in what is called *axial bilateral symmetry.*

If you draw a wedge-shaped plane under the nose, connecting with the centerline, you have just drawn the most difficult part of the face (Fig. 2–88). Look at the shapes at the bottom of Figure 2–89, and try to determine which way the head is turning. Now try to do a drawing yourself using this process, with the head turned and tilted at the same time. Take your time and slowly construct the drawing as suggested in Figure 2–88.

Learning to draw the nose is a good starting point, but in general you should always draw or construct the complete head first, roughly positioning the nose, mouth, and eyes. Figure 2–90 offers a guide to constructing the perspective with basic shapes first and then slowly adding details.

To draw the eyes correctly, think of them as two ping-pong balls set into sockets in the hollows of the skull; then wrap the eyelids over these balls (Fig. 2–91). If you look straight ahead in a mirror, you will see that the upper edge of the lower eyelid almost touches the bottom of the iris. The upper eyelid

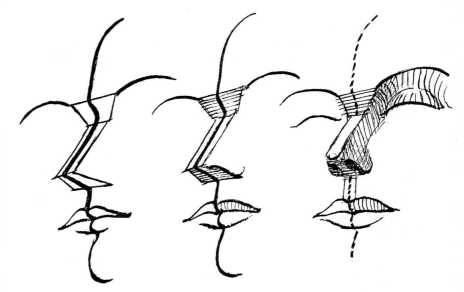

2–88. Positioning the nose and mouth using a central vertical axis line. The tip of the nose must be made three-dimensional and brought out of the drawing using tonal contrast.

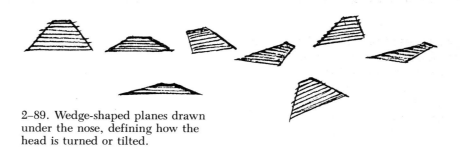

2–89. Wedge-shaped planes drawn under the nose, defining how the head is turned or tilted.

usually covers the top third of the iris. The pupil is not covered.

Because eyelids have thickness, they cast a shadow on the eyeball and iris. Now observe the shape of the eyelashes, which go around and behind the eyeball (Fig. 2–92). This is what makes the eye look three-dimensional.

For the mouth, keep in mind that the upper lip is usually smaller in size and depth than the lower lip (Fig. 2–93). In

addition, the lower lip is usually set back. Figure 2–94 shows how the relationship between the upper and lower lips changes as the head turns and tilts.

Be sure to represent the construction lines of the head correctly in perspective (Fig. 2–95). Most important, notice the spaces between the lines; they help you place and draw the facial features correctly.

2–90. Constructing the complete head using a vertical central axis line, wedge-shaped planes under the nose, and arranging the facial features in perspective.

DIRECTIONS: Practice drawing facial features by doing very slow, careful drawings of each part of the head. Find someone to pose for you; on a sheet of bond paper do twenty drawings of the person's eyes in different views. Then do twenty studies of the nose and twenty studies of the mouth. Friends and relatives want an accurate likeness, so their protests of dismay will force you to try harder and to draw more accurately. Continue doing studies until you can draw the head and face accurately from memory and from any view (Fig. 2–96).

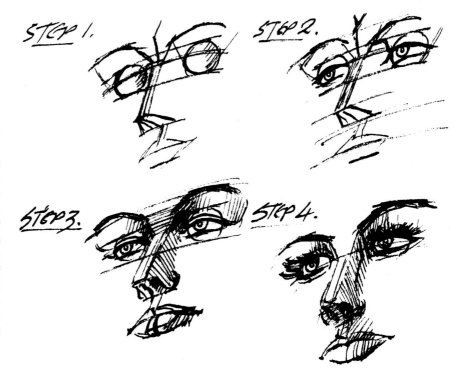

STEP 1. STEP 2.

STEP 3. STEP 4.

2–91. Drawing the human eye.

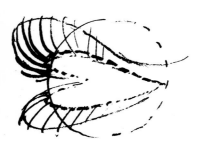

2–92. Position of eyelashes surrounding the human eye.

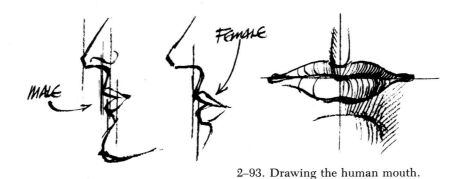

MALE FEMALE

2–93. Drawing the human mouth.

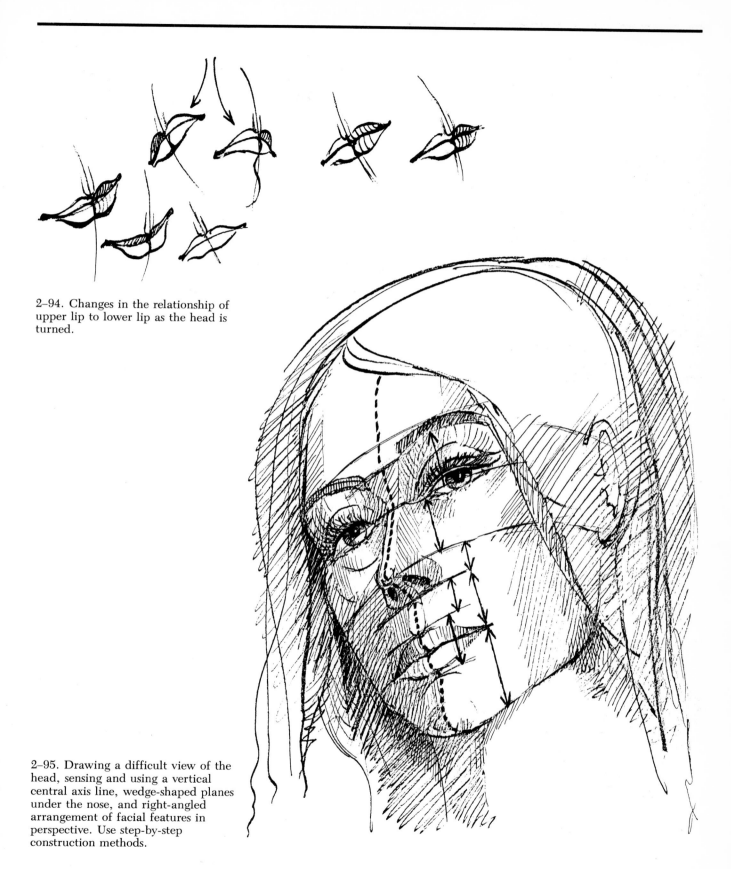

2-94. Changes in the relationship of upper lip to lower lip as the head is turned.

2-95. Drawing a difficult view of the head, sensing and using a vertical central axis line, wedge-shaped planes under the nose, and right-angled arrangement of facial features in perspective. Use step-by-step construction methods.

Rotating the head

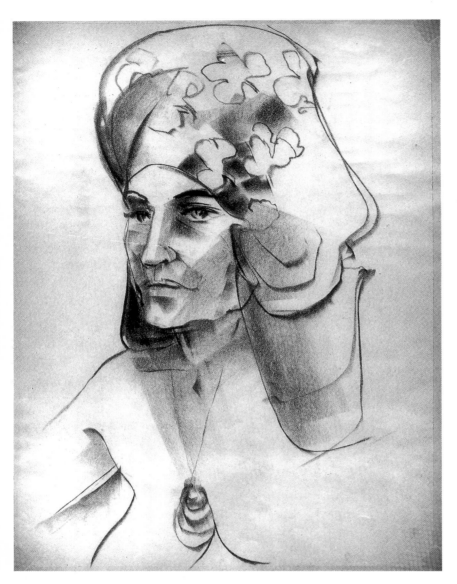

2–96. Finished drawing for Exercise 34.

DIRECTIONS: This memory drawing has a two-hour time limit. Use the sheet of paper horizontally. In the center, draw a front view of a large male or female head, about 14 inches (36 cm) high including the hair. Now draw left and right profile views of the same person to either side of the front view. These drawings should all touch each other.

Next, draw the intermediate three-quarters views, giving you five views in a row of the same head. Finally, draw heads above and below the front view. Make both heads tilt—one looking up, and the other looking down. The tilted head looking up should be drawn above the original front view, and the other should be drawn below it (Fig. 2–97).

2–97. Final drawing for Exercise 35 by Bernard Martin. Black marker felt-tip pen.

Body proportions

If you do not have an anatomy book, check your own bone and muscle structure. Feel your bones and joints, and study yourself in a full-length mirror. When you understand the body underneath, it becomes easier to draw clothed people. Knowledge of the inner anatomical structure will help you make sense of the folds and drape of the garments.

For the beginner, it is best to draw familiar people. Try drawing your relatives and friends; then try people in restaurants, bus stations, and so on. Keep in mind that photographs make subjects appear flat and two-dimensional. The objective in drawing is to make the subject look solid, with a feeling of weight and movement.

To simplify figure drawing, use the standard method for determining correct proportions. Essentially, body height is divided into eight segments (Figure 2–98). These are idealized adult proportions based on a common average. You will find that ordinary people exhibit many minor variations in body dimensions due to age, race, and so on. In the idealized 30-year-old figure, however, the head is one-eighth the height of the body, in both the male and the female. On average, the female's height is less than the male's.

When you draw the figure, be aware of certain gender characteristics. For example, in the male the shoulders are noticeably wider than the hips. Emphasize angularity, straight lines, strong relief, and muscle development. In the female the shoulders are approximately as wide as or slightly wider than the hips. Emphasize curved, flowing lines and minor relief. Also be aware of the relative sizes of body and head at different ages. Study a good anatomy book to further your knowledge of this subject.

Now let's examine the geometric proportions of the body. This approach to drawing the body is not new: the ancient Egyptians used geometry in their depictions of the human figure and in architecture. In any case, knowing the geometric proportions of the body will help improve your drawing skills.

A good place to start is da Vinci's *The Proportions of Man* (Fig. 2–99). This drawing has a purity of structure and an aesthetic sense that pleases the eye. But at the same time, questions arise about the drawing's purpose: Why is the figure inside a square and a circle? Why was the circle swung from the figure's navel? Why are lines drawn across the face, body, and arms? Note the spacing between the lines, particularly across the eyes to the neck and chest and from the hand to the forearm; perhaps these indicate research into the phi proportion or golden section.

The golden section was used in ancient Egypt, where it was called the "proportion of life." Later, the Greek sculptor Phidias used the golden section in relation to a circle swung from the navel to divide the body. In the sixteenth century, da Vinci rediscovered this proportion, as shown in the drawing just discussed. (The drawing also demonstrates the art of squaring the circle: the perimeters of both the square and the circle are equal. In many ancient cultures the square represented the earth with man at the center, while the circle represented the ever-moving universe.)

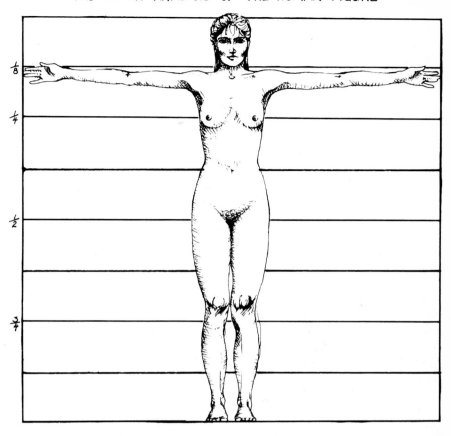

2–98. Dividing the body height into eight equal segments based on the size of the head, by Amanda Northfield. Black felt-tip pen.

2–99. Detail of *The Proportions of Man* (*Uomo Vitruviano*) by Leonardo da Vinci, drawn for geometer Luca Pacioli's book. Notice the lines drawn over the body which represent the phi golden section analysis. Reprinted by permission of the Galleria dell'Accademia, Venice.

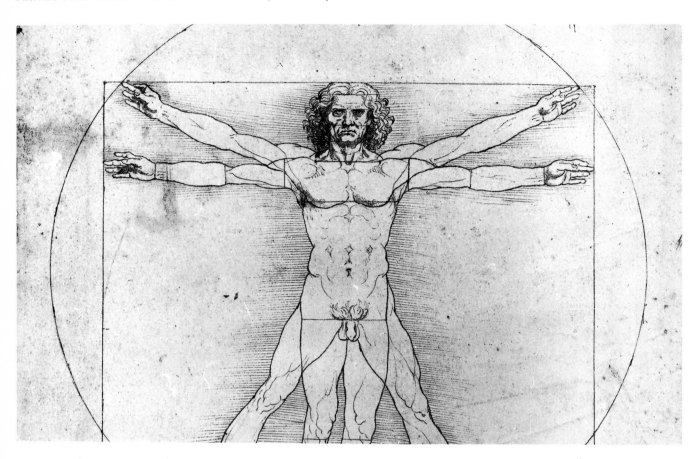

Ideal adult proportions

DIRECTIONS: Work directly from a model or use a photo reference to investigate the body's natural geometry in accordance with two different systems—the divisional and the golden section. Set up the paper horizontally.

STEP 1: On your sheet, arrange two large squares, but leave enough space for a grouping of five small geometric shapes—a circle, an equilateral triangle, a square, a pentagon, and a hexagon. Within each of these small shapes, draw a small nude figure that fits the shape. Refer to Figure 2–100 for ideas.

STEP 2: Now subdivide the first square horizontally into quarters, using a T-square. Draw the lines from edge to edge across the square. Then divide the top section in half to get one-eighth of the square. Centered in this square, draw a male or female nude with arms outstretched. This pose will fit the square, with the head one-eighth of the height. Make sure that the widths of the shoulders and hips are in correct proportion to the body's height. Re-

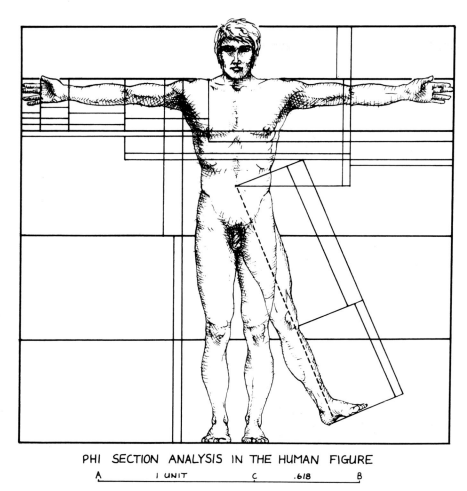

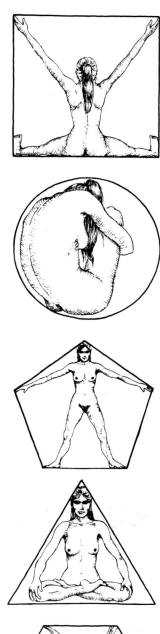

PHI SECTION ANALYSIS IN THE HUMAN FIGURE

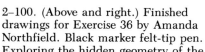

A   I UNIT   C   .618   B

2–100. (Above and right.) Finished drawings for Exercise 36 by Amanda Northfield. Black marker felt-tip pen. Exploring the hidden geometry of the human form.

member that the hip width is less than shoulder width in males and slightly greater than shoulder width in females.

STEP 3: In the second square, draw a figure, also centered, with arms outstretched and one leg raised. Then look at Figure 2–100, which shows how the human body can be subdi-vided into the phi proportions (as was done in the study on the head—Figure 2–86). Using a T-square, draw thin ver-tical, horizontal, and angled lines over your figure drawing, between the joints. The divisions between these lines indicate the phi golden section proportional ratios. Being aware of these constant proportions will help you produce more accurate drawings.

Drawing hands and feet

Hands and feet are almost as difficult to draw as the human head. Many beginners find them virtually impossible—as do many artists and illustrators, both past and present. You would be surprised at how often in realistic figure work the artist has hidden the hands and feet.

DIRECTIONS: Investigate the structure of your own hands and feet. Reduce them to basic shapes, and take careful note of the way the joints are positioned (Figs. 2–101 and 2–102).

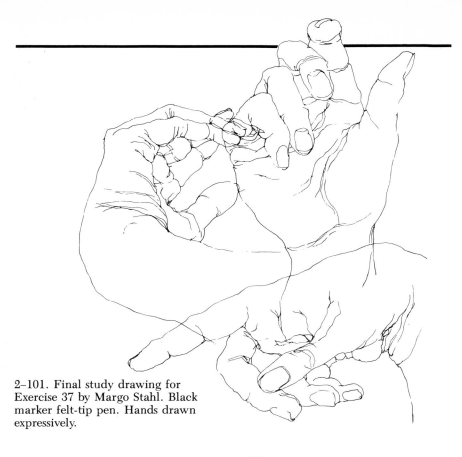

2–101. Final study drawing for Exercise 37 by Margo Stahl. Black marker felt-tip pen. Hands drawn expressively.

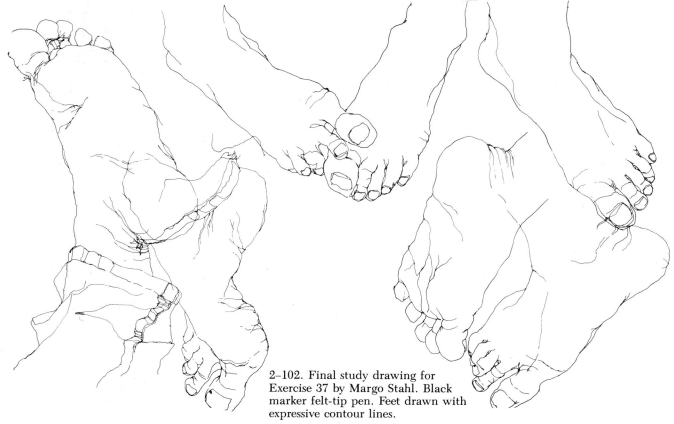

2–102. Final study drawing for Exercise 37 by Margo Stahl. Black marker felt-tip pen. Feet drawn with expressive contour lines.

The figure in perspective

Having investigated the body's proportions, we will now focus on the complete figure in perspective. To do this successfully, you must be able to understand and render action, movement, comparative proportions, and foreshortening.

Drawing the human figure is a definite process involving the following steps:

1. Choose the size and placement of the subject on the sheet.

2. Analyze and capture the action and movement of the pose.

3. Compare proportions, angles, shapes, and dimensions.

4. Search out the geometric proportions of the figure.

5. Decide which parts are closest to you. What advances and what recedes? Remember the drawings of the foreshortened pipes (Fig. 2–33)?

6. Determine how best to express the subject's mood and feeling through your choice of technique and medium.

Action and Counteraction The key to drawing the movement of the figure lies in understanding the movement or shifting of body weight, the subsequent curvature and movement of the spine, and the counteraction of the pelvis to the shoulders and rib cage. Try to capture the basic movement and weight direction of the figure through quick gesture drawings, without worrying about details. Look for the major swing of the spine and establish the angles of the hips and shoulders to it. Then complete the trunk, head, legs, arms, and so on, building and describing as you draw (Fig. 2–103).

Begin with back views, since they are the easiest. Then draw front views. The leg that takes the body's weight is straighter; the pelvis angles one way, and the shoulders angle the opposite way. This is called *counteraction*. Use charcoal pencil or Conté crayon for these drawings and work large.

Comparative Proportions It is a good idea to use an imaginary grid to establish accurate dimensions (Fig. 2–104). Consider height to width, angles and shapes, and the comparative sizes of the limbs. The main vertical line is especially important in establishing features, shapes, and sizes; calculate all dimensions and proportions in comparison to it.

For seated or standing poses, it is helpful to use an imaginary plumb line starting from the nose. Then you can calculate more easily how far a body part projects outward. For example, you might focus on the foot, decide how far it projects from the plumb line, and then begin to draw, starting at the ground and including the foot. As you draw, include any props such as the chair the model is sitting on. The props will thus become an integral part of the drawing and will not appear to have been added later. In addition, the props will help you situate the figure in space.

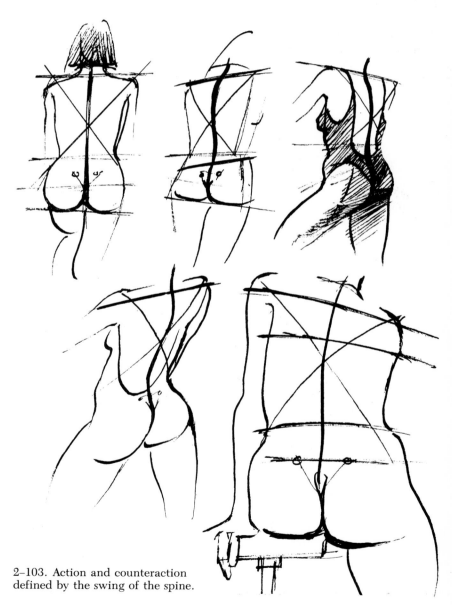

2–103. Action and counteraction defined by the swing of the spine.

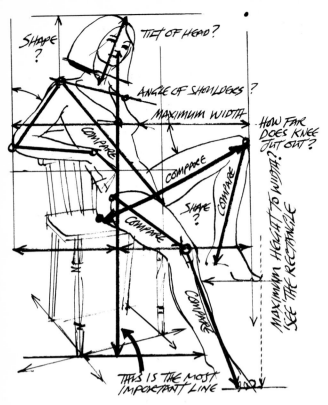

2–104. Establishing accurate dimensions through use of an imaginary grid.

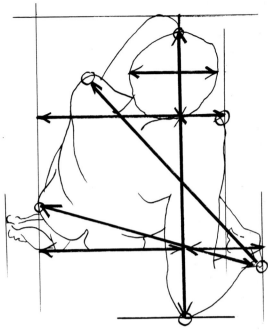

2–105. Use a prime vertical line to compare all other dimensions and shapes.

Foreshortening Foreshortening— the way in which a form appears to shorten as it recedes in space—is the most difficult aspect of figure drawing for the beginner. If you look carefully at a figure, you will see that the limbs taper; therefore, to create the effects of foreshortening, you must thicken limbs that advance and thin limbs that recede (Figs. 2–105 and 2–106). Often beginners make the legs too thin. Remember that the legs support the entire body; you should draw them in a way that shows this.

Keep in mind, too, that you are trying to capture the essence of a living form through your line quality and tones. Learn to draw in a vigorous, lively manner. Vary the weight of your line to describe muscles and limbs, and indicate the parts of the body that are in shadow briskly but accurately. This will create the feeling of solidity that is so important in figure drawing.

To practice foreshortening, begin with seated poses and move on to kneeling and semireclining poses; finally, draw some fully reclining poses. Work in an outline or contour drawing style, defining only the outer edges of the model (Fig. 2–107). Suggest three-dimensionality by varying the thickness of the line. Indicate the body's surface planes with broad strokes of charcoal or Conté crayon.

Inner Contour Drawing An excellent way to learn to draw the figure is to create a series of continuous contour lines, following the volume of the bones and muscles. This method makes you pay attention to the changing diameters of different parts of the body, encouraging you to exaggerate certain areas by diminishing or increasing the volume. Because folds and creases in clothing describe the position or action of the form beneath them you should use

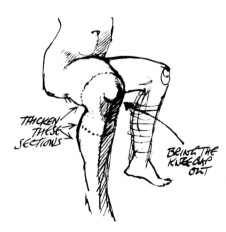

2–106. To accommodate foreshortened limbs, thicken those that jut out and drastically thin those that recede.

them to accentuate the desired parts of the figure (Fig. 2–108).

Planar Drawing Another way to make figure drawing easier to understand is called *planar drawing*. It consists of seeing and representing the surface planes contained within the figure (Fig. 2–109). Concentrating on these changing surface shapes and their corresponding angles will help you give your drawn figures solidity. You can accentuate these planes with various types of hatching or with tonal grays. Understanding the planes will strengthen not only your figure drawing, but also your illustration of any three-dimensional form or subject.

Light and Shadow Many beginners have difficulty representing the light source, often including too many different light sources. To avoid confusion, establish one light source only—either the sun or one artificial light. A single strong light source situated above and to the side of the subject works best to begin with.

Light and shadow can help make your drawing look solid. The first step here is to simplify your subject into basic values: light, middle, and dark. Usually the darkest tone will be opposite the lightest side. As lighting increases or decreases, slide your three values up or down the gray scale. If you wish to use *high contrast*, increase the separation between light and dark (Fig. 2–110).

In addition to representing the main light, you need to look for reflected light—light that is bounced back onto the subject by a surrounding surface or the surface of another object. Reflected light introduces a lighter tone into the shaded side, making it appear even more solid (Fig. 2–111).

Look for cast shadows, too. These are projected onto a surface plane by an object blocking the light source. Be careful not to make the cast shadow more important than either the object itself or the surface it is on. Cast shadows are very important because they anchor the object to the ground plane surface.

Surface Textures Surface textures can make a drawing more interesting and three-dimensional. They can also help describe form and clarify the substance an object is

2–107. Incorporating foreshortening in a contour drawing style. Foreshortening requires knowledge of perspective, structure and form. Begin with the simplest poses before trying more difficult ones.

2–108. Inner contour drawing by Gary Alphonso. Black marker felt-tip pen. A difficult figure pose, with all limbs and body foreshortened.

2–109. Planar drawing by Mark
Hughes. Charcoal. The primary and
secondary surface planes within the
body must be memorized and used
when drawing and painting the
human figure.

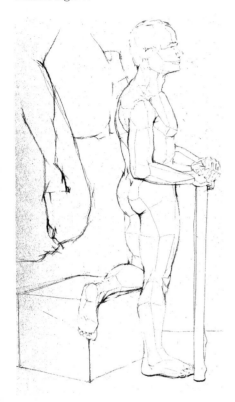

2–111. Drawing defining surface
planes by Mark Hughes. Charcoal
pencil and stick. Light and shade
suggest reflected light.

2–110. Conté stick drawing
emphasizing the planar quality of the
subject. High contrast of light and
dark values (notan) makes a drawing
strong.

made of. Experiment with different surface textures in your drawings (Figs. 2–112 and 2–113).

Purposeful Distortion Now that you have studied the accurate proportions of the human body, try doing some distorted drawings. When used well, distortion adds tremendous excitement and impact to an image. When used badly, it can look amateurish and weaken the drawing. Know your form's correct proportions first; only then create new proportions.

Distortion can be entirely appropriate to an illustration assignment. In fashion illustration, for example, it is quite normal to elongate the figure to accentuate the flow of the garment. In this type of illustration, the size of the head may fit into the length of the body nine to fourteen times, depending on the desired image (Fig. 2–114).

Humorous or whimsical illustrations often distort the form vertically or horizontally (Fig. 2–115). Political cartoons may use distortion to magnify the head in relationship to the body. In animation, the overall scale of objects and figures is often distorted, especially in depictions of fantasy animals.

2–113. Using surface textures.

2–112. Using surface textures, such as cloth, to contrast with the smoothness of the model's skin.

2–114. Elongation adds elegance to a figure drawing by Robin Honey-Morris. India ink, pen, and brush. This technique is especially appropriate for fashion illustration.

2–115. Intentional distortion of form for humorous effect by David Milne. India ink and pen. A strong knowledge of anatomy underlies this type of work.

exercise 38

Draw, draw, draw

Because drawing is of primary importance you should practice it constantly. Practice is necessary to developing and maintaining a high level of proficiency. Eventually you should be able to draw any subject quickly and accurately. Strong drawing is especially important in advertising illustration. (A bad drawing looks much worse when rendered in markers.)

You must also develop the ability to select which subjects (and which parts of them) to draw. Often what you decide to exclude is more important than what you decide to include. It takes some time to appreciate this and to learn to simplify when drawing.

DIRECTIONS: Draw from life, using pencil, Conté crayon, charcoal, black felt-tip pens, or black ink. Choose your medium based on the subject matter you are drawing. If you use a pencil, don't use an eraser.

Do your drawings on separate sheets of paper or in a sketchbook. Vary the time limit for each drawing. Intermix quick gesture, contour, and planar drawings with full tonal renderings of long poses. Include reportage or on-the-spot drawings of objects, figures, and animals done in different locations. First analyze your subject, and then draw it briskly but accurately (Figs. 2–116 through 2–119).

2–116. Reportage figure drawing in contour outline for Exercise 38 by Margo Stahl. Black marker felt-tip pen.

2–117. Contour figure studies for Exercise 38 by Margo Stahl. Black marker felt-tip pen.

2–118. On-the-spot figure drawing for Exercise 38 by Adriana Taddeo. India ink and pen.

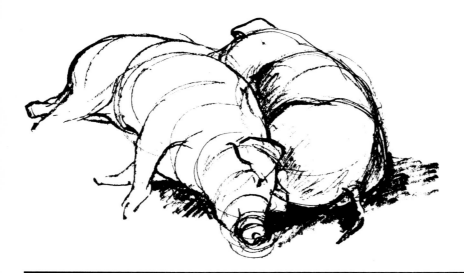

2–119. On-the-spot animal drawing for Exercise 38 by Adriana Taddeo.

Mistakes to Avoid and Keys to Success

In addition to the errors mentioned at the beginning of this chapter, here are some mistakes to avoid:

- Drawing without regard to the horizon line or the eye level

- Not using—or sensing, at least—the vanishing points on the eye level

- Drawing the surfaces of objects and planes to the eye level rather than from the vanishing points on the eye level

- Not using observation and common sense in constructing a drawing

- Weak planning in the preliminary stages of drawing

- Negating the form, function, and structure of inanimate objects and organic forms

- Disregarding the perspective, proportion, and scale of the subject

- Untidy and sloppy work habits—dirt marks, fingerprints, creases in the paper, and buckled, bent, or torn corners

- Timid drawing with too fine a pen or too hard a pencil

- Drawing a three-dimensional subject while using two-dimensional thinking processes

- Copying poorly drawn cartoons and comic books

Conversely, here are some guidelines for success:

- Indicating where the eye level is before starting any drawing, and drawing the subject in relation to it

- Searching out the perspective, and working out where the vanishing points are in relation to the eye level

- Analyzing the structure of the subject, and sensing it as you draw

- Being inquisitive when analyzing a subject, and considering its form, function, comparative proportions, and scale

- Seeing the big shapes first and the minor details last

- Bringing your subject to life through the empathy you feel for it and the expressive manner in which you draw it

- Being sensitive, but not timid, in your drawing. Making definite and meaningful marks on the paper, even when the subject is only lightly indicated

Marker
Rendering

the marker is the most widely used layout medium in the world. It is suitable for idea sketches, roughs, layouts, TV storyboards for commercials, and certain types of finished work such as fashion and architectural renderings. It is the preferred medium of illustrators who work for advertising agencies, art studios, and publishing houses. It is also the standard layout medium of design studios, printing houses, and the art departments of manufacturing and retail businesses. The best, most accomplished marker renderers are in great demand.

Before the early 1960s, the traditional media of the illustrator were still extensively used: graphite pencils, India ink, charcoal, and Conté crayons for black-and-white layouts; and tempera, watercolor, and soft pastels for color layouts. Although effective, these media required time to set and were somewhat difficult to manipulate.

Chemical advances led to the development of the marker pen, which enables artists to produce cleaner, less time-consuming, and thus less costly visuals. Markers have transformed the entire visualizing proc-

ess. In the hands of competent professionals they can produce effects from photographic realism to forceful expressionism. Marker renderings have even been used as finished art. Today marker layouts are the most effective and economical form of visualizing in the rough and rough-comp stages of illustration and design.

Computer graphics have not eliminated the need for marker renderings. Instead, graphic designers use computer graphics in conjunction with illustration. Basically, linear illustrations can be scanned into and manipulated on the computer; however, more elaborate images must still be marker-rendered by illustrators.

Using markers effectively requires sound drawing skills, a sense of design, and a knowledge of color and painting. The strengths of this medium are its freshness, spontaneity, and directness of application. The aims are to capture strong light and shade, evoke an overall mood, and identify form and objects with simplified tones.

The type of dexterity needed is comparable to that involved in Chinese or Japanese brush painting or

Drawing by Gary Alphonso. Gray
wedge-tip markers and black felt-tip
pen.

in Arabic calligraphy. Applying markers has many similarities to applying watercolors—for example, leaving white space where needed and building tonal strength and intensity slowly from light to dark. Another important similarity is the user's ability to overpaint colors, creating subtle nuances. Remember, however, that solvent-based or oil-based markers cannot be removed. In learning how to use markers, it is a good idea to work in black and white first, and then to add grays, before going on to full-color rendering.

Equipment and Materials

Markers

Many brands of markers are currently on the market. The container itself can vary from a thin pen to a stubby canister, and the tip can vary from a fine point to a wide wedge. Illustrators tend to use the latter to cover large areas and reserve fine-point marker pens—either black or brown—for line drawing.

Many companies produce boxed sets of markers, but these are usually impractical and expensive. Sets of primary or secondary colors are generally too intense in hue for illustrators; they are more suitable for designers of posters or packaging. Still other boxed assortments—those in earth, wood, and metal colors—are more useful for architects or environmental designers. Moreover, many colors in packaged sets may never be used. Illustrators usually prefer to select colors individually, creating a palette suitable to their own specialty and color sense.

When buying markers, make sure that the color inside the container matches the color swatch on the printed label or lid. Nothing is more frustrating than to return to the studio and discover that the inside colors are different (usually stronger). Once you have established that the color on the outside matches that on the inside, you can avoid having to test the marker each time before using it. Another reason for testing markers at the art-supply store is that a marker that has been sitting on the shelf for a long time may be dry.

The following colors are the ones most suitable for general layout rendering, including interior, exterior, natural, and man-made subjects:

Black

No. 2 Cool Gray

No. 3 Cool Gray

No. 4 Cool Gray

No. 5 Cool Gray

No. 6 Cool Gray

No. 7 Cool Gray

No. 8 Cool Gray

Light Suntan

Dark Suntan

Beige

Sand

Pale Sepia

Burnt Umber

Clay

Dark Brown

Pale Yellow

Cadmium Yellow

Cadmium Red

Pink

Shock Pink

Pale Mauve

Lavender

Violet

Process Blue

Pale Blue

Cobalt Blue

Teal Blue

Prussian Blue

Forest Green

Olive Green

Pale Olive Green

Yellow Green

Mustard

Aqua

Putty

Some solvent-based markers that show signs of drying up can be rejuvenated if you cut the plastic wrapper, unscrew the top, add a few drops of rubber-cement thinner, reseal it, and then stand the marker upside down for a while. This procedure can almost double the life of the marker—a significant result in these times of soaring costs. The fumes of solvent-based markers can be bothersome, however, so you may prefer to use odorless water-soluble markers.

Caution: Certain solvent-based markers are highly toxic and can be hazardous to your health if used incorrectly. Always work in a well-ventilated space. Do not bend over your renderings for any extended period of time, especially when working in a small, closed room. You will get headaches and may develop nausea.

If you find you are particularly sensitive to solvent-based marker fumes, replace them with water-based markers. You may find that your marker strokes do not blend as well, but the result is perfectly acceptable for layouts. Always keep your marker tops on tightly when the markers are not being used.

Marker stand

To avoid confusion while working, you can make an inexpensive marker stand. All you need is a piece of wood about 18 inches long, 8 inches wide, and 1½ inches thick (47 × 24 × 4 cm). Pencil in three

3–1. Marker stand.

rows of markers; then, using a 1¼-inch (3.2 cm) wood drill, bore holes through the block of wood (Fig. 3–1).

Felt-tip pens

Illustrators seem to prefer hard felt-tip pens to nylon-tip pens. The former come in different widths and with different points, allowing the user to produce different kinds of marks. A fine marker pen can give you a thick to thin line, depending on the angle at which the pen is tilted. If the pen is water-soluble, the lines can be softened with water, creating an exciting line and tone combination.

Most illustrators also purchase pens in two other widths: one, much finer; another, thicker. A felt pen with a chisel point is not only ideal for calligraphy and serif-type indications, but is extremely expressive for line illustration.

A new type of marker pen has a brush-shaped tip and is very flexible and versatile—a big step beyond the chisel-point pen. It can produce lines of the same calligraphic qual-ity but allows much more freedom, since it is closer to a brush. However, it is not as good as a wedge-tip canister marker for laying in large flat areas. It should be used in the same manner as a brush for appropriate rendering techniques.

Drawing table

Illustrators generally use drawing tables that have adjustable tops (see Chapter 11). Two methods of working at the table are suitable. In one method the drawing table is angled at 45 degrees, and you sit on a regular chair, with the markers beside you on a separate low table. Alternatively, if the table has an attached retaining edge, it can be angled 10 degrees off horizontal with the markers arranged to one side of the layout pad or paper. Sitting on a high stool or standing is suggested for this work method.

Layout paper

Whether you are using tracing paper or heavyweight bond, the paper should be fairly transparent, so you can slip the layout under another sheet to polish the drawing. Vellum tracing paper and visualizing layout paper—lightweight and extremely transparent, sometimes with a polished surface—tend to appear grayed owing to their thinness. These papers may buckle in humidity or if stored incorrectly. In addition, certain brands cause marker streaking, so be sure to test.

Bond layout paper is thicker, more opaque, and whiter at the surface. Smooth or semirag paper tends to absorb markers, which dry flat without too much loss in intensity of hue. Generally, bond layout paper of medium weight is preferred.

Depending on the size of the intended illustration, the pad should allow for 3 inches (8 cm) around the illustration area. If you constantly work on small jobs, use 11- × 17-inch (28 × 43 cm) paper. For full-page news ads and most other general types of work, 19- × 24-inch paper is suitable. Larger sizes are rarely required and are uneconomical. Two sheets can always be taped together on the back with transparent tape. Experience will guide you in choosing the most practical pad size.

Developing dexterity with markers

The best way to learn how to use various markers effectively is to experiment, trying out different kinds of line. Only if you know the full range of what your materials can do will you be able to select the most appropriate line for a particular assignment. With practice, you will also develop dexterity and speed—essentials in advertising and other kinds of illustration.

DIRECTIONS: Place a layout pad on your drawing board, turn back the cover (making sure it is clear of the edge), remove the wax-paper sheet from the front or back of the pad, and place it underneath the top sheet. Many people discard the waxed sheet without realizing what its function is. This protective sheet stops markers from bleeding through the next two or three sheets. If a pad does not include a waxed sheet, use a large sheet of tracing paper for the same purpose.

Now practice different strokes, from broad sweeps to light ticks (Fig. 3–2). Draw lines of varying lengths and thicknesses without moving the pad to different positions. Depict different objects, always establishing the correct proportions and perspective. Try fitting short headings, sentences, or even your own name into spaces of fixed length. This will help you develop an eye for proportion.

Next look at Figure 3–3, which is drawn with a "swish and blob" line. Each stroke starts with the felt-tip pen on the paper (blob), moves quickly across the surface (swish), and ends with a pause (blob). This line quality gives slickness and immediacy to the drawing. You must, however, do all the drawing in your head before you make

3–2. Practice line drawing and marker strokes.

3–3. A chisel-point felt-tip has an expressive line quality.

3–4. A hard-tip marker pen drawing. Notice the uniform weight.

your marks. Explore this style of depiction with a subject of your choosing.

Now try working with a hard-tip marker pen, which produces an even, mechanical-looking line (Fig. 3–4). This type of line may lack character, but it is suitable for certain kinds of finished renderings such as technical drawings, blueprints, and ruled-in text body copy on layouts.

Finally, explore the brush-tip marker, which can be handled like a brush. Its flowing thick and thin lines can be very expressive (Fig. 3–5).

3–5. A brush-tip marker has an extremely expressive line quality.

Basic Rendering Techniques

The advertising profession demands realistic, fresh-looking marker layouts for presentations to clients. Layout artists must master drawing with black felt-tip pens and wedge-tip markers in order to achieve high-quality gray tonal or full-color renderings.

A novice at marker rendering may find the permanent nature of the medium intimidating. But a sense of confidence can be gained only through repeated practice.

The following exercises are designed to help you develop the skills you must have if you are to produce effective layouts.

Always use only one pen to create the exact weight of line needed to describe the object you are drawing.

This saves time and helps you avoid imparting an overworked look to the rendering. Wedge-tip markers are similar in stroke thickness to chisel-point brushes used in paint application. The width of these markers enables you to fill in flat areas of tone and color, as well as to define shapes and modeled form. As a general rule, it is acceptable for marker strokes to show when they are used to render a quick layout. Comprehensive layouts require the use of blended strokes, which yield a more polished and realistic result.

To familiarize yourself with the various marker techniques, try rendering scenes from landscape calendars—first in tones of gray, and then in full color. Simplify elements such as buildings, boats, and trees. Don't outline everything with the fine felt-tip pen, or the rendering will lose its three-dimensional quality.

exercise 2

Using a T-square

DIRECTIONS: Fold back the cover of the layout pad, pulling it slightly to one side. This allows the T-square to slide freely up and down the edge of the pad. If the cover gets in the way, the T-square may skip.

Using a felt-tip pen and T-square, practice drawing horizontal and vertical lines, without taking your pen hand off the paper. To do this, hold one hand gently but firmly at the end of the T-square so that it can move freely up and down the pad and yet stop at any point. Your fingers act as a brake. Your other hand (the pen hand) should rest on the moving T-square, with the point of the pen touching the paper so that you can freely draw lines up, down, and across the surface. Practice drawing combined verticals and horizontals *in one continuous motion,* pausing momentarily when changing direction.

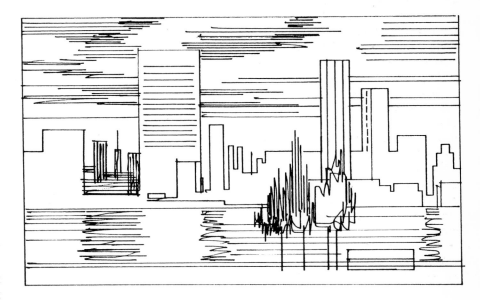

Choose some interesting subject matter, and enjoy manipulating the equipment and media (Fig. 3–6). Use different types of felt-tip pens to give you fine and thick weights.

3–6. Finished drawing for Exercise 2. T-square and felt-tip pen.

Experimenting with basic shapes

There are two methods of drawing squares and rectangles with a T-square and felt-tip pen. One method requires an intuitive sense of accurate proportions, as you draw in a continuous motion (Fig. 3–7). The other method allows for more planning and often greater accuracy. First you draw the two verticals; then you join these with corresponding horizontals (Fig. 3–8). Practice drawing different rectangles and squares. The 2 × 1 rectangle is most appropriate for man-made forms, as you will discover.

To introduce perspective, use a triangle in addition to the T-square. To give your drawing even greater impact, anchor the objects to the ground by means of cast shadows, again using a T-square (Fig. 3–9). When shading, always draw the pen strokes in one direction to keep the drawing from looking busy. Overusing texture confuses the visual effect and negates the clean crispness desired.

After you have mastered squares and rectangles, go on to ellipses and cylinders. Figure 3–10 shows how to draw an ellipse freehand in only four strokes. Use the T-square to indicate the parallel vertical sides of a cylinder. Notice that the lower ellipses of the cylinders are deeper and fuller-looking than the upper ones. This is because they are farther below the eye level (Fig. 3–11).

It is important to practice all these shapes to improve your accuracy — especially because felt-tip pen lines cannot be erased. Try putting the shapes together in a still-life composition. Include a cube, a prism, a cylinder, a cone and a sphere. For now, indicate them in contour or outline only.

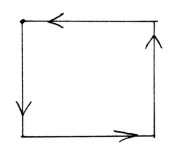

3–7. Continuous-motion method of drawing with T-square and felt-tip pen.

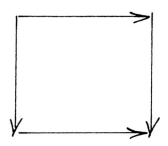

3–8. Vertical-and-horizontal line method of drawing with T-square and felt-tip pen.

3–9. Using a T-square to draw cast shadows.

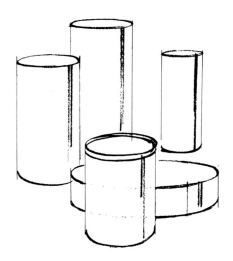

3–10. Four-stroke method of drawing ellipses freehand.

3–11. Cylinders drawn with T-square (sides) and ellipses drawn using the four-stroke method.

Covering an area

When adding color or tone to an area, beginners often use short, scratchy strokes, allowing hundreds of little white flecks of paper to show through (Fig. 3–12). These white flecks become more important than the color itself and give the rendering a fragmented look. To avoid this effect, use long parallel strokes to cover an entire area (Fig. 3–13).

Three methods can be used to render large areas and backgrounds:

1. You can scrub in with multidirectional strokes (Fig. 3–14). This gives the rendering a flat two-dimensional look.

2. You can use a T-square to make overlapping vertical strokes (Fig. 3–15). This method is very fast and gives the composition a fresh and spontaneous look. You must remember, however, to wipe the T-square edge clean.

3. A variation of the second method is to apply overlapping horizontal strokes.

You can also combine all three methods to a limited degree, but be careful: using many different directional strokes creates confusion.

3–12. Wrong way to add color or tone to an area.

3–13. Right way to add color or tone to an area.

When rendering large backgrounds, you can either render just to the edges (Fig. 3–16) or go beyond the edges and cut out your work afterwards (Fig. 3–17).

Practice until you can do methods 2 and 3 freehand in small areas, but

continue to use a T-square for large areas. A wooden T-square works best. It slides more freely over the pad because of its weight, and its thickness makes drawing with wedge-tip markers much easier. If you plan to use a T-square with a

3–14. Scrubbing-in large areas with multidirectional strokes.

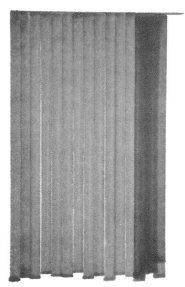

3–15. Using a T-square to make overlapping vertical or horizontal strokes.

plastic edge, you must be careful to wipe the edges; otherwise, ink stays on the surface and can transfer to the next marker, ruining both it and the rendering. Alternatively, you can use a strip of very thick illustration board, which absorbs the colors at its edge (so you don't have to keep cleaning your T-square). Take special care with edges (see Figs. 3–18 and 3–19).

It is a good idea to have on hand two of everything—T-squares, triangles, and illustration-board strips. For rapid work, use one set of equipment strictly for black markers, so you don't have to waste time cleaning it.

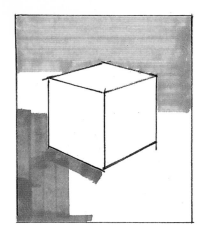

3–16. Rendering backgrounds to the edges of the drawing area.

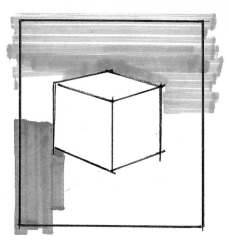

3–17. Rendering backgrounds beyond the edges of the drawing area and then cutting the area out.

3–18. Wrong way to render using wedge-tip markers. Working too slowly causes markers to bleed.

3–19. Right way to use markers to fill in surfaces.

Shading three-dimensional forms

Study the examples in Figure 3–20 to get a sense of how markers are used to render light and shadow, adding to the three-dimensionality of the form. Experiment with your own forms. Use light, medium, and dark gray markers to suggest surface planes. Blending marker tones together creates the finished look required in a comprehensive layout.

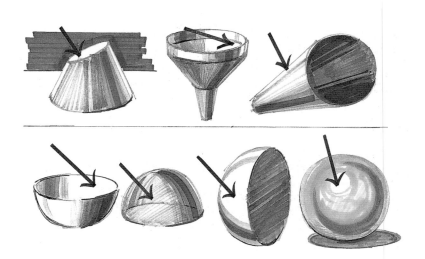

3–20. Using markers to render light and shade.

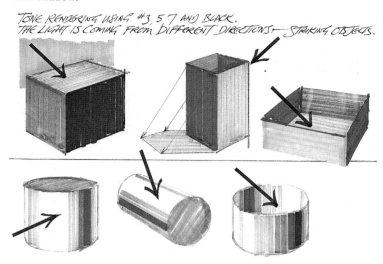

TONE RENDERING USING #3, 5, 7 AND BLACK.
THE LIGHT IS COMING FROM DIFFERENT DIRECTIONS — STRIKING OBJECTS.

Simplifying light and shade

This exercise proves how little rendering is necessary to achieve an excellent likeness and solidity with light and shade.

DIRECTIONS: Use a sheet or two of black paper and a stick or two of square-shaped, hard white pastel. Break the pastel into different lengths—for example 1 inch and ½ inch (2.5 and 1.3 cm). Then follow the example in Figure 3–21, using deft strokes. Work directly; don't rework repeatedly.

To see how effective this technique can be, look at the positive photostat in Figure 3–22. The background is now white, like the paper you will be working on later, and the white pastel has become tones of gray and black.

Do you see how this relates to markers? All you have to do is remember to render the positive forms just as easily. Simplify: that is the key to marker rendering!

3–21. Finished drawing for Exercise 6. Wedge-tip markers should be used in a bold and direct manner.

3–22. Positive photostat of finished drawing for Exercise 6.

Additional Tips on Rendering

So far we have concentrated on capturing the subject's essence in minimal black line work, drawing in quick, direct, deft strokes that describe the proportions and action. We have also worked with different gray tones to create solid forms, although we did not model with grays. Compare Figures 3–23 and 3–24 to see the differences between line and tone rendering.

Now let's try modeling the form with graduated values. Using one marker, you can build up the density of tones by layering the strokes (Fig. 3–25). Practice this technique with different geometric forms, and then render a landscape or similar subject. Vary the speed with which you use the marker itself, using fast strokes for light tones and slow strokes for dark tones.

Remember that dark shapes, heavy lines, and strong textures advance on a white background. Since most illustration work involves daylight situations, rendering is most often done on white paper. For night scenes, dark paper is used.

3–23. Line rendering with markers.

exercise 7

Applying tone

Here are some other techniques worth knowing:

1. Use a paper mask to get crisp edges (Fig. 3–26).

2. Employ partially dried-out markers for textural effects (Fig. 3–27).

3. Create unusual textures by placing paper on rough surfaces (Fig. 3–28).

4. Get lighter tones by working on the reverse side of the sheet (Fig. 3–29).

3–27. Using semi-dried-out markers for textural effects.

3–28. Placing paper on a rough surface for unusual textures.

3–26. Using a paper mask for crisp edges.

3–29. Using the reverse side of the sheet for lighter tones.

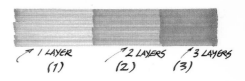

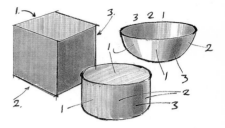

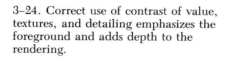

3–24. Correct use of contrast of value, textures, and detailing emphasizes the foreground and adds depth to the rendering.

3–25. Layering marker strokes to build up tone density.

DIRECTIONS: Do a preliminary line drawing of a still-life composition with basic geometric shapes, similar to the one in Figure 3–30. Tear the sketch off the pad, and slip it under the top sheet. On the new sheet, draw in the lines around the objects freehand, with the triangle, and with the T-square. Add tone (with gray markers) to the background, using a T-square, to separate the objects from the background. Tones should be suggested by the application of single, parallel strokes. Layering or blending marker strokes creates a more realistic and modeled form.

Next add minimal strokes of gray to the objects—the cube first, then the prism, then the cone, and finally the spheres. Use a T-square for the cube and a triangle for the cone. Add the shadows or reflections of the objects to the foreground.

3–30. Preliminary drawing for Exercise 7 using T-square. Simple line work and tonal strokes on geometric forms.

Kitchen scene

Set up a kitchen scene with pots, pans, tableware, and so on. These objects have the same basic shapes as the ones rendered in the previous exercise. They involve a few more details perhaps, but nothing too difficult.

DIRECTIONS: Draw the still life with a black felt-tip pen. Work quickly and loosely, but make sure the perspective is accurate.

Tear this sketch from the pad and slip it under the next sheet. Follow the same steps as in the previous exercise to render the scene, but add more detail to the composition (Fig. 3–31). For example, put in lines indicating the handles of pots and pans, using a black felt-tip pen or a black wedge-tip marker. Add gray tones simply, as before. Take care that the tones follow the form. Indicate shadows and reflections if you wish.

Rendering figures

At first figures may seem difficult to render. The secret is to simplify both the lines and the tones.

Think of the body as being composed of basic shapes (Fig. 3–32). Locate the eye level, and determine the main action of the figure. In particular, look for the counteraction of the shoulders and the hips. Pay close attention to creases and folds in clothing, since these provide clues about the underlying form and action (Fig. 3–33).

In most cases you will not be using a live model, so you will need a reference to work from. Professionals often create figures without a reference, but this takes experience. For this exercise you should use either posed photos of friends or photos from magazines (called *swipes*). If you choose a magazine photo, however, use it for the basic pose only, changing all other details. If not, you will be plagiarizing, which is both illegal and uncreative.

3–31. Finished drawing for Exercise 8 using T-square, felt-tip pen, and triangle to make overlapping and layered strokes.

3–32. Drawing the human figure as a combination of simple geometric forms.

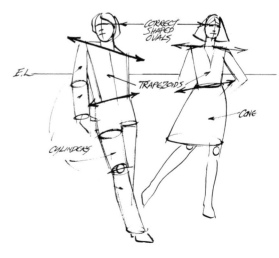

3–33. The underlying forms, pose, and perspective of the figure are indicated by creases and folds in the clothing.

DIRECTIONS: From photo references, draw four to six figures on a sheet in black felt-tip pen. This is just a preliminary worksheet, so you should redraw lines and correct errors in proportion, action, and structure. Make sure, for example, that the perspective of the face is correct for the position of the head. Do two or three sheets of these studies.

Tear the sketch off, and slip it under the next sheet. Now simplify. Break the figures down into a series of minimal black lines. Draw in eyebrows, eyes, nose, and mouth. Add different line qualities to the outside edges of the garments. Don't forget to insert a wax sheet or sheet of tracing paper to prevent the markers from bleeding through the paper.

Select some figures to leave white, and add a gray background to define them. Add tone to the shadow side of the face, body, and clothing.

With other figures, add pale tones for the flesh, leaving the background white. Add grays and blacks to their clothing and darker tones to the shadows.

Finally, add more darks for contrast, further definition, and excitement (Fig. 3–34).

3–34. Finished drawing for Exercise 9 by Gary Alphonso. Wedge-tip markers and felt-tip pen. Simplified light and shade renderings of figures using black and three gray tones. Note the use of the white of the paper.

Focusing on heads and faces

3–35. Final rendering for Exercise 10 by Gary Alphonso. Wedge-tip markers and felt-tip pen. Heads and faces are drawn with a black felt-tip pen and three tones are added to describe the form and structure in a simplified way.

The key to this exercise lies in putting black pen marks in exactly the right places to define the head and then adding gray marker tones to establish the basic shadows (Fig. 3–35). It may help you to think of the head as being similar in shape to a paint can (Fig. 3–36). From this basic cylindrical shape, you can visualize the main facial construction lines. When you are ready to add the hair, remember that it, too, is a basic geometric shape. The hairstyle used can date a person (Fig. 3–37), so look in magazines and newspapers for the latest trends.

3–36. Paint-can method of defining and drawing the human head.

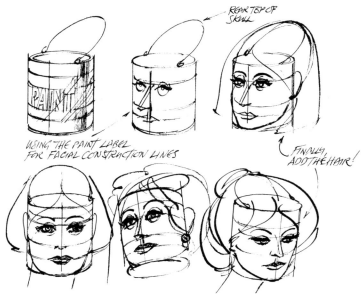

REAR TOP OF SKULL

USING THE PAINT LABEL FOR FACIAL CONSTRUCTION LINES

FINALLY, ADD THE HAIR!

Placing figures in settings

Most often, you will be asked to render figures in a setting. Even the most complex scene is built up from simple geometric shapes. If you can identify these basic shapes first, the rest will fall into place. Another ingredient for success is practice. The five scenes you will draw in this exercise—a beach, a mountain campsite, a farm, a streetside café, and a family outing by a lake—will help you apply and practice all the skills you have acquired so far.

Tackle each subject on a separate sheet. If you make a mistake, keep going. Each exercise can be mounted onto another piece of layout paper, trimmed, and then mounted onto gray or black cover stock for final presentation to the client. Don't forget to use references for the figures and poses, if necessary.

BEACH SCENE WITH SAILBOATS AND WINDSURFERS: First draw a 9- × 12-inch (23 × 30 cm) rectangle, using a black marker pen and a T-square. With the black marker pen, create a seascape or lake scene with sailboats and windsurfers scudding about. Include simplified figures in swimwear in the middle distance. Imagine that it is sunny and windy, with some clouds in the sky. Add objects in the foreground such as sand buckets and beach balls, placed in one or more groups.

Slip this drawing under a clean sheet of paper, and then redraw it crisply, using minimal lines. Before adding tone, remember to insert the wax sheet.

3–37. Hairstyles should be visualized first as geometric shapes.

DIRECTIONS: Find good female and male photos in fashion magazines. The faces should be strongly lit from the upper top side, because this type of lighting reveals the planes of the skull and makes rendering the shadow areas easier.

First use a few black lines to identify the placement of the head and facial features. Next to these heads, do tonal gray studies, sensing the planes of the head. Use only one gray on the face and one for the hair.

Now combine the steps, starting with the black line drawing, then adding two grays for facial planes and shadow areas, and finally introducing two or three grays for the hair. If you are to get a good likeness, your initial black marks must be accurate.

3–38. Final rendering for Exercise 11 (beach scene) by Gary Alphonso. Wedge-tip markers and felt-tip pen. Contrast, tones, textures, and detail soften with increasing distance.

Using a no. 4 gray marker, tone in the water, leaving the white of the paper for the sand and sail shapes. Now add tone for the sky, using a no. 2 or no. 6 gray marker. Use different gray tones for the sail stripes and dark tones for figures in the sailboats.

Finally, add a few black lines for definition on the sailboats and windsurfers. Add grays for fleshtones on the figures, and put shadows on and under the objects on the beach. Keep everything simple (Fig. 3–38).

CAMPSITE IN THE MOUNTAINS: Draw a 9- × 12-inch (23 × 30 cm) rectangle, using a T-square and a black marker pen. Design a composition that includes tents in the foreground and small figures by the edge of a lake in the middle ground. Across the lake, create an interesting arrangement of high mountains, adding a thin waterfall. Place some trees in the middle distance. Create a mood by making the scene predominantly light or dark.

Slip this linear composition under the next top sheet, and draw in the foreground with a black felt-tip pen, using many lines. Draw the details and textures of grass and rocks. After inserting the wax sheet, tone in the grass around the trees, and add simple tones to the shaded side of the tents.

With a minimum of faint black lines, indicate the figures. Add tones to their hair, clothing, and so on. Simplify everything in the middle distance.

Using gray markers, suggest the mountains as tone shapes only. Reflect the mountains in the lake, but be sure the reflections are lighter in tone.

Give the trees light or dark tones to connect the distant view to the middle ground. Finally, add small areas of tone to the figures, and add line or tone where needed to heighten the mood (Fig. 3–40).

3–39. Final rendering for Exercise 11 (street scene) by Gary Alphonso. Wedge-tip markers and felt-tip pen. Curvilinear figures contrast with rectilinear buildings.

FARM SCENE: Once again begin with a 9- × 12-inch (12 × 30 cm) black rectangle. Then create a linear composition of a family getting out of a white car parked in a driveway near a farmhouse. Their friends who own the farm are coming to meet them. Someone is working on farm equipment in the middle ground. The farmhouse is surrounded by trees and other buildings—perhaps a barn, a silo, and a shed. It is late in the afternoon and sunny.

Work out the perspective and eye level of the road, driveway, car, and buildings first, and then draw in the figures. Note that the buildings are tall prisms, cubes, and cylinders.

After completing your black linear drawing, slip it under the next sheet. Then redraw the scene with black pen, using minimal linework. Simplify everything. Use more lines and texture in the foreground and less in the middle ground, where tone will hold the shapes.

After inserting the wax sheets, start rendering the gray tones of the sky, and then of the buildings and streets, up to the middle foreground. Leave the driveway pale gray. Add a figure on the farm equipment, using simple tones and very little contrast.

For maximum contrast of black and white, render a black cast shadow on the driveway from the car, and put a middle gray on the car's shadow side. Define the figures with various grays, white, and black. Finally, add linework where needed to create stronger definition.

STREET SCENE WITH FIG-URES: Using the same size rectangle as before and the T-square method, place a café in the foreground, with people variously seated and standing. Place cars in the middle ground and buildings in the background. You may need to do several preliminary line drawings to work out the composition.

When you are satisfied, tear the sketch off the pad and put it under the next clean sheet. Render objects on the tables by accurately drawing their outlines. Then simplify the figures, using a minimum of line. Draw in the clothing, hairstyles, and hands as shapes; and draw in the faces—eyebrows, eyes, nose, and mouth. Add lines to indicate fingers, where appropriate.

Move on to the basic shapes of cars, again using a minimum of line. Then begin to build tones, introducing more tone than line in order to obtain less contrast and softer details.

Finally, add simplified tones to the buildings, trees, and so on. Define these further with a few lines. You should also render the sky, figures, and clothing in tone (Fig. 3–39).

FAMILY BY A LAKE: In a 9- × 12-inch (23 × 30 cm) area, draw a family being picked up at a lakeshore wharf by a person in a motorboat. Show the wharf from an interesting angle. Include some luggage and sports equipment such as water skis and fishing rods. Add islands in the middle ground and in the far distance, with houses on some of them. It's a sunny day. Concentrate on the action and figures.

Do one or two preliminary compositions in line only, using a black marker pen. Organize your layout so that it features the actions and poses of the people. Begin by drawing the wharf in correct perspective. Then draw the boat beside it, and add the islands. Next add the figures in the boat, and plot other figures, some overlapping. Finally, introduce the sports equipment and any other details.

Tear off this sheet, place it underneath the next sheet, and redraw everything using minimal black linework. Don't draw around the entire edge of anything. Just suggest the forms and objects. Accentuate only the folds and creases of limbs, clothing, and facial features.

With the wax sheet in place, separate the figures from the background by using a middle-tone gray for the water. Add dark tones to the islands and light tones to the sky. Leave the houses white. Using gray and black markers and perhaps a pen, add details to the clothing and sports equipment. Where necessary, add minimal linework to the figures. Finally, add tonal details, darkening all the tones on everything in shadow.

VARIATIONS: Practice drawing figures in various settings. For example, depict students at a college, in either a classroom or a gym. The more you practice, the better you'll be prepared to handle assignments later.

3–40. Final rendering for Exercise 11 (mountain-campsite scene) by Gary Alphonso. Wedge-tip markers and felt-tip pen.

Presenting Marker Renderings

You may wish to mat your marker renderings in order to protect them and to show them to clients. Do not rubber-cement them to a board because, in time, the glue will turn yellow and stain the paper. Moreover, with temperature changes, the layout paper will bubble and lift, as will the mat if it has been rubber-cemented.

Here is the professional way to mat your renderings (Fig. 3–41):

Trim your rendering so that you leave about 1 1/2 inches (4 cm) of paper around the rendering itself.

Tape the rendering to thick white matboard by stretching the paper a bit as you go, and placing pieces of tape in each corner and at the center of the top, bottom, and sides.

(This method of attaching the rendering to the board allows it to expand or stretch with temperature changes without ruining the look of the presentation.) Note that the size of the backing board should be larger than you want it to be when finished (you will trim it later).

Cut a mat of either dark gray or brown board. It should be 3 inches (8 cm) at the top and sides and 4 inches (10 cm) at the bottom. The inside window should allow about 1/2 inch (1.3 cm) of paper to be seen around each marker rendering. Use double-sided adhesive tape to stick the mat down onto the white board. Now press this down firmly, and trim the board to the exact size of the mat.

Guidelines for Marker Rendering

For basic marker renderings, keep these simple guidelines in mind:

- In the preliminary stages, drawing briskly yet accurately with a black felt-tip pen; effective marker renderings are achieved through a minimum of line, with the form suggested rather than completely drawn or defined

- Always sensing the structure and perspective of any subject, and indicating it accurately

- Giving your work a crisp professional look by using the T-square and triangle where appropriate, rather than relying exclusively on freehand rendering

- Empathizing with the subject, and making your linework expressive

- When rendering figures, using a thick-and-thin line to maximum effect to give the subject life

- When rendering inanimate objects, using strokes that follow the contours of the form

- Suggesting three-dimensional modeling by using the correct values

- Wherever possible, accentuating dramatic lighting through contrast of tone

Mistakes to Avoid

Here are several mistakes that should not be allowed to mar your work:

- Drawing inaccurately, using a poor design, and not observing perspective

- Doing drawings that look tight and traced rather than drawn

- Allowing the markers to bleed over the linework

- Trying to model form realistically, rather than creating an impression of a subject (which is the real function of marker rendering)

- Overworking the rendering with too many busy lines or too many little bits of the white paper showing through, leading to a lack of freshness and clarity

- Acquiring slovenly work habits such as working on messy drawing boards, working on buckled (improperly stored) paper, and letting markers get dry or dirty

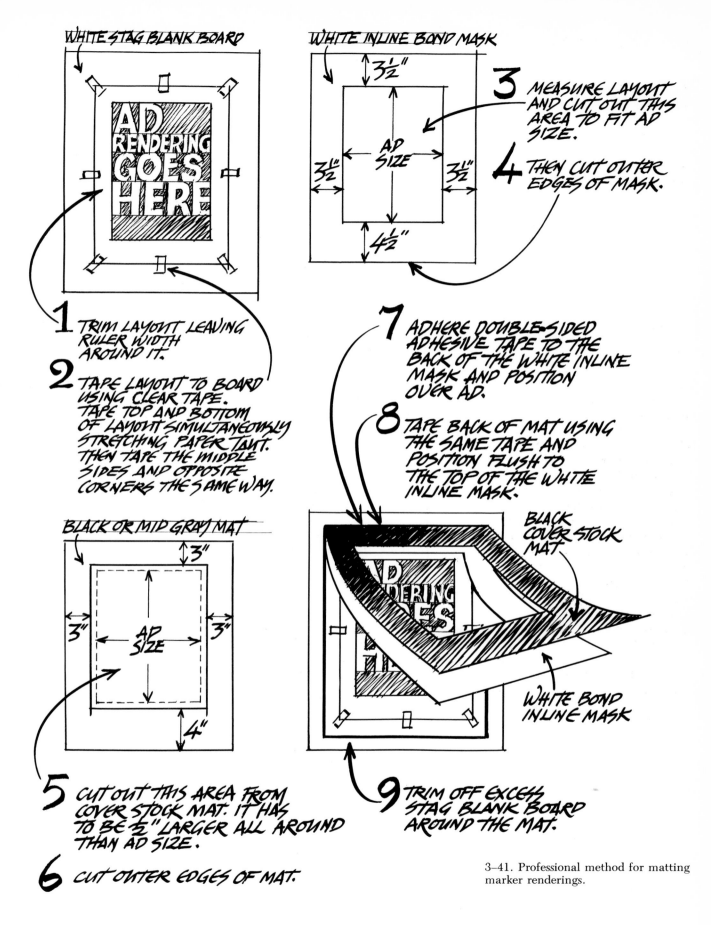

WHITE STAG BLANK BOARD

AD RENDERING GOES HERE

1 TRIM LAYOUT LEAVING RULER WIDTH AROUND IT.

2 TAPE LAYOUT TO BOARD USING CLEAR TAPE. TAPE TOP AND BOTTOM OF LAYOUT SIMULTANEOUSLY STRETCHING PAPER TAUT. THEN TAPE THE MIDDLE SIDES AND OPPOSITE CORNERS THE SAME WAY.

WHITE INLINE BOND MASK

$3\frac{1}{2}"$ $3\frac{1}{2}"$ AD SIZE $3\frac{1}{2}"$ $4\frac{1}{2}"$

3 MEASURE LAYOUT AND CUT OUT THIS AREA TO FIT AD SIZE.

4 THEN CUT OUTER EDGES OF MASK.

BLACK OR MID GRAY MAT

3" AD SIZE 3" 3" 4"

5 CUT OUT THIS AREA FROM COVER STOCK MAT. IT HAS TO BE $\frac{1}{2}"$ LARGER ALL AROUND THAN AD SIZE.

6 CUT OUTER EDGES OF MAT.

7 ADHERE DOUBLE-SIDED ADHESIVE TAPE TO THE BACK OF THE WHITE INLINE MASK AND POSITION OVER AD.

8 TAPE BACK OF MAT USING THE SAME TAPE AND POSITION FLUSH TO THE TOP OF THE WHITE INLINE MASK.

BLACK COVER STOCK MAT

WHITE BOND INLINE MASK

9 TRIM OFF EXCESS STAG BLANK BOARD AROUND THE MAT.

3–41. Professional method for matting marker renderings.

Color Basics

Students sometimes find the theory of color confusing. They may have read a book on color theory, but find it difficult to relate the theory to the actual use of color in art. It is possible for an illustrator to use color without knowing anything about color theory. But to do this is to miss out on an exciting field of study. You must become sensitive to the natural laws of color all around you; and by learning about these, you will develop a color sense.

Have you ever wondered why color in nature always seems right? Only when people start to arrange colors does the possibility of color disharmony arise. Artists in the past learned about color by observing nature, and we will do the same.

One of the most important points to keep in mind is that color should be used selectively. In other words, you should not feature all colors equally. Decide to let certain colors predominate, and then add other colors sparingly so as not to overpower the main ones. If you introduce a color that just does not fit into the existing color scheme, it will look harsh or jarring. As in music, you have hit the wrong note — one in a totally different key — and it has changed the whole mood.

Characteristics of Color

Before we begin analyzing color in nature, a few color terms should be clarified.

Hue refers to the name of a color — for example, yellow, blue, red, or violet. Every color in the color spectrum falls into a specific hue category. Hue is important to the illustrator because of its psychological impact on the viewer or consumer. An artist can create specific moods by using a certain range of hues.

Intensity or *chroma* refers to the degree of a color's brightness or dullness. When colors are fully saturated, they are described as being more intense than duller colors of the same hue. By controlling the intensity of a hue, an illustrator can create an illusion of depth. Contrast of hue is heightened by the use of undiluted colors at maximum intensity. The luminosity and brilliance of colors are most noticeable when hues of similar value are positioned side by side.

Value refers to how light or dark a color is. Yellow is high in value, almost white, and violet is low in value, almost black. Red and blue

Experimenting with different color
schemes.

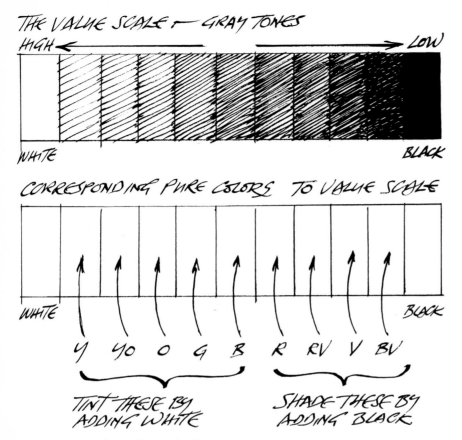

THE VALUE SCALE ← GRAY TONES

HIGH ← → LOW

WHITE   BLACK

CORRESPONDING PURE COLORS TO VALUE SCALE

WHITE   BLACK

Y   YO   O   G   B   R   RV   V   BV

TINT THESE BY   SHADE THESE BY
ADDING WHITE   ADDING BLACK

4–1. Corresponding value scales for gray tones and pure colors.

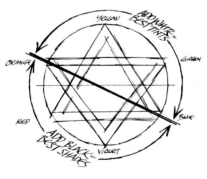

4–2. Guide to tinting and shading.

fall into the middle range of value (Fig. 4–1). Value is one of the most important aspects of color, since an illustrator can suggest form through contrasts in light and shade. Contrast of value makes colors appear darker on a white background, but lighter and more brilliant on a black background.

In addition to using the natural value of a pure color, you can create modified colors by adding white or black to them. Adding white to a pure color creates a *tint;* adding black to a pure color creates a *shade.* The process of mixing black and white together to create a gray and then adding that gray to a pure color creates a *tone.*

To produce harmonious color, you must pay special attention to tints, tones, and shades. Remember that it is usually best to add white to high-value (light) pure colors and to add black to low-value (dark) pure colors (Fig. 4–2). For example, when painting the effects of a warm

sunny blue sky as it appears from mid-morning to mid-afternoon, you should select the lightest pure blues to begin with and add white to them. These hues include pale or light blue, turquoise, cerulean blue, sky blue, process blue, and azure blue. You should not use ultramarine, indigo, or Prussian blue for a sunny sky, because they are dark in value and lean toward the blue-violet range. When white is added to them, the effect is quite unpleasant.

The Color Wheel

For illustrators, the three primary colors (those from which the other hues can be mixed) are yellow, blue, and red. The printer uses the same three colors, plus black, in the printing process. Every color image you see in a magazine is actually made up of dots of yellow, blue (cyan), red (magenta), and black. You can verify this by inspecting such a picture with a magnifying glass. Instead of seeing the individual dots, however, our unaided eye mixes the different-colored dots and sees the combined colors of the original subject.

Georges Seurat, a French Neo-Impressionist, used this type of color mixing in his paintings. He created the same visual effect by using tiny paint dots of pure color that the viewer's eye would mix to produce the intended final color. This technique is called *pointillism.*

Let's return to the three primaries. If you mix any two primaries—yellow + red, red + blue, or blue + yellow—you get the *secondary colors:* orange, violet, and green. The *intermediates* are hues between a primary and a secondary, such as yellow-orange. The first twelve hues identified in this way can be arranged in a circle, forming a color wheel (Fig. 4–3).

Knowledge of relationships on the color wheel can be helpful in devising a pleasing color scheme. The formulas in Figure 4–4 may seem confining at first, but they offer a useful starting point. As you gain more experience, you can experiment with more complex combinations. The basic schemes are as follows:

- Achromatic — black, gray, and white

- Monochromatic — one color only, plus black and white

- Adjacent — three colors that appear side by side on the color wheel; for example, yellow, yellow-green, and green

- Complementary — colors directly opposite each other on the wheel; for example, orange and blue

- Split complementary — similar to complementary, but instead of using the direct opposite, using the two colors on either side of it; for example, orange with blue-green and blue-violet

- Triadic — an equilateral triangular arrangement of three colors; for example, the secondaries of orange, green, and violet

- Dominant tint — a tint of any one color (usually a transparent layer added at the end to cover an entire painting), which automatically makes all the colors in the painting harmonize with each other

Color Studies

For color theory to become meaningful to you, you must study the way color works in nature. Keep all that you have learned about color theory in the back of your mind; don't let it dictate what you do. Instead, concentrate on the color you see. Evaluate its brightness or dullness, and find an equivalent color in whatever color medium you choose.

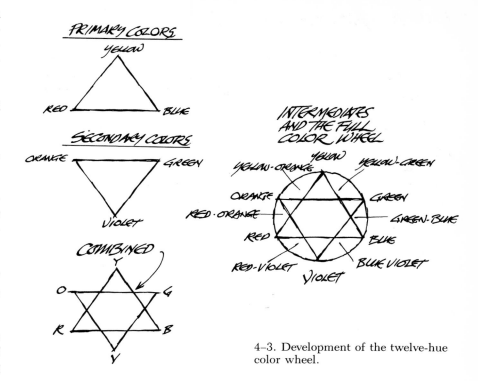

4–3. Development of the twelve-hue color wheel.

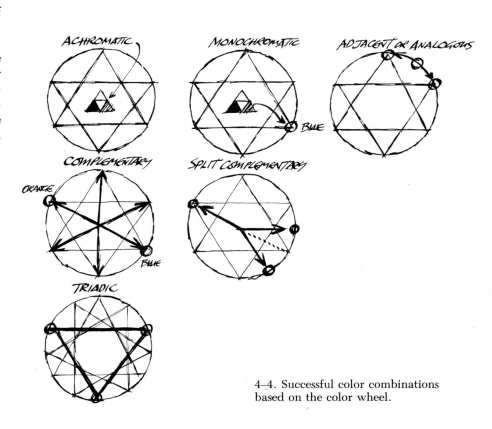

4–4. Successful color combinations based on the color wheel.

Color changes during a day

The native people of the American Southwest state that "the sun paints the land." This exercise investigates that statement. The idea is to paint a series of studies at regular intervals through the day, starting at dawn and continuing to sunset and nightfall.

It is particularly interesting to watch what happens with the warm/cool and dark/light aspects of color as sunlight increases or decreases. It is also worthwhile to see what happens when the sun shines from different directions and how this affects the natural color of various landscapes. The sun may appear to change color, but in fact it does not. It seems to do so only because of the changing angle at which its light passes through the earth's atmosphere.

Notice that the sun bathes the landscape in predominantly warm tints, changing from yellow-orange to yellow, yellow-white, white, yellow, yellow-orange, orange, red, and red-violet. As the sunlight increases, its color shifts toward yellow; and as the sunlight decreases, its color shifts toward blue-violet.

After you have spent some time studying how sunlight changes, experiment with different colored backgrounds, using orange for the sunlit views and dark gray for stormy and moonlit sequences. For this sequence, use your imagination and memory recall. Squeeze two or three pure colors onto the board; then blend and manipulate them to define the landscape. If necessary, add white to the light hues to tint them. Try restricting your palette to various pure reds, blues, and yellows, and create all other colors with these.

Look at your own studies as well as at those in Figures 4–5 and 4–6 on page 130. What have you learned about color? Here are some of the conclusions you will probably reach:

1. Color has temperature—warm (reddish) or cool (bluish).

2. The eye perceives warm color more readily than cool color.

3. Warm colors advance or appear to come toward you; cool colors recede.

4. On a white background, dark shades advance and pale tints recede. This is reversed on dark paper (which would be used to depict a night scene).

5. Contrast lessens with increasing distance.

6. Texture loses definition with increasing distance.

7. The color found on forms and objects ranges through colors that are adjacent on the color wheel.

8. Light colors emphasize the depth of dark colors, while dark colors emphasize the airiness of light colors.

9. Complementary colors (opposites on the color wheel) have an exciting visual quality.

10. Analogous colors (a range of colors in sequence, either warm or cool) are highly emotional or moody.

11. Contrast in value or hue increases the impact and interest of an area.

12. Adding blue to colors can make them recede, indicating distance.

13. The color and value scales range from warm, dark colors in the foreground to light, cool colors in the background.

14. The amount of light (low, normal, high, or high contrast) changes the value and intensity of colors.

In sum, the color in a landscape changes with the transit of the sun. A smooth progression of colors around the color wheel occurs during a twenty-four-hour period. In general, the movement is from pink/orange, orange, and yellow at dawn to yellow/white, yellow, and yellow/orange in the daytime to orange, red/orange, red, and red/violet at dusk. At night the colors shift to violet, blue/violet, and indigo, and then to violet, red, and orange at dawn.

Contrasting day and night

Draw or paint one day and one night scene, with particular attention to contrast. The objects in the far distance, for example, are generally close to the sky in value, while the objects closest to the foreground are farthest in value from the sky or background color.

Notice that in daylight warm colors and dark colors advance. At night this is reversed: light colors advance against the darkness. The same principles apply on dull or cloudy days, but there is less contrast.

As you do this exercise, start modifying colors by mixing them on the board, rather than using them straight from the tube. To get a tint (lighten a color), add white to it. To get a shade (darken a color), add black to it. Finally, obtain tones by adding gray to pure color. Remember to add white only to light-value colors and black only to dark-value colors.

Creating depth and space

An easy way to create depth and the sensation of space in color work is to translate colors into black, grays, and white. In the illustration business, color artwork sometimes has to be reproduced in black and white. In such cases artwork with the greatest contrast of values and colors reproduces best. Artwork with little tonal contrast tends to appear flat, dull, and confusing in black and white. Thus contrast can be a key to understanding color. Warm or cool color, light or dark—it is all a question of contrast.

In a landscape, color, texture, and details soften and lessen in contrast and value with increasing distance. Diminishing contrast can also be found in other subject matter, such as street scenes, crowds, portraits, and still-life arrangements (the latter two, of course, to a lesser degree). In other words, to suggest depth and space using color, you must adjust colors and values according to their position in space. If you do not, the result will be quite two-dimensional.

Another aspect of color to consider is the warmth or coolness it conveys. Adding a certain amount of blue to colors cools them, making them recede. The more blue is added, the more the colors will recede. To create even more depth, add both white and blue to the color. Or try neutralizing the original color with its direct opposite on the color wheel. If you are using violet, for example, add yellow first and then some blue and white.

Experiment with atmospheric depth, emphasizing blue-grays and blue-violets.

Studying shadows

Shadows possess a definitely bluish cast that is especially noticeable, for example, in the shaded areas of snow banks. An excellent experiment involves taking a sheet of white paper and laying it on the grass so that half is in the shadow of a tree and the other half is in direct sunlight. Compare the blue of the shaded side to the yellow-white side.

Because shadows in a sense describe the absence of light (direct light), the best way to paint shadows is to neutralize your lighted color. In the case of the grass, you would add red (green's direct opposite or complementary color on the color wheel) to the green, mix the two to the correct value required, and finally add a touch of blue. Try to keep the paint application semitransparent and full of life, not muddy and opaque.

Putting color theory to work

In our discussion of color theory, the use of a dominant tint was mentioned. After painting a subject in the local colors, you may want to give the piece a specific mood—to warm it up or cool it down. To do this, put a glaze of *one* transparent color over the entire piece: yellow or orange for warmth; blue, green, or violet to cool the mood. This technique works well with transparent painting media, such as acrylic glazes, watercolors, or colored inks. It also works well in marker rendering. It is in precisely this way that the sun paints the land with a dominant color. The same effect is also noticeable in indoor situations, especially with artificial lighting.

Explore other ideas from the color wheel in relation to nature. Find adjacent color harmonies, complementaries, split complementaries, and triadic relationships (Figs. 4–7 through 4–9).

To make both the working process and the end results more exciting and interesting, do your paintings from imagination and paint them upside down on the canvas so that the sky is at the bottom and the landscape at the top. This makes it easier to see the landscape as a group of shapes and colors rather than as a collection of details.

Further color explorations

The four steps in this exercise will teach you a great deal about the application of color theory and color mixing, and about the use of light and shade.

STEP 1: Select a photograph of an interesting outdoor subject, and cut it diagonally. Paste down one-half only onto a piece of illustration board. Next to it, render the other half of the image in flat shapes and flat colors.

STEP 2: Repeat the previous exercise, only this time use an interesting photo of an animal, bird, or insect. The shape of the subject you choose must be exciting. Crop the photograph to vary the size of the background shapes, and make the placement of the subject itself asymmetric. Accentuate the negative spaces or counterforms.

STEP 3: Now do a four-part color study in which the parts are placed in a row or side by side to form a square. First find an interesting photograph of a still life of fruit or other food. The lighting must be dramatic. Paste this down on a sheet of illustration board. In the next rectangle paint the same composition exactly, using a complementary color scheme (orange/blue, yellow/violet, or red/green). Render the photo image in flat shapes and flat colors. Don't model it. Intermix the two colors to create other values. Now repeat the process in the third rectangle, but this time add white to the colors to create tints. Try to retain the same value relationships as in the original. Finally, repeat the process in the fourth rectangle, but this time add black to create shades. Again, try to maintain the value relationships that exist in the original photo.

STEP 4: Choose a complicated photograph of an outdoor or indoor scene that includes figures and objects. Use a black felt-tip pen to divide the photo into a grid of 1-inch (2.5 cm) squares. On a piece of illustration board, resize this photo on a grid of 1½-inch (4 cm) squares. Draw the image from the photograph within the new grid, working one square at a time. Then carefully duplicate the photograph in color, tonal values, and lighting. It should perfectly match the original.

Keeping a Color Notebook

It is a good idea to use a notebook or sketchbook to record your color observations (Fig. 4–10). Do a quick line sketch, and use an abbreviated letter code—for example, Y for yellow, YO for yellow-orange, YG for yellow-green, and so on. For light or dark colors, simply put an L or a D in front of the color (L/BV, for example).

Basic Color Guidelines

Here are some general suggestions and recommendations for the handling color:

- Restricting your color palette, using a fixed, harmonious arrangement from the color wheel

- Controlling the amount of light illuminating the subject you've chosen

- Using high-key, low-key, normal, or high-contrast lighting

- Determining the contrast in values, colors, and textures

- Using a predominantly warm or cool scheme

- Creating depth by adding blue to colors and by lightening with white

- Intermixing colors to increase subtlety

- Using opposite colors—which can be visually dynamic in large areas—but featuring one more than the other

- Using colors close together in an analogous scheme, creating a warm arrangement, a cool arrangement, or a combination of both

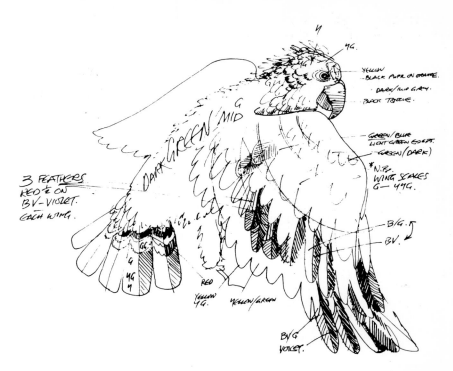

4–10. Recording color observations in a sketchbook.

Mistakes to Avoid

- Overusing texture, which tends to provoke confusion

- Creating discordant color schemes by ignoring the harmonies found in nature and harmonious color-wheel arrangements

- Working only with colors as they come straight from the jar or tube

- Starting a painting without first choosing a color scheme

- Muddying colors by doing too much intermixing

- Adding too much white to colors, thus making them chalky

- Using too many colors in one piece of artwork

- Making all colors equal in importance

- Mixing white into dark pure colors to lighten them when a lighter color should have been selected in the first place

- Mixing black into light pure colors to darken them when a darker color should have been selected in the first place

- Not having a wide enough range of colors to work with

4–5. Finished studies for Exercise 1.
Gouache. Color investigations of early
morning light.

4–6. Finished studies for Exercise 1.
Gouache. Color investigations of
late-day sunlight.

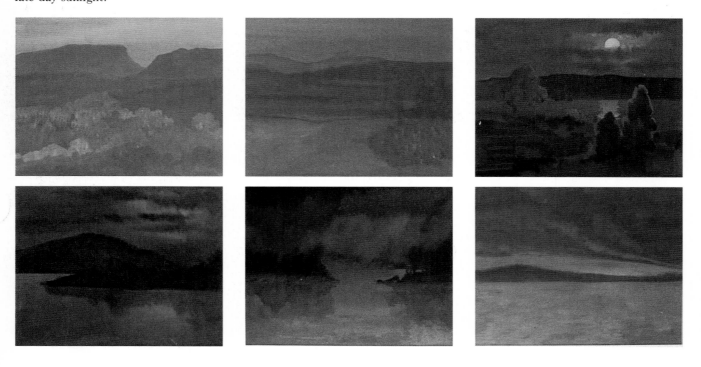

4–7. Finished painting for Exercise 5. Acrylics. Using a restricted color scheme from the color wheel guarantees harmonious color work.

4–8. Finished painting for Exercise 5. Acrylics. Pairing of colors opposite each other on the color wheel will also create color harmony.

4–9. Finished painting in acrylics for Exercise 5. Acrylics. Using colors which are analogous or adjacent to one another on the color wheel creates a strong mood.

Basic Painting Techniques

painting brings together all that you have already learned about design, drawing, marker rendering, and color theory. The very act of painting is exciting and satisfying. It should be fun.

Contrary to what you may have been told, techniques come last — not first — in learning how to paint. Using slick techniques will not help if you have no ideas, cannot draw well, and have no sense of color and composition. Beginners often assume that, if they use the same medium and technique as a well-known illustrator, they will automatically get the same results. It just does not work that way.

Another common mistake is to start with a complicated subject and then get lost in the details, ignoring the overall scale, proportions, colors, and so on. You must build a painting step by step, making sure that the basic structure is correct before you pursue the details.

Here are some guidelines (some of which you already know) to help you get started:

1. Decide on the mood you wish to create.

2. Restrict your color scheme, selecting a minimum number of colors to work with.

3. Think in terms of black and white tones for clarity, simplicity, and contrast.

4. Feature one predominant color or tint, and do not let other colors compete with it.

5. Dark colors work best on a light or white background, and light colors work best on a dark background.

6. Warm colors advance, and cool colors recede. Therefore, adding blue to a color can create an illusion of depth or recession.

7. Bold textures, extreme value contrasts, and heavy detailing also appear to advance.

8. To create a feeling of depth, soften textures and value contrasts. Use no details, just shapes, in the extreme background.

There are, of course, many different ways of painting (Figs. 5–1

High-contrast painting by Paul
McCusker. Gouache, glazing medium,
and acrylic chisel-point brushes.

through 5–3). With illustration, however, you are dealing with a client, so your work has to be functional. You should use color and other aspects of painting to enhance the client's message or product.

Materials and Equipment

Most art supplies, particularly painting materials, contain highly toxic chemicals and can be hazardous to your health: acrylic paints and glazing media contain polymer plastics, certain gouache paints and watercolors contain gum arabic, and oil paints contain lead. Always work in a well-ventilated area and exercise caution and common sense regarding the handling, use, storage, and disposal of your painting supplies.

Paints

Theoretically, with the three primaries—yellow, blue, and red—plus black and white, you can mix any color. In reality, however, you need two of each primary to achieve a full color range. Specifically, you need a greenish yellow and an orangish yellow—one slightly cooler and one slightly warmer than primary yellow. Likewise you need a warm blue (cobalt or ultramarine) and a cool yellowy blue (turquoise or cerulean blue). With reds, you need an orange-red and a cooler red with some blue in it, such as scarlet or geranium. You cannot mix an orange-red with a yellowish blue and get violet. You must use a bluish red and a reddish blue to start with.

Buy your paints and painting media in plastic squeeze bottles, so the containers will not break if accidentally dropped. Tube paints are also recommended.

If you do buy small jars of paint, store them upside down until you want to use them. That way, the gum arabic binding agent will not sink to the bottom of the jar, and as a result the top of the paint will be

5–1. Painting by Wendy Losee-Orr. Gouache. A fixed harmonious color scheme. High-contrast lighting using tints and shades only, and blended sable brushstrokes.

easier to work with, with no streaking or high gloss areas when dry. You should still stir the paint well, though, before using it.

Sometimes, previously used paint or medium containers will not open. The material dries hard around the inside of the lid, sealing the top tight. If it is a plastic squeeze bottle, simply squeeze it firmly between

your hands, all around, and force air into the top. For a glass container, tap the lid all around with the metal handle of a kitchen knife. If it still will not budge, soak it in hot water for a few minutes. For tubes of paint, rotate the plastic top over a match or lighter. Allow it to cool slightly, and then remove the top with your fingers or with pliers.

5–2. Painting by Brenda Clark. Gouache. Bold, chisel-point brushwork, analogous color scheme, and high-contrast lighting.

5–3. Watercolor. Semi-wet colors are blended within specific areas. Placement and elements of line and shape are emphasized.

Palettes

The best type of palette to use for acrylic or gouache, with or without a glazing medium, is a butcher's tray—a metal tray with an enamel surface. Buy a fairly large one, such as, 12 × 18 inches (30 × 46 cm). After painting, you can run hot water over the tray, and the paint will wash or peel off as a skin.

To make an inexpensive palette, wrap a piece of illustration board with acetate. To clean it, run water over it and then wipe it. With this palette, as with the butcher's tray, dried paint (except acrylics) can be rewet and used again.

Brushes

Invest in good brushes. With care they will last a lifetime. The most commonly used brushes are round, pointed sables and synthetic brushes with chisel points. You will need three different widths of the synthetic brushes: ¼, ½, and 1¼ inches (0.6, 1.3, and 3 cm). You also need a large 2½-inch (6 cm) brush for applying gesso to untreated surfaces such as raw canvas and Masonite. Buy a good-quality 2½-inch (6 cm) house-painting brush at a hardware or paint store, since art shops charge too much for a brush this size.

You can make your own soft, chisel-point brushes by wetting no. 2, 4, and 7 pointed sables, placing them against a cardboard surface, and then cutting their tips off with a sharp knife or razor blade (Fig. 5-4). A chisel-point brush is excellent for adding precise details to a painting.

After painting with them, wash all your brushes immediately—especially those that have been used with acrylics, gesso, or glazing medium. Otherwise, these fast-drying materials will collect in the bristles and soon make the brush inflexible. While you are working, keep the brushes you have used in a jar of water. After you finish painting for the

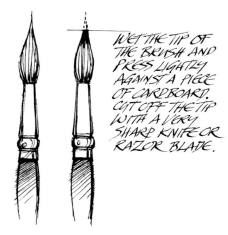

5-4. Making a chisel-point sable brush.

day, rinse them all in warm water. Then put some liquid detergent in the palm of your hand, rub the brushes around in it, and when the brushes are free of paint, rinse them under running water.

Gouache and tempera

Gouache and tempera paint—also called designers' colors and poster paint—are opaque painting media. Using them forces you to model with the paint, lightening or darkening it, and this experience will increase your understanding of light and dark in work with acrylics and watercolors, which are transparent media. The white of the paper shows through transparent media to create light tints; only the intermediate and darker areas are modeled.

Here are some gouache colors to start with: flame red, scarlet, Bengal rose, marigold orange, golden yellow, lemon yellow, raw sienna, burnt sienna, raw umber, burnt umber, permanent green light, viridian green, cerulean blue, cobalt blue, turquoise or azure blue, ultramarine, sky blue, Prussian blue, spectrum violet, permanent white, and lamp black. The two greens, however, should hardly ever be used. Far more interesting greens can be obtained by mixing any yellow, orange, or earth color with a blue.

As a beginning exercise, squeeze some paint directly onto illustration board or canvas. Do not use a palette, and do not premix the desired color. Instead, push, manipulate, and mix the color on the surface as you paint. If you are intimidated by holding a brush in your hand, loosen up by painting with your fingers. It's amazing how accurate this technique can be—and how much freedom and confidence it engenders (Fig. 5-5).

The basic instructions are as follows:

1. Don't use a palette to mix the paint. Apply the paint directly to the surface by squeezing it from the tube.

2. Squeeze out other colors where desired.

3. Now mix the pure colors on the surfaces with brushes.

4. To lighten or darken an area, first squeeze out the appropriate colors and then blend them together with a brush.

5. Add white or black if necessary, and use appropriate brushwork.

To give your painting a dramatic look, apply the skills you learned in earlier chapters. For example, use asymmetrical balance in the composition. Try using tight cropping in arranging the composition. Accentuate the counterforms, and vary the size and area of background spaces. Emphasize color and value contrast.

Generally, beginners expect too much of themselves. No artist—not even a great one—produces a perfect painting every time. Just relax and enjoy the process. Expecting too much will only lead to frustration; try to be realistic in your objectives.

To learn, you have to be willing to experiment with different kinds of brushstrokes and different compositions (Figs. 5-6 through 5-9).

Painting Terminology

Here is a list of terms commonly used in painting and illustration:

Achromatic: Artwork in black, gray, and white only, without color.

Glaze: Color diluted or thinned to a transparent state.

Gouache: Opaque watercolors that use white to create tints.

Highlight: The brightest area of reflected light.

Impasto: A technique in which paint is used very thickly, creating texture and relief effects.

Medium: The actual material used for a painting or drawing, such as acrylics or charcoal. Also, any substance added to paint to thin it, thicken it, or make it transparent.

Monochromatic: Using one color only, usually with all its values—light, middle, and dark. (Black and white can be added to the color.)

Underpainting: A preliminary stage, before the glazing or final layers of a painting.

Wash: Color applied in an extremely fluid and transparent way.

Brushwork

The best way to learn to use a brush expressively is to start with a large brush and to work boldly. Many beginners think that small brushes will be easier to handle. But because small brushes encourage tight, fussy brushwork they tend to inhibit the artist. Instead, begin with large brushes and then move on to smaller ones for detailed work.

Choose a brush that gives fast coverage, such as a 2¹/₂-inch (6 cm) brush from a hardware store. A large brush of this kind is very flexi-

ble and works particularly well when the bristles are splayed or separated. It can be used for various strokes, including a broad stroke when used flat and parallel to the surface, a thin stroke when held sideways, and a slightly broader stroke when the corner edge is used.

With a 2¹/₂-inch (6 cm) brush, you can also create various surface textures, such as those of grasses, rocks, wood grain, fabric, and concrete. Simply move your wrist in different rhythmic ways—dragging, stabbing, rolling, twisting, and dabbing the brush's bristles. Look at Figure 5–9 again. This painting was done entirely with this size brush, except for the facial features, which were done with a no. 4 chisel-point sable. The time for execution of this painting was two and a half hours.

The trick to using the big brush is not to worry about staying within shapes. You can always clean up the background with white or color around the subject. Besides, you will get interesting brushwork around it.

Using synthetic chisel-point brushes

Besides working well with designers' gouache and tempera, synthetic brushes are used with gesso, acrylic paint, oil paint, cassein, and egg tempera. They come in many widths, from ¹/₄ inch (0.6 cm) to 1¹/₄ inch (3 cm). The characteristic stroke is of uniform width, but it can be varied according to the way the brush is held. Large shapes and areas can be painted in very quickly. Synthetic chisel-point brushes tend to apply pigment in a streaky manner, particularly when acrylic paints are used transparently. This effect can be used to advantage in your painting or illustration.

Using custom-made chisel-point brushes

As was described on page 136, you can make your own chisel-point

brush from a round sable brush. The advantage of these brushes is that they combine the precision of the chisel-point with the sable's flexibility and capacity to hold paint. Such brushes can be used for either thick or thin even lines, depending on the angle at which they are held.

As a practice exercise with your chisel-point sable, angle a thick, 24-inch (60 cm) metal ruler against an illustration board or paper surface by placing your fingers between the ruler and the surface. Your thumb should press the bottom edge of the ruler tightly to hold the ruler at the desired angle. Let the hand holding the brush rest on the ruler so that the tip of the brush touches the paper. By sliding your hand along the ruler, you can make a perfect brushed line (Fig. 5–10). This technique does require practice, however. Eventually, you can use it to reproduce chrome strips on cars, beams on buildings, or any other object with straight edges.

Using pointed sable brushes

Studying Arab, Chinese, and Japanese calligraphy and painting, will enable you to learn about the many different types of marks and strokes that can be made possible with a pointed sable brush. The tip, heel, and sides of the brush can all be used with varying rhythmic movements and changing pressure. The resulting brushwork is most suitable for gouache and watercolor painting. The pointed brush will not give you a constant parallel line, however, even when used with a ruler.

Using stencil brushes

The bristles of the stencil brush are densely packed and very short. Hold the brush vertically and dab the paint onto the surface with the tips of the bristles. Build up color or tone by dabbing over and over until the desired strength is achieved. Be careful not to pick up too much

5–5. Painting by Michael McKeever. Acrylics. Finger-painting can lessen your inhibitions and result in very expressive work. Use pigment opaquely and enjoy!

5–6a. Painting by Daniel Kewley. Gouache. Impasto (thick) painting is done by applying paint in blobs, dots, or layered streaks, with brush, palette knife, or by squeezing paint from the tube. This is a good technique for expressing texture, rhythm, and movement.

5–6b. Pigment can also be applied sparingly with the tip of a small, fine-point sable brush and then spread in diagonal one-directional stokes across the entire surface. This creates a feathered effect, which is more subtle than the impasto method.

5–7. Painting by Henry Van Der Linde. Acrylic. Paint is applied fluidly for the background, which contrasts with the more modelled brushstrokes of the objects in the foreground. Emphasis is by contrast, line, and shape.

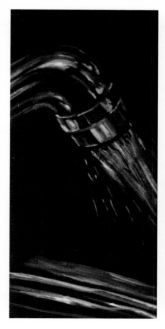

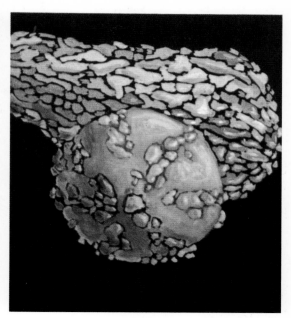

5–8. Painting by Dan Kewley.
Gouache. Experimental variations in
the mixture of water and paint. Paint
applied expressively with a
chisel-point sable brush. Emphasis by
contrast and placement, stressing
shape.

5–9. Gouache. Large brushes and
broad strokes achieve dynamic results.
Paint large areas first and define
details and facial features with
smaller brushes later. This painting
had a 2½-hour time limit.

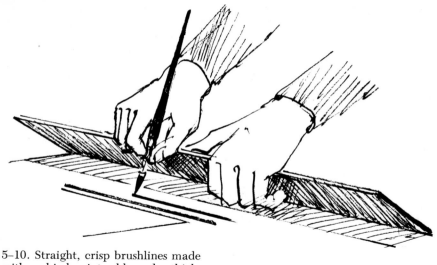

5–10. Straight, crisp brushlines made with a chisel-point sable and a thick metal ruler are ideal for product and architectural renderings.

Using Acrylic Glazing Medium and Gesso with Gouache

Acrylic glazing medium in gloss or matte finish may be added to designers' color or poster paint to create a type of acrylic paint. Since you decide how much of this medium to add to the paint, you can control the final product's degree of transparency—something you cannot do with ready-made acrylic paints.

To get a semi-transparent effect, you can combine the acrylic glazing medium with matte white gesso. You can also add gesso alone to designers' colors as a tinting base.

In sum, there are three possibilities:

- Color + gesso for tints of color

- Color + glazing medium for transparent tints

- Color + glazing medium + gesso for semitransparent or semiopaque tints (depending on the amount of gesso added)

Combining these techniques results in a layered approach in which the user under- and over-paints until the desired result is achieved. This technique also allows you to start with dark, pure colors and then lighten them by means of layering glazes.

Figures 5–17 and 5–18 show examples of this technique. To produce similar pieces, begin by drawing strong two-dimensional shapes on a white background and modeling them slightly to suggest form, light, and shade. You can draw with a charcoal pencil, a felt-tip marker, or a brush, using a pale neutral color. Now add acrylic glazing medium to the colors on your palette, and build up progressively darker values, letting each coat dry before applying the next. (Remember that acrylic glazing medium dries extremely quickly.)

paint on the brush. There should only be a little dot of paint at the end of each bristle. If mastered, this stipple technique can give compositions an airbrushed effect.

Applying Paint

Gouache and tempera are meant to be used opaquely and thickly. You can apply them flat, by diluting them with water; build them up, through the drybrush technique; or use them extremely thickly and dimensionally by squeezing them from the tubes directly onto the surface. You should not, however, dilute gouache too much and use it as if it were watercolor, because the result will be flat, dull color. Instead, add an acrylic gloss or matte medium to the gouache so that it takes on the properties of acrylic paint and retains its brilliance even if used transparently. This glazing technique is especially useful in rendering highly reflective surfaces such as glass, metal, satin, and silk. Another trick is to add acrylic medium to black gouache to create a gray halftone.

Students often wonder which brush works best with each technique. Here are some guidelines:

- *Flat painting:* chisel-point or pointed sable

- *Drybrush:* any brush

- *Impasto:* any brush

- *Planar rendering:* synthetic or sable chisel-point

- *Glazing:* any brush

- *Blobs, swirls, and streaks:* any brush or paint tube

- *Feathering:* round, pointed and chisel-point sable

Take a look now at Figures 5–11 through 5–16. Notice the boldness and simplicity of much of the brushwork. Try to imagine what kind of brush was used in a certain area and how it was held. Studying other paintings—even other students' paintings—can teach you a lot about the possibilities open to you.

5–11. Painting by Paul McCusker. Gouache. Small and medium acrylic brushes were used to apply paint both fluidly and with the drybrush technique. Emphasis through contrast of value using strong shapes.

5–12. Gouache. Use a big brush to quickly establish lighting and basic shapes. Emphasis is on contrast of value and color.

5–13. Painting by Robert McPhail. Tints and high-contrast values painted with strong strokes on a black matboard. Acrylic 1½-inch chisel-point brush was used. Emphasis on placement and contrast.

5–14. Gouache applied with a 1-inch acrylic chisel-point brush. Short, definite strokes.

5–15. Self-portrait by Cheryl Watson. Gouache. Loose brushstrokes with an acrylic, chisel-point brush.

5–16. Painting by Peter Malaguiti. Acrylics. Various acrylic chisel-point and sable round-point brushes were used. Brushstrokes were blended on the face only.

5–17. Tree studies done by layering glazes over dark, pure colors. The actual tree shapes were painted last (the "cutting back" method).

5–18. Wildlife painting by Henry Van Der Linde. Glazes layered over dark pure colors.

Another technique is to wipe off the paint just before it dries, so that only a tint of color remains. Yet another approach is to apply broad areas of pure color and medium very transparently. By adding gesso to the glazing medium, you can create very opaque tints to contrast with the glazes of pure color.

Don't worry about mistakes. If you make a mistake, let it dry, paint gesso over it, and then reapply the correct glazes. You can also paint gesso over the whole piece and start again.

Four Painting Methods

Before examining other painting media, let's consider the four main ways of producing a painted image. The first method builds from big basic shapes, through intermediate shapes and details, to minute details, and finally to the center of interest or focal point.

The second method consists of working on parts of an image—connecting, building, and joining as you go—always keeping the finished whole in mind. This approach is somewhat like working a jigsaw puzzle.

The third method is indirect. It involves feeling your way through various random stages of overpainting and underpainting until the image appears. The image is defined very slowly, emerging from a negative into a positive.

The fourth method (also indirect) takes a reverse approach to imagery. The subject is painted fully and broadly in dark colors and tones. Then the highlights are wiped out and the light areas are worked in with glazes. Finally the paint is cut back to define the basic shape of the form. (Cutting back is the method mentioned on page 140.)

The different methods can be linked to different paint media, although such associations are not absolute. The first method invites almost any medium, while the second lends itself more to acrylics and watercolors. The third method is particularly suited to gouache, either by itself or with acrylic glazing medium and gesso. The fourth method favors acrylics and oils.

Examples of these four methods are given in Figures 5–19 through 5–22. The woman in Figure 5–19 was painted directly. Lines of paint were used for the drawing, and the areas were filled in as basic shapes. Then values were added, and the final colors were built up to create tonal contrast. Finally the facial features—the focal point—were defined.

Figure 5–20 was done in portions, which were joined and built with the whole kept in mind. In contrast, Figure 5–21 was done with layers of under- and overpainting. Finally, Figure 5–22 shows the method of wiping out highlights and tint areas.

Acrylics

Acrylic paints, which can be used either opaquely or transparently, have their pigment suspended in a polymer emulsion base. Although acrylics can be used directly on paper or board, they perform best on a prepared surface such as Masonite or canvas whitened with gesso. For best results, paint the surface with three coats of gesso, allowing each coat to dry before applying the next. The first coat should be painted horizontally, the second vertically, and the last horizontally. If you are in a hurry, apply one very thick coat to the surface. Allow plenty of time for it to dry.

Certain brands of acrylics do not mix. Stick to brands that have the same base—either alkaline or vinyl. Here is a list of other substances that can be mixed with acrylic paints:

Matte medium varnish: This increases color transparency and is good as a final varnish or as a glue for collage.

Gloss medium varnish: This also increases color transparency and can be used as a final varnish. It is also good for collage.

Gel: This gives a highly transparent and even impasto effect. It is best for collage and montage, especially when heavier pieces need to be glued down.

Slowing medium: This slows down the drying time of acrylic colors. (They normally dry within ten minutes; even faster if thinned.)

Gesso: This is used for surface preparation. It makes a sensible replacement for white paint, too, because it is cheaper.

Modeling paste: This is used to create three-dimensional tactile effects and low relief. It can be used on its own or with acrylic color added. Thin it with water or an acrylic medium.

Glazing medium (gloss or matte): This is used with acrylic or with designers' gouache colors to increase the transparency of colors.

Working on canvas

Canvases can be bought ready-made, but these are expensive. If you want to make up your own, buy wooden stretchers and get the canvas off a roll. After you put the stretchers together, lay the assembly on top of the canvas and staple each edge of the canvas to the back of the frame. The canvas should be firm but not taut; otherwise, it may warp the stretcher frame.

Illustrators, however, usually work on canvas board, rather than on stretched canvas. If stretched canvas is used, the composition must be taken off the stretchers to be photographed for reproduction.

Watercolor

Watercolor is a beautiful and expressive painting medium. Its characteristic transparency and fluidity make it ideal for rendering light and shade. There is no point, however, in using watercolors to model form opaquely and solidly; tempera and gouache are far more appropriate for this. In watercolor, the effect should be fresh and spontaneous. It should never look overworked. Study traditional Chinese and Japanese watercolor paintings. The images are rendered precisely but in a style full of expression and fluidity. It takes a great deal of practice to master watercolor in this way.

It is important for you to know how much water the paint-loaded brush you are holding contains, how wet or dry the paper is, and how the combination of these will affect the results. You must experiment with variations of these possibilities to learn the potential of the watercolor medium (Fig. 5–23). You must also develop the dexterity needed to handle the brush with full control (Fig. 5–24).

The very essence of watercolor is lost through reworking or overworking. Try to visualize the entire painting before you start. Then you will know exactly which areas to leave unpainted and exactly where to place the desired colors. Tints may be produced by diluting the paints so that the paper can show through them. All such activity, however, must be planned.

Materials and equipment

There are two basic types of working surface for watercolor. The first is a heavyweight paper or watercolor board that will not buckle when water is applied to it. Regular illustration board can be used, but it lacks the "tooth" or texture of traditional watercolor paper or board. Smooth illustration boards are unacceptable because they make it impossible to obtain smooth gradations of wash.

The second type of preferred surface is thin watercolor paper, which must be stretched as described. Three different textures of watercolor paper are available: hot-pressed is very smooth; cold-pressed is slightly textured; and rough finish is heavily textured.

Sable brushes are preferred by many watercolorists, although soft synthetic brushes can also be used. A no. 12 sable is best for general work, while nos. 3 and 8 are best for small detail. To lay in a large flat wash, use a 1- to 3/4-inch (2.5–1.9 cm) flat sable.

In addition to brushes, you will probably want a synthetic sponge, a blotter or paper towels, and a utility knife or razor blade to create textural effects in your painting. To mask out certain areas while you paint, so that the paper remains white, you will need a liquid masking agent or rubber cement.

Watercolor paints are available in cakes and in tubes. A complete palette might include cadmium yellow pale, cadmium red, alizarin crimson, light red, French ultramarine blue, cerulean blue, cobalt blue, yellow ocher, burnt sienna, burnt umber, Payne's gray, and ivory black.

Stretching paper

Soak light- or medium-weight paper in about 2 inches (5 cm) of water for 10 to 15 minutes. Use a large sink or flat pan for this; the paper should lie flat on the bottom of the container.

Then lift the paper out of the water, and hold it up to let the excess water run off. Since paper fibers expand when wet, the paper will be slightly larger than it was when dry.

Lay the paper on a clean, dry wooden drawing board, and smooth out any air bubbles by wiping the paper with a clean wet sponge. Cut four long pieces of 2-inch-wide (5 cm) brown paper tape, wet these with a sponge, and use them to tape the wet paper to the board. Wipe firmly over the pieces of tape with the wet sponge just once.

At this point you can apply the first washes of paint, if you want to work on wet paper. If not, allow the paper to dry. After the paper has dried, you can rewet any part of it and it will not buckle.

Basic watercolor techniques

There are three basic methods of painting with watercolor:

1. *Wet color on wet paper:* This method creates soft, fusing effects. As the paper gradually dries, you can work with wet paint on the semidry surface to achieve slightly crisper definition.

2. *Wet color on dry paper:* This method allows for sharp definition and great control. You may want to pencil in the composition lightly before starting to paint. This method can be combined with working wet on wet — achieving soft effects by wetting specific parts of the paper.

3. *Dry color on wet paper:* In this method, water is applied to specific areas where you wish to paint. Crisp shapes and diluted washes are then created by applying fairly dry paint to the wet areas and blending where necessary.

Figures 5–25 and 5–26 illustrate these methods, as well as the drybrush technique, where a touch of dry color is applied to a dry area. Drybrush, however, should be limited to certain textural effects. Watercolor — as the name implies — is basically a wet medium.

If you wish to leave crisp white shapes on a broad wash of color, you must use a mask to prevent the paint from coloring the paper. Frisket paper is excellent for this. It comes in

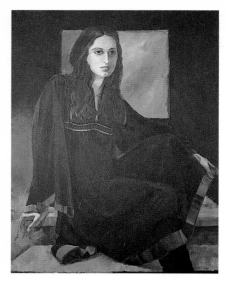

5–19. Painting method #1: building from big basic shapes, to small details, to the focal point. Acrylics applied with blended brushstrokes.

5–20. Painting method #2 by Michael McKeever: working one part at at time, keeping the whole in mind. Gouache, acrylic glazing medium, and gesso.

5-21. Painting method #3 by Eric Colquhoun: using layers of overpainting and underpainting until the image appears. Gouache, acrylic glazing medium, and gesso. Avoid an overworked result.

5-22. Painting method #4 by Paul McCusker: wiping out highlights and tint areas. Oils.

sheets that have an adhesive on the back. The areas that you cut out can be burnished onto dry watercolor paper to block the paint. Alternatively you can use a liquid masking agent, which is applied with a brush and later rubbed off. Thinned rubber cement is another possibility.

Because watercolor is a difficult medium to master, start with easy subjects. You might begin with a small landscape (Fig. 5–27) before moving on to still lifes, figures, and finally figures with props in action

poses. You can use photo references, but life studies are preferable.

To gain a better understanding of the medium, practice painting simple three-dimensional geometric forms. The approach is similar to the one described for markers in Chapter 3, except that here you are drawing the form with watercolor on a brush. Use the white of the paper for highlights, and build the other values by working from light to dark. Remember that with watercolor the amount of paint in relation

to the amount of water used determines the lightness or darkness of the color. Try layering light washes of watercolor to work up to your darks.

One of the strongest features of watercolor is its ability to create a mood. This is often obtained by working on wet paper with very wet paint. Experiment with painting wet on wet, wet on dry, and dry on wet. Figures 5–28 through 5–34 show you a few of the many effects that can be achieved.

5–23. Watercolor studies experimenting with different concentrations of paint and different degrees of wetness and dryness of paper.

5–24. Watercolor by Les Marubashi exhibiting complete brush control.

5–25. Watercolor studies using wet-on-wet, wet-on-dry, and semi-dry techniques.

5–26. Watercolor composition using wet-on-wet technique for the sky (background), semi-wet technique for the middleground, and drybrush used in the foreground.

5-27. Landscape by Les Marubashi
Watercolor. Wet-on-wet techniques
work well for clouds and water.

5-29. Painting method #2 by Peter
Malaguiti. Watercolor. Unadorned,
white areas contrast with the
dramatic, painted surface. A mask of
frisket paper was used to block out
paint.

5-28. Painting method #2 by Kevin
Breen. Watercolor.

5–30. A very controlled watercolor by Michael McKeever.

5–31. Painting method #3 by Adriana Taddeo. Watercolor and wax color pencils.

5–32. Painting method #1 by Sharon Matthews. Watercolor. Wet-on-wet technique was used to establish large, gradated areas. Then, semi-wet pigment was used to define colored shapes, values, and positive and negative forms.

Additional Media for the Illustrator

Although gouache, acrylic, and watercolor are the most popular painting media for illustrators, other possibilities exist. All of the following media reproduce well when photographed. It is a good idea to buy and experiment with a range of these products.

Colored inks

Water-soluble colored inks soak into a board surface. They come in a great variety of colors, which are relatively permanent unless exposed to sunlight for an extended period of time. If the colors are too intense, you can dilute the inks with water. If after painting an area you decide that the color you used is too strong, you can lighten it by applying household bleach with an old brush and then using a paper tissue as a blotter to pick up the excess color.

Dr. Martin's watercolor dyes

These dyes come in a wide range of brilliant colors (Fig. 5–35). They can be used straight from the bottle, mixed, or thinned with water. The main difference between watercolor dyes and colored inks is that when the dyes have dried, painted areas can be rewet and reworked. Moreover, the color can be lifted up, creating an interesting negative effect.

The cadmium yellow in these dyes can be painted over other colors to make them glow. The blue-black is excellent for painting halftones (the gray mid-values between light and dark) in black-and-white illustrations.

Luma dyes

These water-soluble dyes are extremely intense and vibrant. When they are dry, however, they cannot be reworked or lightened. Luma dyes are particularly good if you want large, flat, even areas of vibrant color. They are most appropriate for two-dimensional graphics. Because of their flat, smooth quality, they can produce effects resembling those of a silkscreen print.

Oil paints

Techniques such as oil painting and egg tempera are sometimes used by illustrators. If you are interested in these techniques, consult one of the many books that deal exclusively with them. Remember, however, that oil paints can be used for illustration only if they are applied in thin washes of color that have been diluted with turpentine or a thinning and cleaning agent for oil-based media (such as Varsol). The reason for this is that an illustration usually has to be done within a short time frame and oil paints take a very long time to dry. A painting whose surface is still drying can easily smear, either when it is taken to the client for approval or while it is at the printer. Consequently, most printers will not take responsibility for shooting an oil painting in this state.

If you want to use oil paints for an illustration, you should paint on a canvas board. As noted, if instead you work on a stretched canvas, you will have to take the canvas off its frame and staple it onto illustration board in order for it to be photographed for reproduction.

Combining media

Experimenting with different media is one of the most exciting aspects of the whole visual arts process. The following list suggests some of the other materials you can combine with conventional painting media.

- *For spraying and spatter effects:* spray diffuser, toothbrush

- *For textures:* sponges, sandpaper, rubber cement, soap mixed with inks, different drawing-paper surfaces

- *For collage:* newspapers, tissue paper, cloth, feathers, sequins

- *For drawing:* grease pencils, Conté crayons, colored pencils, wax crayons, pastels, graphite pencils, chalk

Painting Exercises

The exercises that follow are designed to improve your painting skills. As with drawing, the more you practice, the better you will become. You may even want to repeat these exercises several times, varying the subject matter or the composition.

To begin, use gouache or poster paint as your medium, since this is easy to work with. (It is also one of the most popular illustration media.) You do not have to purchase all the colors mentioned on page 136, but use at least two reds (warm and cool), two blues, and two yellows, along with black and white. Take some practice sheets and try out different color combinations. Also experiment with different kinds of brushstrokes, as described on pages 137–40. Once you have a feel for how to apply the paint, you're ready to begin.

Applying color theory

Before you do this exercise, study the information on color in Chapter 4. This exercise encourages you to investigate thoroughly the harmonious schemes of the color wheel. Do the parts of this exercise in order; they are arranged from the simplest to most complex. As you will discover in the first few frames, you need to determine the correct sequence of values and then translate this into cool or warm color relationships. Remember that warm color advances and cool color recedes. In addition, dark colors advance on a light background, and light colors advance on a dark background.

DIRECTIONS: To begin, work with gouache on 20- × 30-inch (51 × 76 cm) illustration board. Do not add any acrylic medium to the paint. Use nos. 2 and 4 chisel-point sable brushes.

First divide the board into twenty frames. As you perform the instructions that follow, design each composition as a landscape with trees. Use simple shapes rendered in flat colors.

FRAME 1: (Achromatic) Work with black and dark, middle, and light grays on a white background. Paint a daytime landscape, with the black in the foreground and the grays showing gradations from dark in the foreground to lightest in the background.

FRAME 2: (Achromatic) Now use white and light, middle, and dark grays on a black background to suggest a night scene. In this case the white should be in the foreground, with the grays showing gradations from lightest in the foreground to darkest in the background.

FRAME 3: (Monochromatic) Use one color only. Add black, gray, or white to the color to create different values.

FRAMES 4–9: (Complementary Colors) Do a frame of each of the following complementary pairs: (1) orange and blue; (2) red and green; (3) yellow and violet; (4) red-violet and yellow-green; (5) yellow-orange and blue-violet; (6) red-orange and blue-green.

FRAMES 10–13: (Triadic Colors) Paint four frames, using the following colors: (1) the primaries red, yellow, and blue; (2) the secondaries violet, orange, and green; (3) the intermediates red-orange, yellow-green, and blue-violet; (4) the intermediates yellow-orange, blue-green, and red-violet.

FRAMES 14–19: (Split Complementaries) Render any six of the following color schemes: (1) red, yellow-green, and blue-green; (2) orange, blue-violet, and blue-green; (3) yellow, blue-violet, and red-violet; (4) green, red-violet, and red-orange; (5) blue, red-orange, and yellow-orange; (6) red-orange, blue, and green; (7) yellow-orange, blue, and violet; (8) yellow-green, violet, and red; (9) blue-green, red, and orange; (10) blue-violet, orange, and yellow; (11) violet, yellow-orange, and yellow-green; (12) red-violet, yellow, and green.

FRAME 20: (Full Color) Choose any color combinations.

NOTE: In the complementary, triadic, and split-complementary color arrangements, you should use pure colors and then intermix these colors to create others. Mixing neutralizes the pure colors and can introduce subtle refinements.

Using warm and cool colors

Many beginners experience difficulty in painting three-dimensional subjects realistically in full color. Yet they may have no difficulty in drawing a figure or object and modeling it in light and shade, using different values of black and white. It is important to be aware that color not only has tonality but also temperature. That is, color has a definite warm or cool aspect.

It may be helpful for you to translate color temperature into tonal values. Since warm color advances against a cool background color, surfaces receiving direct light should be painted in tints of warm color. Similarly, surfaces in shadow should be painted in cool colors. Painting in this way increases the solidity and dimensionality of the subject.

DIRECTIONS: Using a black-and-white photo as a reference, paint a person in an outdoor setting. Show either the full figure or the head and shoulders only. Begin by drawing the subject on tracing paper, using a black felt-tip marker pen. Then, using a hard pencil, trace the subject twice onto a piece of illustration board.

Now draw over the penciled compositions with a brown water-soluble felt-tip pen, and erase the pencil lines. Then start to suggest volume by adding hatched lines to the areas in shadow. Next, using a wet brush, wet the lines of the felt-tip pen drawings wherever you want to introduce tone. Do this on both drawings. You now have line and tone drawings in a warm monochrome color.

To introduce cool colors, apply a semitransparent blue-green wash to both drawings in the parts of the figure that are in shadow. Use the same blue-green in a very pale wash over both backgrounds. Leave one rendering as it is; it is now complete. It shows modeling in light and shade, using color in its simplest form: the direct contrast of warm and cool color.

In the second composition, to play off warm colors, add very warm highlight tints of semiopaque color to the side of the face and body that is receiving direct light. Use a very pale tint of yellow-orange to do this, adding a small amount of white to the pure color.

Add more warm tints of color or pure warm colors to the lit side of the figure. Now look at the relationship of warm and cool colors. You may want to add cool bluish colors to the side of the figure that is in shadow. You may also decide to add cooler color to the background, in lighter-value washes than those used on the figure.

Bridge the meeting point of light and shade by rewetting certain areas and then brushing vigorously to mix the warm-colored penwork and the cool-colored paint. Mixing neutralizes these colors, since they are opposites or complementaries on the color wheel.

The principles you have learned in this exercise apply to all color work to a greater or lesser degree—although, of course, you must take the actual or local color of the subjects into account.

Composition

Good composition is essential to good painting. Review the composition terminology and diagrams given in Chapter 1. In this exercise you will explore various compositional devices and then compare them. Since composition should support your ideas, not fight them, you must carefully choose the device that is best suited to your subject matter.

DIRECTIONS: Use a 19- × 24-inch (48 × 60 cm) sheet of layout paper and a black felt-tip pen. Work on the sheet vertically, and leave a 1-inch (2.5 cm) border all around. Divide the sheet into twenty equal areas, with margins between each row. (A simple way to keep the margins even is to put 1-inch—2.5 cm—masking tape in this area.) Each frame will be approximately 4½ × 3¼ inches (11 × 8 cm).

Choose any subject matter, using separate subjects for each frame or treating the exercise as a theme with related subjects. In either case use a different compositional device for each frame, and note the compositional device you have used under each composition.

From marker roughs to paintings

DIRECTIONS: Start with small color roughs, using markers to develop the concept, to strengthen the composition, and to decide on colors. Work in small rectangles of approximately 4 × 6 inches (10 × 15 cm) and use restricted color schemes.

For each rough, make the listed art elements and principles dominant and all others secondary. When the rough is satisfactory, do a painting on either 20- × 30-inch (51 × 76 cm) illustration board or 24- × 32-inch (60 × 81 cm) Masonite. Coat the smooth side of the Masonite with gesso and let it dry before painting on it. Work either vertically or horizontally in gouache or gouache with acrylic medium; using large brushes such as a 2½-inch (6 cm) gesso brush and a 1-inch (2.5 cm) acrylic chisel-point brush.

ROUGH 1: Make the design asymmetric or off-centered; make the principle emphasis be by contrast and action; make the elements shape, line, and color; make the color scheme complementary.

Work with two interlocking figures. Leave these figure shapes white, and use color in the counterforms and background areas only.

ROUGH 2: Make the design asymmetric or off-centered; make the principle emphasis be by action and rhythm; make the elements line and area; and make the color scheme all the primary and secondary colors.

Create a composition based on a combination of numerals (for example, your age, telephone number, and ad-

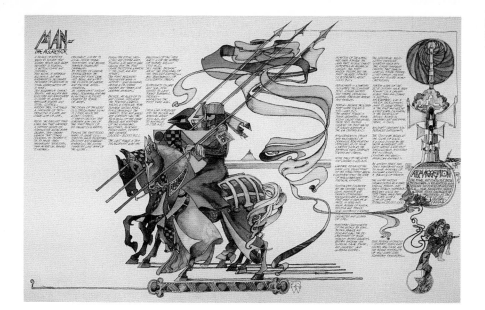

5–33. Painting method #2. Watercolor. Small areas were painted using the wet-on-dry technique.

5–34. Painting method #3 by Peter Malaguiti. Gouache and acrylic glazing medium, with different types of brushes.

5–35. Symmetrical composition done using Dr. Martin's watercolor dyes. Colors are more intense and vibrant than watercolor pigment.

dress) as an abstract arrangement. Vary the numbers' size, the position, and style.

ROUGH 3: Make the design asymmetric; make the principle emphasis be by contrast and rhythm; make the elements pattern, texture, and shape; make the color scheme analogous color (warm or cool).

From your imagination create an aerial landscape highlighted by a river with streams running into it. The ground is cultivated in some areas and not in others. By accentuating pattern, this rough should emphasize the graphic abstraction of the subject.

ROUGH 4: Make the design asymmetric; make the principle emphasis be by rhythm through placement and progressive repetition; make the elements shape and transparency; make the color scheme monochromatic.

From your imagination compose a still life of bottles. Vary the sizes and shapes. Create interesting overlaps and semiabstracted imagery. Do not model the bottles realistically.

ROUGH 5: Make the design asymmetric; make the principle emphasis be by contrast; make the elements shape, value, and texture; make the color scheme analogous.

Study one vegetable, cut apart in different sections. Arrange the sections into an interesting, balanced composition. The accent here is on shapes and counterforms.

ROUGH 6: Make the design asymmetric; make the principle emphasis be by contrast and action; make the elements mass and shape; make the color scheme split complementaries (mainly cool, with a touch of warmer color).

Base your composition on a man-made object, such as a shoe, typewriter, chair, or bicycle (refer to Fig. 5–7 on page 138). Provide a closeup view of the object, with tight cropping, and place the object within the rectangle in a graphic way.

ROUGH 7: Make the design asymmetric; make the principle em-

phasis be by actual-size proportion; make the elements shape, line, and pattern; make the color scheme triadic secondaries (violet, green, and orange).

Select an interesting variety of man-made objects. Accentuate the variety of the shapes and objects, to make your composition interesting.

ROUGH 8: Make the design asymmetric; make the principle emphasis be by action; make the elements texture and shape; make the color scheme warm analogous colors.

Design a composition consisting of one figure and one or two supporting elements (organic, man-made, or both). Stress the textural quality through the method of paint application. Use brushes, not a palette knife (a tool that restricts your range of textures), and use definite illumination—for example, high-key, low-key, or normal lighting.

The complete series, from start to finish, should demonstrate your developing understanding of form, design, and color. Painting techniques are inconsequential in this series.

exercise 5

Painting a still life

Now do six or eight still-life paintings, using any subject matter that appeals to you (Fig. 5–36). Here again, it is important to set up some definite guidelines before starting to paint. Decide on the type of composition, the color scheme, and the method of applying the paint. All of these depend on what you are trying to say about the

5–36. Experimental piece for Exercise 5 by Michael McKeever. Gouache and acrylic glazing medium. Painting method #2.

subject or on the mood you are trying to project.

Use large brushes to paint expressively and smaller brushes to add detail. Model objects by emphasizing light and shade. Try to complete each painting within four hours. Often paintings are more exciting if they are not too "finished" or slick.

Experimenting with brushwork

The key to successful painting and illustration lies in knowing what your brushes and paint media can do. This exercise is designed to expand your repertoire of brushstrokes. Before beginning, you may want to review the information on brushes given earlier in this chapter and to try out all your brushes on a practice sheet (Figs. 5–37 and 5–38).

For this exercise you will be painting several different compositions, applying the paint with a brush in the manner most appropriate for expressing each idea. The subjects are as follows:

- A still life of basic geometric forms—cubes, cones, cylinders, prisms, and spheres—done in a cool analogous color scheme and modeled solidly by means of light and shade

- A still life of either geometric forms or household objects, with the emphasis on warm analogous colors

- A figure in action

- A figure with objects

- Still lifes of your choice

Begin with marker roughs in color, to establish the composition and color scheme. Save the actual rendering technique, however, for the final paintings. For now, just indicate the basic shapes.

Vary the lighting within the compositions. And most important, vary the brushwork. In one painting you might use an impasto technique; in another you might lay on glazes for a transparent effect. Other possibilities include feathering with diagonal strokes; blobs, swirls, and streaks; planar strokes; and drybrush.

STEP 1: Draw up six equal-sized rectangles on layout paper. Sketch in the first two compositions. Then select the subjects for the last four composi-

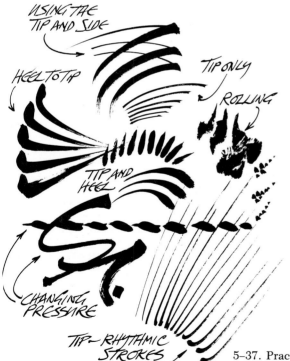

5–37. Practicing different brushstrokes and hand pressures.

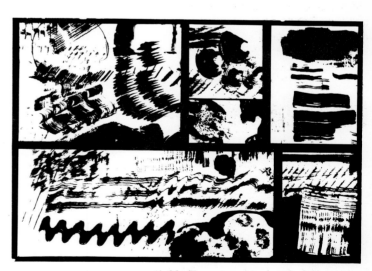

5–38. Experimenting with different brushes.

tions, find photo references for each, and draw the compositions with a black marker pen. After you have decided which color schemes and rendering techniques are appropriate, use markers to add color to the black-and-white linear layout.

STEP 2: For the finished art, use four pieces of 15- × 20-inch (38 × 51 cm) illustration board. (Save one in case you make a mistake.) In pencil, draw six rectangles, all the same size, two to a board.

STEP 3: Begin with the two still lifes in cool and warm color schemes. Apply a cool blue color over the first rectangle, out beyond the edges. Now paint in an orange overall background in the second rectangle.

STEP 4: Pencil in the composition in each rectangle. Then paint the basic forms in the first rectangle. Use a ruler and a chisel-point brush to follow the straight-edge forms with strokes in light, middle, and dark values, but paint the sphere freehand. Paint out a little beyond each form, except where they touch or meet.

STEP 5: Using a foreground color, cut back to define the outer edges of the forms (see page 140). Use the same method to define the outer edges of the geometric forms. (When working on the second rectangle, you should reverse the order so that you paint the background first.)

STEP 6: Paint the last four compositions, using whichever techniques you feel are most appropriate (Figs. 5–34 and 5–38). Use expressive brush strokes to bring out the character of each subject. Be as experimental as you can. Paint two subjects using direct methods of applying paint, and paint two additional subjects using indirect or layered applications of paint.

Rendering different materials

Illustrators need to develop their technical abilities so that they are better able to create the illusion of reality. In the illustration business you must be able to render realistically. Working from this sound base, you can then stylize, interpret, and distort.

In capturing a likeness of any subject, you must analyze the figure or object—its structure, weight, surface textures, and so on. Then you must decide which paints, materials, and tools will work best in simulating those qualities. This calls for a thinking and decision-making process. The actual rendering is easy after a thorough analysis has been completed.

Product rendering constitutes a large part of advertising and technical illustration work. In addition to wanting a realistic rendering of their product, clients expect you to give the rendering extra interest and life.

To do this, you must have the technical skills necessary to render different materials such as glass, leather, steel, chrome, concrete, and fur. Following are some tips:

If the object is heavy and quite dry in texture, such as a concrete block, try applying paint in a very thick, dry, impasto manner. If the object has an extremely shiny, lustrous surface, such as chrome, try working with a fluid medium.

If the color of your subject matter is primarily light, with small dark areas—for example, concrete (which has little pitted areas), grainy wood, or corn on the cob—lay in a dark background color first and then paint the lighter colors on top. This leaves the dark areas, the shadows, or the linear texture, as

negatives and makes them sit more effectively with the overpainting. They are not little dots and lines added later, which may seem to jump off the surface. If an object is very dark, with tiny light shapes or detail textures, first paint the lightest color overall. Then paint the exact darker colors needed on top of that, more thickly, to achieve a credible likeness of your subject. Subjects such as a wicker basket, an old suitcase, or a cane chair need a combination of light and dark underpainting for a good likeness. You must experiment.

For any rendering, ask yourself the following questions:

1. Should I paint light on dark or dark on light?

2. What type of brush is best, and do I need any other equipment?

3. How should I apply the paint—fluid and wet, fluid and crisp, feathered, impasto, or drybrush?

4. What other effects might I try? (Consider applying the paint with a sponge, sanding or scratching with a knife or razor blade, or holding the painting under running water. Some of these techniques can be used to create an aged, weathered effect. Free experimentation is the key to discovering new techniques.)

DIRECTIONS: Take a look at Figure 5–39. The techniques used are not complicated; the key lies in careful observation and analysis of the texture. Practice is also important. Use your knowledge of brushwork, and experiment with new tools such as a sponge and a razor blade to render the following ten subjects: (1) glass; (2) chrome metal; (3) satin or silk fabric; (4) steel;

5–39. Finished painting for Exercise 7 by John Hurley. Gouache.

Correcting errors

Rendering errors can be corrected in several ways:

1. If the art is on illustration board, cut through the top layer of the white board surface, remove it, and replace it with a patch from a fresh piece of illustration board. Lift up the new piece and sand the back, which is coarse. Then glue it onto the final illustration. The joint can be hidden by thick paint or by a heavy line (if it is an ink drawing).

2. To correct charcoal, ink, or pencil lines on illustration board, use a fiberglass eraser, even if you have already sprayed the drawing with fixative.

3. Bleach will remove certain colored dyes and inks from illustrations rendered in black ink on illustration board. Pick up the color with a paper tissue. Use an old brush to apply the bleach, since the brush will be damaged.

4. When using paint on colored papers or other glossy surfaces such as acetate, photographs, or photostats, mix a binding agent with the paint or ink. This will prevent crawling, bleeding, and chipping. Saliva can be used as a binding agent with paint; but *never* put a paintbrush in your mouth.

5. Use bleed-proof white paint to cover blots and similar errors. Typists' white correcting fluid also works well.

(5) leather; (6) polished wood; (7) plywood; (8) burlap; (9) fur; (10) concrete or brick.

These subjects are arranged in order from high-contrast, highly reflective surfaces to low-contrast, dull and matte surfaces.

Now try to render various other objects or effects—a basket, reflections in a pool or puddle, rope or twine, animal skin, clouds, rocks, grasses, tree bark, crumpled paper, crumpled tin foil, a fruit or vegetable, feathers, or other interesting things.

Rendering animals, birds, and insects

Forms in nature are exciting to paint. With the skills acquired in the previous exercise, you will find it easy to simulate fur, feathers, hides, and the like.

The most important aspect of this type of work is to draw the animal, insect, or bird anatomically correctly. Photo references are useful, but doing study drawings of live animals is preferable. Failing that, you can draw the stuffed animals in museums. The weakness of photo references is that they are flat and two-dimensional, and often paintings done from them reflect this flatness. Photos are good, however, for action poses, for accurate details such as coloration, and for basic shapes.

Many renderings of animals lack impact because the artists were too concerned with fine details. Such renderings look overworked and stiff, and they usually lack a strong underlying design.

DIRECTIONS: Choose an animal, bird, or insect, and render it in designers' gouache. Select a subject that has interesting textures and either bold or very subtle coloring. Avoid cute, cuddly animals that may entice you to fall into the trap of cliché images.

After you have rendered several animals, create a poster entitled "Survival," featuring a particular animal species. Work in gouache and in a restricted color scheme. Figure 5–40, for example, was done in black and white.

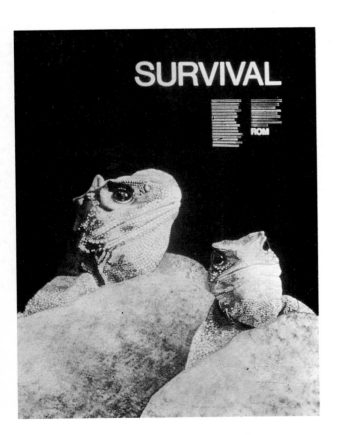

Experimenting with gesso and glazing medium

Once you feel comfortable working with gouache alone, begin exploring work with gesso and acrylic glazing medium as described on page 140.

STEP 1: Paint a thick, streaky coat of gesso on a piece of illustration board. Draw a complete composition of a subject of your choice—either a figure or a still life—on the board, with a charcoal pencil. Then apply a coat of clear glazing medium over the entire drawing. This process streaks the charcoal, which can be deliberately brushed in certain directions. At the same time, it fixes the entire drawing.

STEP 2: Apply colored glazes, using acrylic glazing medium with paint over large areas. When that is dry, add gesso to the paint and glazing medium mixture. The more gesso you add, the more opaque the paint will become. You can build up highlights with pure gesso and paint, or you can cut back to pure white if necessary (by painting light background areas last) and then tint these with the acrylic glazing medium and a touch of color.

STEP 3: Now try another illustration. At first treat your artwork as a basic black-and-white drawing. Using charcoal as in Step 1, do a line drawing of your new subject. Leave the gray glaze over the entire work, and then cut back with white paint in the background. At this point you have a black-and-white painting (Fig. 5–41). You

5–40. Finished painting for Exercise 8 by Debbie Walker-Crowle. Gouache and a small chisel-point brush.

can also apply one color over the top of it—for example, a gray—with the black line, plus perhaps a violet tinted with medium in certain areas.

The original line drawing can be painted out simply by applying paints in a very opaque manner. The result can be quite painterly, as in Figure 5–18.

5–41. Finished painting for Exercise 9. Charcoal drawing, gouache, glazing medium, and gesso.

exercise 10

Landscapes in acrylic

Let's banish these forever: chocolate-brown tree trunks, institutional-green grass and leaves, and mid-gray roads and paths. If you think back to your first days in elementary school, you may remember doing some of the most creative artwork of your life. There seemed to be no limits to your creativity. As you got older, however, you began to feel pressure to conform. Trees could not be pink or blue; they had to be brown, with green leaves. Under such duress, without realizing it, children begin to conventionalize their artwork to the point where it becomes a formula. Sometimes adults find that they have never taken note of the true colors of so common an object as a tree. Look for yourself. Tree trunks come in many varieties of colors; as well as different grays and even white. You will have to search a long time for that chocolate-brown, though.

To succeed as an illustrator, you must open your eyes and really look at what is around you. Is grass the same color all year long? Of course not. It even appears different at different hours of the day. True grass greens cannot be achieved by using a green paint straight out of a tube or pot. You will get more vibrant and realistic results if you mix yellows, oranges, or ochers with different warm and cool blues.

Spend time observing everything in a landscape. Look at a road at different times of the day. It can be yellowish or grayish white or blue-violet. Note any special effects you see, such as a highway that appears orange because the setting sun is reflecting off its icy surface. Imagine the drama of this image in a snowy landscape. The French Impressionists were masters at observing and recording the effects of changing light in nature; study their work.

After you have closely observed the colors in nature and perhaps made some sketches with color notes, you are ready to work on a series of landscape color studies based on memory. Remember that illustrators often have to meet tight deadlines. It pays to be able to paint from memory.

The paintings in this exercise should be very basic, painted expressively with lots of free brushwork. They are also good vehicles for experimenting with acrylic paints.

DIRECTIONS: Stretch several canvases, or use canvas board or Masonite. Gesso the surfaces. Work with the canvas upside down; painting upside down can make ordinary subjects more interesting and exciting. Instead of sketching in the subject, draw with the brush. Keep in mind that the top of the landscape is situated at the bottom of your canvas and that the ground is situated at the top of your canvas.

Remember that warm colors, value contrast, and heavy textures advance; try to emphasize this at the top of your surface. Use rhythmic linear intervals in studies of trees, rocks, and the sky.

Most important, really enjoy the painting process. Return to your pre-school state of mind. But don't forget the structure and form of the objects you're painting.

Toward the end of the working process, place your painting rightside up and use smaller brushes to refine it. Then do another quick painting rightside up. Has your thinking about landscapes changed?

Outdoor architectural rendering

Landscapes and buildings form a large part of an illustrator's work. You may need to render an architect's concept or existing buildings, historical or contemporary. To be able to do this you must practice architectural rendering.

This exercise makes use of what you have learned in Chapter 2 about the structural drawing of trees, water, and other landscape elements. You must pay attention to basic perspective, scale, and proportion, decreasing everything in size with distance. In addition, you need the maximum contrast of color and value in the foreground, less contrast in the middle ground, and much less in the background. Following are some additional tips:

When you paint a warm blue for the sky, add white to it near the horizon and work the white up into the blue so that the sky shows gradation from a very pale blue at the horizon to a slightly more intense blue at the top of the painting. You might try the same technique with the grass in the foreground. The grass can be a very pale blue-green at the horizon. Then use less blue in the green in the middle ground, and add yellow to the green in the foreground. This creates a sense of depth.

Wherever you locate the building, light it from one side only. Add a very small amount of blue into the color of the building on the shadow side. Add a pale yellow tint to the color of the building wherever it is not in shadow. Work out your composition, if necessary coloring in a marker rough.

DIRECTIONS: Go outdoors with a 20- × 30-inch (51 × 76 cm) illustration board, and in pencil draw the building of your choice accurately and in perspective. Think about adding interesting clouds and introducing or eliminating trees. Decide on the direction and angle of the light.

Beside your rendering of the building, draw six or eight different types of trees in a layout of small squares (Fig. 5–42). Introduce the same trees into the building setting.

Now begin your rendering, using either acrylics or designers' colors with glazing medium and gesso. Work from largest to smallest shapes and details. Use large brushes for the sky, grass, and foliage. Use smaller brushes for the building, the details on the trees, and so on. Above all, make sure that your color scheme emphasizes warmth; an architectural rendering must appeal to potential tenants.

In rendering the windows, depict the glass as transparent and reflective by using diagonal brushstrokes and contrasting tonal values. Use your brushwork to make brickwork and concrete solid and opaque, and to make foliage, grass, and shadows semiopaque. Finally, add crispness to the building by using a ruler and a chisel-point sable. (All the rendering at this stage should be done at the drawing board, so you can be very precise.)

This is a very difficult subject to paint so don't expect to get it right the first time. It is a good idea to do this exercise twice, to learn from your mistakes. You may choose to render the same building both times or to try different ones.

5–42. Finished architectural rendering for Exercise 11 by John Hurley. Gouache, gesso, and glazing medium.

Basic figure painting

Now it is time to translate what you have learned about drawing the figure into painting the figure. Start with a clothed model. Set yourself a time limit of two and one-half hours. This time restraint will force you to make decisions quickly and to paint directly. Consequently it helps promote gutsy paintings that are full of vitality.

At the beginning, use the simplest lighting possible. Let the model pose and then shine just one strong light on him or her. Work on a board of a dark color such as a brown, gray, black, or even blue; then you can paint only the highlights or tint surfaces of the subject. In doing this, concentrate on the planes or surface shapes, and paint vigorously with a large brush. The results can be dramatic, as in Figure 5–12.

After doing a few of these paintings, go on to paintings that involve strong contrast, where one side of the model is brightly lit and the other side is in darkness. Then do some paintings in a high key, with hardly any dark areas.

Experiment with other kinds of lighting. Notice that, as the amount of light increases or decreases, the shadows and details are strengthened or softened. Adjust the values and color intensities accordingly.

Most of the work should be completed within the time limit; but if the painting is not finished, you may work on it at another time without the model. Often the facial features, hands, and costume details need refining. It is important, however, to avoid overworking the painting—to learn when to stop.

MATERIALS: Use 22- × 28-inch (56 × 71 cm) matboard and leave a 1-inch (2.5 cm) border all around so that the image is 20 × 26 inches (51 ×

66 cm). Work with designers' colors or poster paint, beginning each painting by using the largest brush you have. (This will help in blocking out the big shapes and the placement of the lighting striking the figure.)

LIGHTING: At first, place the light source to the upper left or upper right of the subject. Avoid frontal lighting, because this makes the figure look flat.

MODELING THE FORM: When you rendered with markers, you followed the form with your marker strokes. But that was for a geometric form with a smooth surface. The human figure and its clothing have complex, broken-up planes, not smooth surfaces. To capture this effect, use multidirectional brushstrokes. Even arms cannot be painted smoothly, because they consist of subtle planes.

5–43. Incorrect and correct method of figure painting.

Study Figure 5–43 carefully, and avoid the most common error in painting the figure: following the form with the brush so faithfully that the figure looks as if it were composed of smooth plastic piping.

PAINTING FLESH COLORS: Flesh coloration varies greatly. In the beginning it may be easier to stay with earth colors such as ochers, umbers, and siennas, but more pleasing combinations can be achieved by using ultramarine plus cadmium yellow orange, or viridian plus cadmium red light, or permanent green light plus cadmium red medium. All of these can be tinted with white; without white, they can be used for shadow areas.

Shadows tend to contain some elements of the complementary of the flesh color. The receding planes in the figure, even in light areas, should be painted in colors of lower intensity to

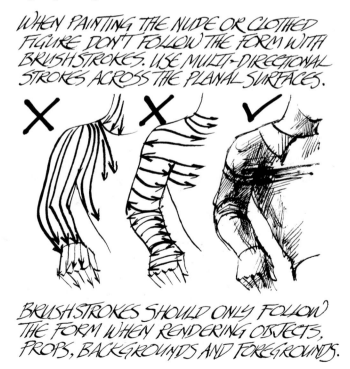

WHEN PAINTING THE NUDE OR CLOTHED FIGURE DON'T FOLLOW THE FORM WITH BRUSH STROKES. USE MULTI-DIRECTIONAL STROKES ACROSS THE PLANAL SURFACES.

BRUSHSTROKES SHOULD ONLY FOLLOW THE FORM WHEN RENDERING OBJECTS, PROPS, BACKGROUNDS AND FOREGROUNDS.

create illusions of roundness and depth without changing the value.

PAINTING HIGHLIGHTS AND SHADOWS: When a figure or object is viewed under a single light source, three distinctly different values are apparent: light, middle, and dark. In normal lighting, the light area will have a value of 1, 2, or 3 on a nine-value scale. The middle tones will have a value of 4, 5, or 6; and the dark or shadow areas will have a value of 7, 8, or 9. It is best to allow at least two steps in value between these tones in normal illumination — for example 3, 5, and 7. As lighting diminishes, so does contrast in value and in intensity of hues. In high-contrast lighting, allow three steps between values — for example 2, 5, and 8 (Fig. 5–44).

To mix the correct color for a shadow, first establish the subject's basic hue. Then mix this color and its complementary color to create darker, less intense values of both hues, and use these in the shadow areas. For cast shadows, mix the basic background color and its complementary color.

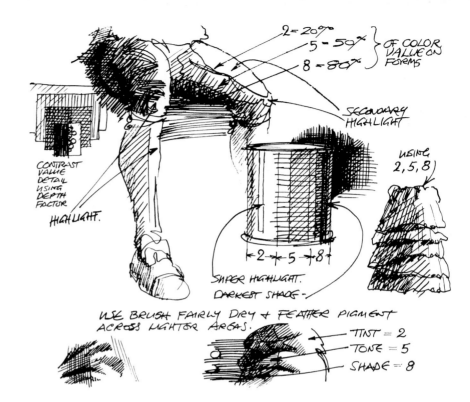

5-44. Color or grayscale value guide.

More figure painting

You cannot do too much figure painting. This exercise continues your study of the play of lighting on the figure. Paint both half-figures and full figures, tightly cropped within the rectangle.

On dark surfaces, paint a few figures in high contrast, using tints and tones only. The background can be left unpainted as a dark. Then, again using a dark surface, show some contrast on the figure. Use only tints, tones (middle values), and shades. Here you will need to lighten the background. Finally, on a white surface, feature the figure in high-key lighting with tints and tones only. All the shadows and contrast should be softened.

DIRECTIONS: First, set up your board on an easel. Don't draw the model on the surface with pencil; instead draw it with a neutral-color paint.

Instead of using a palette, select pure colors of the correct value and squeeze them into the appropriate areas. Use all paint thickly and opaquely.

Work with a 2½-inch (6 cm) brush, and mix the colors as needed. Add white for tints, black for shades, and gray for tones.

Using smaller brushes and multi-directional brushstrokes, model and define the planar surfaces. Finally, refine the facial features.

Painting figures in a setting

Exercises 12 and 13 concentrated on depicting figures on a flat, colored background. Now we will incorporate "props" and take a storytelling approach suitable for book, magazine, or advertising illustration.

Working in gouache or acrylics, begin with seated poses; then move to standing, semireclining, and finally fully reclining poses. (The latter two require extensive foreshortening.) The lighting can be normal, high-contrast, low-key, or high-key. Remember, though, that high-contrast lighting simultaneously simplifies the subject and (often) lends drama to the scene.

After painting the figure (either from a costumed life model or from a photo reference), use a photo reference to add a background. Choose a background that ties in with the pose of the figure, so that the situation is believable.

Regardless of the clothing or furniture details, everything should be depicted quickly. Paint only what is really necessary. Never overpaint or paint entirely from edge to edge. It is much more interesting to leave something to the viewer's imagination, inviting the viewer to complete in his or her own mind what hasn't been painted.

High-contrast painting

Strong illumination—with pronounced light/dark contrasts—can help you find the essentials in a composition. The two paintings in this exercise should help you refine your skills.

PAINTING 1: Do a self-portrait, looking at yourself in a mirror. Use only one light source.

Starting with a dark background, paint the darkest colors first. Add multidirectional brushstrokes of a mid-value color. Finally, add touches of the lightest value to create highlights. Paint these areas in lively strokes and flecks.

In most paintings of three-dimensional forms, tones of 80, 50, and 20 percent are sufficient along with extreme darks and lights (refer to Fig. 5–15).

PAINTING 2: Find a photograph of a musician performing in a nightclub. Using a ruler, draw a ½-inch (1.3 cm) checkerboard grid over the photo with a black marker pen. Then draw a 1-inch (2.5 cm) checkerboard grid on a piece of illustration board, using a ruler and pencil.

Decide on the size and placement of the subject by cropping the photo in a new way. Then, copying the photo square for square, use a brush in a dark neutral color to draw the figure, props, and background. Heighten the sense of excitement by slightly exaggerating the movement and pose.

With a large brush, paint the warm and cool solid areas. Then paint the highlights on the planes of the subjects. Try to accentuate the quality of strong artificial light. Next, paint the contrasting tints and shades (light and dark colors). Finally, define the details (Fig. 5–45).

5–45. Preliminary stage of a high-contrast painting for the second part of Exercise 15 by Michael McKeever. Watercolor using painting method #2.

Multiple-image painting

An interesting type of illustration consists of many pictorial images arranged in a balanced but asymmetrical manner (see Fig. 5–34). Multiple-image painting can be used effectively to tell a story. For example, images can be arranged to represent certain stages of the plot or to show growth, change, or metamorphosis. This type of composition is excellent for depicting social concerns, political problems, environmental and ecological subjects, psychological states, and historical events. It is particularly valuable in depictions of complex subject matter.

The first step is to collect appropriate reference material—photographic or otherwise—and to work out the composition in a color-marker rough. In the composition you might try using different types of perspective or unusual viewpoints, changing the scale and altering proportions, or mixing two-dimensional and three-dimensional imagery. Overlapped images and shapes can yield intriguing new colors and shapes. Pay attention to the negative shapes created by the placement of the various images.

The best way to design the composition is to draw each element on a separate piece of tracing paper with a black marker pen. Then move the drawings around, overlapping them. When you have hit upon an arrangement that pleases you, tape the drawings together and place them on a light box. Then lay a piece of paper on top, and trace the final composition.

Although any medium and technique can be used in multiple-image painting, it is best to begin with a single medium and a single technique. Too much of a mix can produce a disjointed and confusing piece.

Experimenting with different media and techniques

Experimentation with new media and techniques will keep your work from becoming stale and will provide you with new ideas. Often an art director must decide between using an illustration and using a photograph. If you are merely doing average representational productions, your work may not stand out from a photograph. Experimenting will expand your repertoire and give the art director more of a choice.

DIRECTIONS: Choose a well-known personality, either contemporary or historical, and find references to use as a basis for an experimental multimedia painting. Draw a 16-inch (41 cm) square on a 20- × 20-inch (51 × 76 cm) illustration board. Subdivide the square into sixteen equal areas. Then experiment with all the media and tools described in this chapter, combining different materials and techniques, to find an approach that expresses what you are trying to say in your painting. Work illusionistically, and use any black-and-white or color techniques. The more you experiment, the better (Fig. 5–46).

5–46. Finished mixed-media painting for Exercise 17 by Martha Staigys.

Painting Guidelines

Here are some suggestions for effective painting:

- Empathizing with the subject you are painting

- Before starting, deciding on art principles that suit your subject and stress certain elements

- Deciding which medium and technique to use

- Deciding whether a symmetrical or asymmetrical compositional balance will best suit the subject; think about the placement and cropping of the subject within the rectangle

- Choosing a fixed color scheme from the color wheel — at least at the very beginning

- Establishing the light source and type of lighting: normal, high-contrast, high-key, or low-key

- Letting warm colors with a touch of cool color prevail, or vice versa

- Using various shapes, spaces, and areas in both a positive and negative way

- Using large brushes to start a painting and small brushes to add details

- Using brushes expressively, allowing each to show its characteristics

- Letting brushstrokes follow the form of three-dimensional inanimate objects, describing their contours and surface planes, but not doing this with figures and clothing — in these instances using multidirectional strokes

- Except with watercolor, using a colored board or surface to work on (when appropriate)

- Studying the works of well-known painters and their use of color and line. Learn about art history and the different art movements

Mistakes to Avoid

You should try to recognize and avoid the following mistakes:

- Being overly concerned with technique, at the expense of everything else

- Applying paint a section at a time, as if you were painting by numbers

- Overusing textures

- Using the wrong brushes for the media selected

- Following the form and drapery on a figure with brushstrokes

- Using the wrong medium for transparent work — in particular, diluting opaque paints to the consistency of watercolors

- Using watercolors opaquely instead of transparently

Typography and Layout

Invitation poster for an art exhibition. Printed using the split-fountain technique.

Imagine that an art director phones you and asks, "Can you also handle the typography and layout?" In other words, you are being asked to do the complete job. Illustrators always did this in the past, but in the 1930s graphic design became a separate profession from illustration. Nonetheless, illustrators today need to know something about graphic design in order to work effectively with graphic designers. When both the lettering and the illustration are designed at the same time, a greater sense of unity prevails in the finished work.

Just as illustration grew out of illuminated manuscripts so typography developed from calligraphy. It then evolved through handset type to the present forms of computerized typesetting.

The art of typography is complex. One might compare indicating letterforms on a layout to drawing objects, especially the figure. Both require an exacting eye for proportion and form, as well as manual dexterity. Indeed, the ability to design skillfully with type requires years of experience.

Although you do not need to become a type expert, as an illustrator you may wish to incorporate letterforms into an interpretive illustration creatively. Pick up the catalogs of companies that make transfer type (also called press type), and keep these beside your drawing board. They can be valuable references when you want to choose an appropriate typeface or lettering style for a job. It is also a good idea to read an explanatory book about typography, to become better acquainted with the subject.

Knowing about type is just one aspect of the layout process—the way visual ideas are presented to a client for approval. As an illustrator, you may be asked to show a client various stages of a design or illustration, from a rough sketch to a polished layout. How to do this is the focus of this chapter.

When designing with type it is perfectly acceptable to select an appropriate typeface that is similar in nature to the characteristics of the featured illustration. A second school of thought suggests that type which contrasts with the illustration has a stronger visual impact. The decision is made by the designer and the subject matter often dictates the final choice.

Understanding Type

One fundamental distinction in type is between *serif* letters, which have tails (top example in Fig. 6–1), and *sans-serif* letters, which lack tails (second example in Fig. 6–1). Regularweight upright letters are called *roman*, in contrast to *italic* letters, which are slanted (third example in Fig. 6–1), and *boldface* letters, which are heavier.

Many different typefaces are commercially available: Times Roman, Baskerville, Helvetica, and Futura are common ones. The main text of this book is set in *California* (a version of *Caledonia*). In any illustration, lettering and type must be legible. Correct spacing must be maintained between letters and words so that the eye reads them easily. The overall effect should be one of even color—that is, an even grayness when you look at the type from a distance or squint at it.

Capital letters are called *caps* or *uppercase*, and small letters are called *lowercase*. Other typographical terms are shown in Figure 6–2.

Measurements in typography are given in *points* and *picas*. There are 12 points to a pica and approximately 6 picas or 72 points to 1 inch (2.5 cm). Typefaces come in many different point sizes, but 9- to 12-point type is most common for text. Sizes larger than 14 points are usually referred to as *display type*.

Figure 6–3 shows some text layout styles. In A, the text (also called *body copy*) has been arranged *flush left, ragged right*—that is, aligned on the left but not on the right. In B, the body copy is *justified:* the copy aligns on the left and on the right. In C, the arrangement is *flush right, ragged left*. In D, the copy is *centered*—a formal arrangement often used for invitations. E and F show two possibilities for a *logo* (the symbol for a company): either the name in a specific type style or the trademark (a pictorial device).

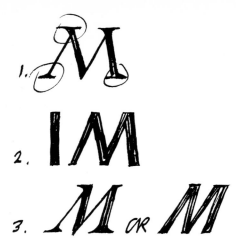

6–1. Serif, sans serif, and italic letterforms.

6–2. Typographical terms.

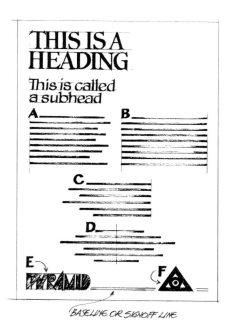

6–3. Type components of an ad.

Dummying Type

To indicate type on a rough layout you can simply use parallel lines, as in Figure 6–3. These lines indicate the x-height (the height of the lowercase letters) rather than the cap height (the height of the uppercase letters). The spaces between these lines should always be bigger than the lines themselves.

For practice, try this exercise. First draw two parallel horizontal lines on a layout pad. Make up a heading, and use the parallel lines as guidelines to letter the heading in all capitals. Do a rough drawing freehand. Then tear this sheet off, and put it under the next top sheet. Use a T-square and triangle to position the sheet. Following the instructions in Figure 6–4, use a T-square and tri-

1. T-SQUARE LETTERING ~ STEP BY STEP.
   VERTICALS FIRST...

2. THEN ALL HORIZONTALS

3. DIAGONALS USING TRIANGLE

4. FINAL SEMI-CIRCLES / CIRCULAR STROKES & SERIFS.
   ADDED FREEHAND

Sont so sontisont
son sonti so sontiso
so sont son sont
sontisont so son so

DUMMY TYPE BODY COPY.

6–4. Use T-square and felt-tip pen to indicate large headings. An even grayness is important when rendering lines and blocks of dummy type.

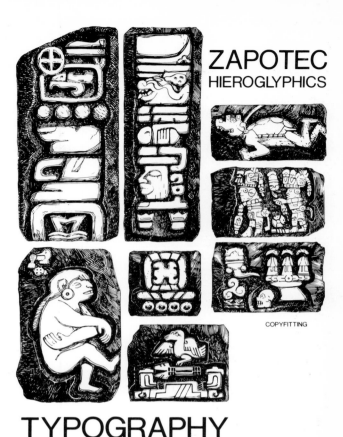

ZAPOTEC
HIEROGLYPHICS

COPYFITTING

TYPOGRAPHY

6–5. Finished comp by Alex Hawley. India ink and adhesive rub-down type. A finished comp usually combines type and illustration. In this example type has been set in caps only.

angle to draw in the vertical, horizontal, and diagonal lines.

Now go on to the body copy. Before type is set, you may be asked to dummy (or "greek") the copy in. The idea is to draw in meaningless words that simulate the weight of the desired type. Dummy type should appear to be an even gray when you squint your eyes, with no irregular or heavy black spots that jump out in the line or white open spaces caused by having the words too far apart. To do this, you must practice. Keep in mind that the average English word contains six characters and that one letterspace falls between any two words.

The more you know about how illustrations and type work together, the more aware you will be of the art director's or graphic designer's needs. In most designs either the type or the illustration predominates. Spend some time studying different designs. For example, consider Figure 6–5. What would happen if the type were italic? How might that interact with the illustration?

Layout Techniques

A *layout* is an arrangement of fixed elements, usually pictorial and typographic, within an area of a specific size. Attention must be paid to the requirements and limitations established by the client concerning size, number of colors, final production process, and type of publication in which the artwork will appear.

A layout converts the client's verbal instructions into a visual solution. It must contain all the requested information and at the same time strongly convey the client's message to the viewer or consumer. In essence, it is a prototype that the client must approve before production of the final artwork can proceed.

Several steps are involved in the layout process although not every piece goes through all of them. The actual sequence of steps depends on what the client wants.

Small roughs

At the beginning of the process, the artist puts his or her ideas down on paper, indicating the format and the different elements to be used. Small roughs (also called "thumbnails")

6–6. Preliminary small roughs (or minis) establish the artist's concept.

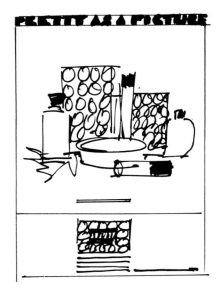

6–7. Slick small roughs finalize concepts more clearly.

should be done in a size approximately proportional to the final size. Use a felt-tip pen or marker for this. The best approach is to let your ideas pour out. Sketch a number of these ideas side by side for comparison, covering the whole sheet of paper (Fig. 6–6). Each idea should be different, not just a variation on a theme. Sometimes it helps to write a list of associated words on the side of your pad and let these trigger ideas.

Rough roughs (slick small roughs)

The next step is to choose the ideas that seem workable and to render them more precisely in exact proportion to the size of the final ad (Fig. 6–7). The design may have to be changed somewhat to fit the exact proportions specified. And it may take many of these roughs to find the correct balance of elements.

Layout linear

This layout, as its name implies, is drawn in black outline only, either in the actual size of the final artwork or at half that size (Fig. 6–8). Definite shapes or type elements should be rendered solid black, like silhouettes. Consistency of handling

6–8. Layouts organize both type and pictorial elements. Linears should be rendered in black and white only.

should be your goal here. Nothing is more distracting in a layout than drawing variations in the illustration or in the type. Make sure that the spelling of headings and subheadings is correct before presenting this layout to the client. You might also add one gray tone or one color very briskly to the layout, increasing its dimensionality.

Clean or slick rough

The client may request a slightly more finished layout at this point. Tear approximately 1 inch (2.5 cm)

off the top of your layout linear, insert it under the top sheet of your layout pad (the bottom and sides of the sheet should align with the pad), and place the waxed sheet under the layout linear to prevent the markers from bleeding through. Depending on the client's wishes, you may simply be asked to clean up the previous linear, possibly adding a flat tone or color to it. Alternatively, you may be asked for a slick rough, with *no* black showing except black that will appear in the finished art.

Semicomp

The next type of layout that may be requested is a semicomp, short for *semicomprehensive rough*. This stage is more elaborate than the slick rough, with precise drawing, clean and legible type indication, and good overall craftsmanship in the use of the rendering medium (usually markers).

The semicomp should simulate the look of the final printed piece. It

6–10. Comp layout for a charitable organization. Black marker and felt-tip pen and rub-down type. The layout was pasted onto an actual newspaper.

should indicate whether the final art will appear flat and two-dimensional or will give the illusion of three dimensions by using gradations of tone. Black felt-pen linework should be used only if it represents the finished art technique, as in a design using black line and flat color.

Comp

In the comp (short for *comprehensive*), the illustration may require a bit more polishing, but the focus shifts to the typographic elements. Transfer type or even typeset copy is used for the headings and subheads. Depending on the client's budget,

body copy may either be simulated by adhesive dummy type (the sheets of greeked-in—nonreading words lettered quickly—body type that can be burnished onto a layout) or be set in a chosen typeface.

Any medium—including markers, of course—can be used to render a comp. The important point here is that the type and the illustration are both given the same degree of finish. The comp should be a close representation of the printed piece as it will appear in a publication (Figs. 6–9 through 6–11).

Keep in mind that every art director or client has a different definition of what constitutes a clean rough, a semicomp, and a comp.

6–9. Comp layout for a food processor advertisement by David Milne. Markers and black felt-tip pen. Note the type indication.

6–11. Comp layout for a cable channel advertisement by Gary Alphonso. Black and white mixed media.

6–12. Negative photostat of a super comp.

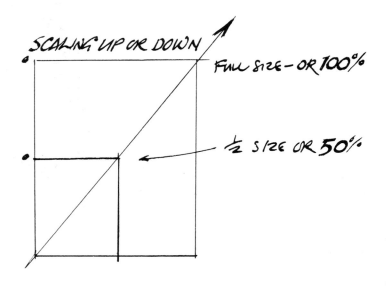

SCALING UP OR DOWN

FULL SIZE - OR 100%

½ SIZE OR 50%

One client's clean rough is another's semicomp. When you first start working with a person, ask for very specific guidelines to avoid a misunderstanding.

Super comp

The super comp is simply an extension of the comp. The rendering is virtually the same but the presentation approaches its finished state. Thus, whereas the comp and earlier layouts are usually trimmed and matted, using a neutral-colored cardboard window mount, the super comp's presentation simulates that of the final version. In the case of a book, magazine, or newspaper, the super comp would be pasted into a dummy publication to create an authentic look. In other settings, particularly three-dimensional advertising displays and technical models, the layout is pasted onto a unit constructed to simulate the final product (Fig. 6–12).

Resizes

Resizing involves adapting the original art so that it can be used in a range of publications, as in an advertising campaign. Often the original illustration can be enlarged, reduced, or cropped without further alteration. The type elements, however, may require more adjustment so that the text remains readable. Figure 6–13 demonstrates one method of scaling in situations where the art remains proportional. If you draw a diagonal through the original art, any proportionate rectangle will have the same diagonal. Thus, if you know the width or height you want, you can easily figure out the other dimension.

6–13. Layouts or finished art can be resized by using a diagonal line and scaling up or down from the original size.

Layout exercise

In this exercise you will go through all the necessary steps of presenting an idea to a client. Remember, however, that these are layout renderings, not finished art; so keep your renderings direct and impressionistic. You may want to review Chapter 3 on marker techniques before proceeding. You may even want to practice the line and T-square exercises given there.

There are certain objectives to keep in mind when indicating type headings and subheadings in marker layouts:

- Keep the thicks and thins of the type style constant and of uniform weight and color. This demands a very accurate and disciplined form of eye/hand coordination and drawing ability.

- Make sure you do not vary the size, weight, and stress of repetitive letterforms. (Make letters which are the same, look the same.)

- Pay careful attention to legible letter spacing. Once you have decided on tight, normal, or open/loose spacing, keep it constant throughout.

SPECIFICATIONS: The client is a retail department store that has just acquired a new look, including new packaging and shopping bags. They want to announce this in a full-page newspaper advertisement of 15 × 21½ inches (38 × 54 cm). The ad should be black and white only, with the heading "We have a New Look" and room for 200 to 250 words of body copy plus the logo or store name.

STEP 1: First put all of your ideas onto paper, in line only, using a black felt-tip pen and a black wedge-tip marker. To facilitate comparison, it is best to put everything on one sheet of paper.

Keep your roughs proportionate in size to the final ad size. If you don't do this at the start, you will probably have to do some redesigning later. It is not necessary, however, to measure the small rectangles for each rough. Just be sure to work in more or less the correct ratio to the finished size.

A good method for drawing the rectangles is to use a T-square. First draw the horizontal lines for the top and bottom edges of the small rough rectangles. Then, starting at the left or right edge of the paper, draw the verticals.

As you fill in the rectangles, try different compositions and totally different approaches. Make sure that the pictorial and typographic elements work together in each idea.

STEP 2: Select an idea to be developed as half-up roughs (roughs half the size of the finished art). Draw this idea within a half-size rectangle, using a black felt-tip pen. Work loosely, since you are simply resizing the elements from the small rough. Render both the illustrative elements and the type elements in equal detail.

STEP 3: Tear the half-size layout you have just done off the pad, and tear about 1 inch (2.5 cm) off the top of it, using a ruler. Then slip it under the next sheet. Redraw the half-size rectangle with a T-square, drawing the two horizontals first and then the verticals. Now draw the composition very accurately, working both freehand and with mechanical tools. To draw perfect circles, tape a felt-tip pen to a compass. For very accurate and smooth curves, use plastic French curves. For shapes or lines that repeat, use a snake—a rubberized lead strip that bends to and then holds any shape.

Your drawing should all be done in black line. If you want to create the effect of tone, hatch in free diagonal lines. Solid black areas should be filled in with a wedge-tip marker.

STEP 4: Now indicate the type. Decide on the cap height for the heading, and draw two thin guidelines. Plan the heading and a few lines of body copy on a separate piece of paper. Then slip this under the first sheet and position it accurately.

Using a T-square, draw all the verticals of the heading. Next, still using the T-square, draw the horizontals of the heading and rule in the body copy. Use a triangle to draw the diagonal lettering strokes in the heading. And finally, render the circles and semicircles of the heading in freehand.

You have now rendered a half-size layout linear, similar to the one in Figure 6–14. Even if you were working with markers in flat colors, this would still be referred to as *line only*.

6–14. Half-size, semi-comp layout rendered in line only.

STEP 5: Using the layout you have just finished as a guide, redraw the half-size rectangle with a T-square, and redraw all the black outlines, giving them an interesting line quality. You can add solid blacks now or wait until the end to do so. Do not add any hatching for tonal areas, however; you will be using gray markers for tone, combining line and tone.

In adding tone, remember to leave white paper where you want highlights to appear. To create a strong mood, let one tone predominate and emphasize contrasts in lighting.

Use only three tones for the objects you render: light, middle, and dark. Concentrate on drawing the pale values first, and add the dark tones and shadows last. Use black only if it is a local color.

To add the tone, use very fresh markers. Work about 1/16 inch (1.6 cm) from the black felt-tip pen lines. The color will run to the lines by itself. If you draw too close to the lines, they will bleed and create a messy look.

Insert the layout linear under the next sheet on the pad. Then insert the waxed sheet or a sheet of tracing paper between the top sheet and the layout linear. Using the T-square and the lightest cool gray marker, fill in any large shapes in vertical or horizontal strokes, overlapping them slightly so that no white paper shows through. In other areas you may want to scrub in the tone freehand. A very flat effect (which is sometimes desirable) can be achieved by scrubbing in all the shapes.

Now, working freehand and with mechanical tools, indicate all the middle-gray tones with a cool gray wedge-tip marker. Finally, add all the dark gray tones with a cool gray marker. If you did not render the solid blacks previously, do so now. Use the T-square for drawing final accents — for example, to strengthen black lines or to bring out details.

6–15. Tone-only layout rendered in gray and black markers.

STEP 6: At any point in the rendering process, the client may ask you to make changes in the artwork. This does not usually mean that you will have to start all over again. You can often introduce the changes by using patches and tape.

To do this, take the rendered layout off the pad and remove a fresh sheet of the same paper. Place the rendered marker layout over this clean sheet, and tape both sheets together at the top so that they won't move.

With a sharp scalpel knife, cut around the shapes or elements to be changed, making sure that you cut through both sheets. Follow the inside of any black felt-tip pen lines and cut around solid black areas where there is a joint. You can also cut shapes out of white areas, but the cut lines will show unless you cover the seam of the patch with a line or with white paint.

When you have cut out the patches, lift up the old rendered areas and dis-

card them. Keep the new white patches. Flip the layout over, and fit the new white patches into the holes. They will fit exactly because they were cut with the same strokes at the same time.

It is important at this point to wash your hands. They may have some marker ink on them, and this will transfer to the clean patches and to the tape. Using transparent tape, tape each patch carefully into place. To ensure a good fit, tape the shortest cuts first and the longest last.

Flip the layout sheet over to its right side and re-render the elements in the white areas, matching tones and stroke directions and adding black lines over the seams. It is practically impossible to detect patches that are done well.

STEP 7: You have now completed either a slick or a clean layout in line and tone. Now you will render a tone-only layout, consisting of all grays plus

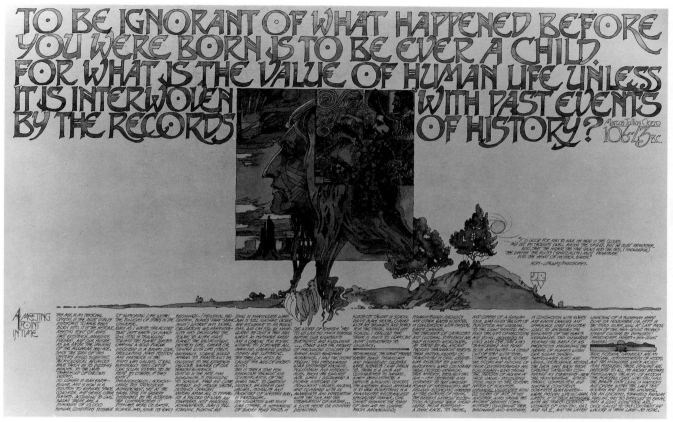

6–16. Super comp rendered in markers and black felt-tip pen for half-page institutional news ad layout.

black (if that is the color of an object in the rendering). No black linework is to be used around objects and shapes. Instead, gray markers will hold and define the total composition, with the white of the paper left for white subject matter and highlights.

This type of marker rendering most closely resembles the look of halftone illustrations of black-and-white photography (Fig. 6–15). To begin, insert your layout linear from Step 3 under the top sheet of the pad. Then insert the protective waxed sheet between the linear and the top sheet.

Draw the outside border of the layout in a very faint pencil line. Use the same process as in Step 5, adding grays in sequence from light to dark. You may want a wider range of gray markers at this point, especially if you need a higher degree of realism. However, you should never render with both warm and cool gray markers. The effect of such a mix is quite unattractive.

After rendering the basic values, add details where desired. A small amount of black linework can be used if the subject has lines on it. You have now completed a half-size tone-only semicomp.

STEP 8: To render a full-page lay-out with markers, like the one in Figure 6–16, simply repeat Step 7, but this time work at full size. First draw the composition into a full-size rectangle with a black felt-tip pen. Then lay this under a fresh sheet, and render the tones as in Step 7. Since this is a larger rendering, it requires more drawing, modeling, and refinement. The lettering also has to be crisper and more accurate, to match the quality of the pictorial image.

When rendering with markers, try to relax and be confident. If you do not, it will show in your work. Remember not to overdraw; instead, simplify wherever possible.

Additional Exercises

For additional practice, rework existing advertisements. Using the same wording for headings and the same amount of body copy, completely redesign the ads, putting your own concepts to work. Remember to make your ideas as functional as those in the original ads.

Now develop your own ad layouts for a variety of subjects. Here are some suggestions:

1. *Fashion:* Feature clothing, accessories, or cosmetics in a black-and-white newspaper ad and in a single-page magazine ad.

2. *Cars and automotive products:* Feature automobiles and accessories in a double-page magazine or newspaper ad and on an outdoor poster such as a highway billboard.

3. *Food products:* Choose a range of products such as garden produce, dairy products, or packaged goods. Render these in rectangular formats of different sizes for possible use in newspapers or magazines. Do them in black and white, full color, or both.

4. *Mechanical or heavy equipment:* Render on-site construction or farm equipment for use on posters, brochures, or folders.

5. *Sporting goods:* For a specific sport, show equipment in use. This will include figure work. Design the ads for newspaper, magazine, or poster use.

6. *Home furnishings and appliances:* Lay out a full-page newspaper ad for a retail department store. Show furniture and accessories, linens and towels, or kitchen appliances.

7. *Garden equipment and outdoor furniture:* Lay out a full-color double-page magazine ad for the product of your choice.

8. *Rendering people:* Design a poster or full-page newspaper ad for a charitable organization. Incorporate a heading and body type with a large portrait of a child or elderly person. Use a photo reference (Fig. 6–17).

Layout Guidelines

The following guidelines will help you perform tasks efficiently and professionally:

- Setting up your drawing table, layout pad, and equipment in a clean and orderly manner

- Organizing your markers in a marker stand

- Always working to the correct final proportion in scale or full size

- Using a calligraphic felt-tip pen or medium felt-tip pen—do not draw with a pencil—and developing flair and dexterity in drawing by using a thick-and-thin expressive line

- Using correct perspective for all objects and figures

- Making marker layouts crisp and professional by using the triangle and the T-square

- Combining accurate freehand marker strokes with mechanical strokes where appropriate

- Using the T-square/marker combination when rendering backgrounds, foregrounds, and mechanical forms

- Keeping your layouts fresh and spontaneous; they should not look like finished art

- Simplifying all forms when you draw and working economically

Mistakes to Avoid

Beware of the following pitfalls in doing layouts:

- Not using design principles to organize the elements of an illustration

- Disregarding the correct proportions of an advertisement in the layout stages

- Not using the appropriate tools and equipment for layout

- Destroying the unity of a layout by overworking separate parts at the expense of the whole or by using incorrect perspective or proportions

- Using felt-tip pens of uniform thickness unexpressively or drawing timidly

- Overworking a layout by modeling too much with the markers instead of using the correct tonal or color markers to indicate light and shade

6–17. Marker layout for a full-page
news ad comp by Kent Burles.
Markers and black felt-tip pen.

Reproduction and the Printing Process

Line drawing with black marker felt-tip pen. Progressive repetition showing movement.

a fine artist can use any medium and technique, because the artwork does not have to be reproduced for mass publication. An illustration, however, requires a knowledge of printing processes, because the illustration may have to meet specific production criteria. Six main factors must be considered:

- Where the illustration will appear

- The print run

- How many colors are needed to print it

- The cost of reproduction

- The type of press

- The paper size and quality

These factors help determine the most effective medium and techniques; they also have an impact on the client's specifications to begin with.

The illustrator is usually not directly involved in the budgeting of a job and in the production specifications. These aspects are the concern of the client, the advertising agency account executive, or the art director. In the case of a small business client, however, a freelance illustrator who is knowledgeable about production may be able to help by getting quotes from a typesetter and printing house. The client must pay a fee for this extra service.

Generally, the more you know about production, the more chance you have of controlling the quality of the end result. Of course, you have to be careful about stepping on someone's toes, but most art directors and graphic designers welcome an illustrator's input. Most important, you will know how to prepare the artwork so that no question will arise about how it should be reproduced.

Reproduction Techniques

Let's begin with the simplest type of illustration, line art, which also happens to be the cheapest to reproduce. Then we will work our way to full-color illustration, which is the most complicated to create and the most expensive to reproduce.

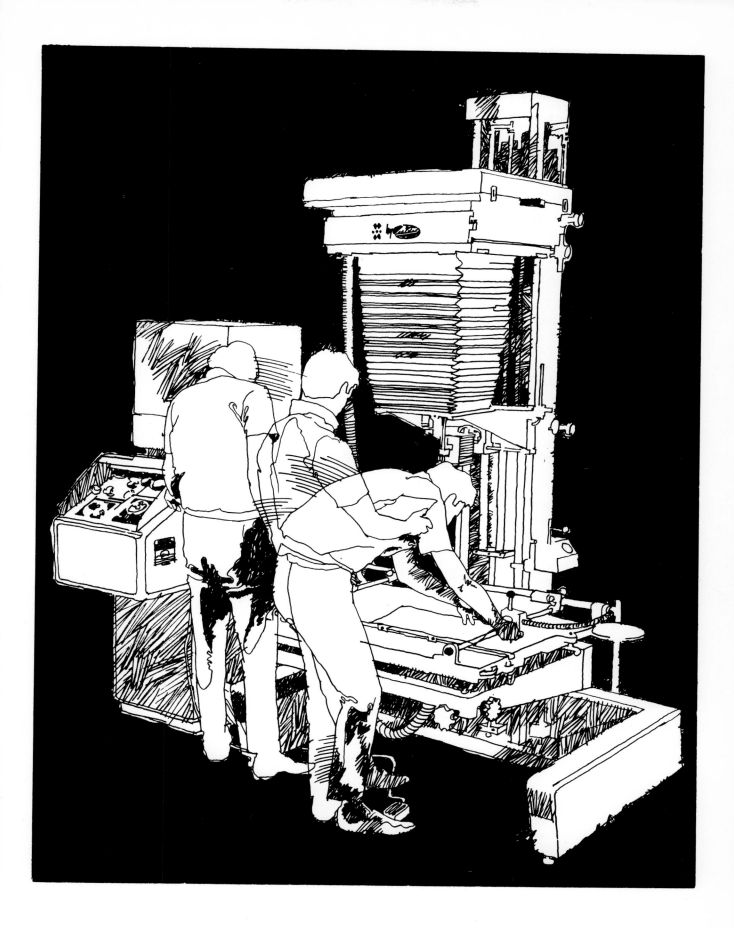

Line art

An illustration consisting of solid black lines, areas, or dots, but lacking tones, is called *line art*. Rendering techniques based on using a pen or brush and ink, stippling, crosshatching, rules, lines, scratchboard, grease pencil, linocuts, wood blocks, and the like are considered forms of line art. Figure 7–1 shows two different ways of rendering a scene, but both pictures are line art. Each mark is black; there are no grays.

Continuous-tone copy

Drawn or painted illustrations that use gradations of tone or combinations of line and tone are called *continuous-tone copy*. (The word *copy* refers to any material that is to be printed.) Pencil and pastel drawings, paintings in all media, tonal marker renderings, airbrush, pen, and wash illustrations, and photographs are all forms of continuous-tone art (Fig. 7–2). For reproduction, the grays in these artworks must be translated into black dots of varying sizes by means of a halftone screen. If you look at any tonal illustration in this book through a magnifying glass, you will see that it is actually composed of many black dots. The amount of grayness you see is determined by the ratio of white paper to black dots in a given area.

Line and tone combinations

Often illustrators use both line and tone. If an illustration is screened as a halftone, the black lines in it will be composed of black dots and may therefore have a slightly irregular edge. This is particularly problematic with type, which may appear fuzzy in a halftone. As long as the type or other line areas in an illustration are discrete, the work can be shot as a combination of line and halftone. This involves photograph-

7–1. Drawing by Patrick Sayers. India ink and pen. One scene rendered two ways, using line, high-key, and high contrast.

7–2. Continuous-tone art.

ing the line and tone areas separately and then recombining the two.

Flat tints and self-adhesive screens

By specifying to the printer that you want a tint in a certain area, you can convert a solid black to any percent-

age of black—that is, to a particular gray. As in the halftone process, the printer screens the black so that it becomes a series of black dots with the white paper showing through in between. But a tint is a uniform and constant pattern of black dots, whereas a halftone is built from irregular black dots that create different densities of tone. In fact, a tint does not have to be gray; it can be a tint of any color or color combination of printing inks being used. Illustrators may also be interested in self-adhesive sheets of different screens available in art-supply stores. Numerous types of dot and line patterns are marketed, as well as grids, textures, perspectives, and special optical patterns. Figures 7–3 and 7–4 show a few of the effects you can achieve with these screens.

Square halftone

The square halftone is the simplest and most commonly used type of halftone illustration. It is rectangular or square, and the entire image is covered with dots. Essentially no solid blacks or pure white areas are present (Fig. 7–5).

Silhouette halftone

An illustration that consists of an irregular outline shape on a white background is called a silhouette or outline halftone. A complete range of grays appears in the illustration itself, but all the dots outside the image's edges have been removed, leaving the background white (Fig. 7–6).

7–5. Square halftone by Louise Andison. Gouache, glazing medium, and gesso.

7–4. Using self-adhesive screens.

7–3. Composition by Henry Van Der Linde. Self-adhesive, rub-down mechanical screens.

7–6. Silhouette halftone by Henry Van Der Linde. Grease pencil, India ink, and pen.

Dropout halftone

In a dropout or highlight halftone, the dots have been removed in the pure white areas or highlights within the illustration so that only the white paper shows (Fig. 7–7). The dots may be eliminated by photographic techniques, or they may be manually opaqued on the film.

Vignette halftone

In a vignette halftone, the illustration is given an irregular shape, with a shadow or soft edges fading out to white. The dots on the edges become progressively smaller until they eventually disappear. This imparts a soft, blending tone to the edges (Fig. 7–8).

Duotone

A duotone is produced by overprinting two halftones of the same original art work in two colors, usually black and one color; for example, cyan or magenta. The halftones are shot at different screen angles, thus achieving tonal contrast of maximum highlight and shadow. This enriches the illustration by giving it a fuller tonality.

Four-color process

Printed full-color illustrations are made up of dots of four colors: yellow, cyan (blue), magenta (red), and black. If you look at any of the color illustrations in this book through a magnifying glass, you will see that it is composed of red, yellow, blue, and black dots. The range of color you see is the result of optical mixing, much as in pointillist paintings such as those of Georges Seurat. All colors can be created by varying the percentage of dots of each color in relation to each other.

The best four-color printing reproduces color almost without diminution of quality. Any two-dimensional medium and technique will reproduce. What you see in the artwork is essentially what you get in the printing, although there may be some loss in subtle color shifts.

Printing Methods

There are four basic ways of printing an illustration: letterpress, silkscreen, rotogravure, and offset lithography.

Letterpress

Also referred to as *relief printing*, letterpress is used for small to medium print runs. The image is in relief—that is, raised up from the background—and the paper is pressed onto the raised inked surface. This method is suitable for such jobs as folders, flyers, invitations, and calling cards.

Silkscreen

Silkscreen—also called *serigraphy*—uses a camera and light-sensitive emulsion to produce a stencil. Alternatively, the image may be cut directly out of a paper stencil attached to a mesh screen. The ink goes through the clear screen and onto the surface to be printed. Silkscreen images can be printed onto almost any surface. Silkscreening, however, is used only for very small print runs—for example, 2,000 posters. It is not the best process to use for fine line illustration.

Rotogravure

In rotogravure the image is cut or etched into the surface of a metal plate, which is then inked and wiped clean. When the paper is pressed onto the plate, it absorbs the ink in the depressed areas. This intaglio printing method is used for magazines, newspaper color supplements, packaging, postage stamps, and fine art reproductions. It is good for big print runs (100,000 and up).

Offset lithography

Probably the most popular printing method is offset lithography. The plates are made photographically. A light-sensitive emulsion coats the

7–7. Dropout halftone by Timothy Stevens. Charcoal pencil and Conté stick.

7–8. Vignette halftone by Henry Van Der Linde. India ink, line and wash drawings.

plate, and when the image is exposed and the plate cleaned off, the image is left as a greasy surface that retains ink. The image is transferred (offset) to a rubber plate and from the rubber plate to the paper. This method is primarily used for printing magazines, newspapers, and books in substantial runs.

Preparing Artwork for Printing

The line art and type are put in position on illustration board, making up what is commonly called a *mechanical*. Any halftones or pieces of four-color art are kept separately, but their position is noted on the mechanical by a photocopy, a photostat, or simply an outlined area. The person who prepares the mechanical is called a *pasteup* or *mechanical artist*, and the process is referred to as *pasteup*.

The number of colors to be used sometimes makes a difference in how the material is prepared. If the printing is to be done in one color, (usually black), all the material can be placed on the same board. If there are two, three, or more colors, however, some of the art may have to be preseparated and placed on overlays of transparent vellum or acetate. This is particularly true if specific printing inks are being used rather than the four-color process. Because different printers have different requirements for what needs to be separated, be sure to ask the production person how best to prepare the art for the printer.

In general, preparing preseparated art involves the following steps:

Step 1. The artwork that is the most complex (usually black) is placed on the illustration board. Trim marks are indicated to show the paper edges. Folds are indicated with a fine dotted line. Photostats or photocopies are put into position, if photographs are to be used. Crop marks and sizes are indicated on the original photos (Fig. 7–9).

FOCUS 81
an exhibition of photography

When Charles Hill, Assistant Curator of Post-Confederation Art at the National Gallery of Canada, was in the process of organizing the exhibition Canadian Painting in the Thirties, he came across a little-known artist of the period, the photographer John Vanderpant.

Charles Hill has followed the evolution of the artist's work through the many stages of his career. Vanderpant devoted himself to the cultivation of themes derived from his natural surroundings to give an undeniably national character to his photographs. Well aware of technical developments and wishing to transcend the pictorial aesthetic, Vanderpant pursued his experiments to achieve a new vision - the expression of a very essence of form. His explorations led him to a conception of beauty that is a result of the approach of the observer, the treatment of the subject, and balanced relationships in the work of art. The most modest of subjects - a grain elevator, a vegetable, a plant - offered Vanderpant the opportunity to reveal a harmony of precision in the immediacy of the object itself. The artist's vision relied upon his own eye and not on the manipulation of negatives or prints.

John Vanderpant is, without doubt, an important photographer and this exhibition will, we hope, make him better known and appreciated.

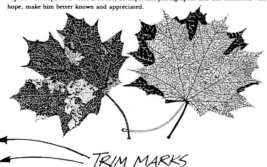

TRIM MARKS
REGISTER MARKS

7–9. Preparing preseparated mechanical art by David Milne: sizing and positioning of photos, type being assembled on board, and indicating trim marks.

Step 2. If an additional color is to be printed, any areas that overlap the black plate must be placed on a transparent acetate overlay. (It used to be that everything in the additional color had to be placed on an overlay, and a few printers still prefer this.)

Step 3. An overlay must be registered to the art on the board with small cross-shaped register marks, to ensure perfect alignment when the colors are printed one on top of the other.

Step 4. The mechanical is flapped with a sheet of tracing paper. Instructions to the cameraperson and printer are indicated on it (Fig. 7–10).

Step 5. It may be necessary to mark the color breaks on the tissue with felt-tip pens and colored markers, to show how the colors will look when printed (Figs. 7–11 and 7–12). If you are using specific inks, you may need to attach small color swatches on the board surface.

If all of this sounds complicated, keep in mind that normally the illustrator is not required to know everything about complex reproduction and printing processes. Such expertise is primarily the responsibility of other professionals — production managers, graphic designers, and pasteup artists. Generally, the art director, client, or production manager will tell you exactly how he or she wants the artwork prepared for reproduction.

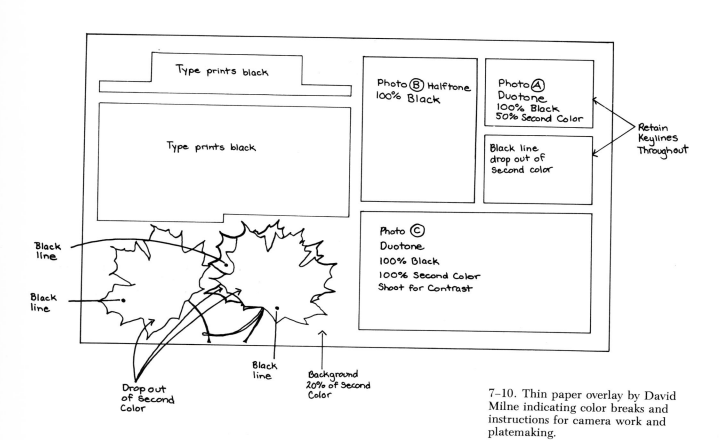

7–10. Thin paper overlay by David Milne indicating color breaks and instructions for camera work and platemaking.

7-11. Final proof of the rotogravure-printed piece.

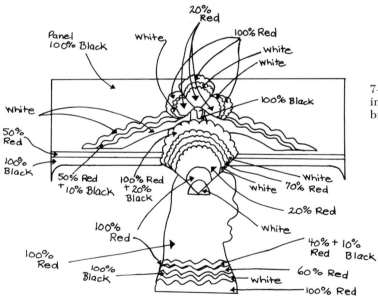

7-12. Thin paper overlay indicating instructions to printer for color breakdown and percentages.

Illustration

the vast majority of illustration is reproduced in black and white—as black line, line and tone (grays), or continuous tone (grays that show gradation). An illustrator thus needs to develop a repertoire of black-and-white techniques. Although most drawing or painting techniques can be done in black and white, certain techniques reproduce better than others. Study black-and-white illustrations in magazines to see what works. Also look at black-and-white prints such as linocuts, woodcuts, etchings, and lithographs. Some of these techniques can be simulated for reproduction.

An arbitrary or flashy technique alone, chosen for effect only, cannot save a poor or weak drawing. Technique should support the concept or idea and reinforce the design and content. The choice of technique and medium should be based on their appropriateness to the subject matter and to the type of image that the client wishes to project. Illustrations have a function to perform, and this must be the key consideration in deciding on media and techniques.

Practical Considerations

In applied illustration, the choice of technique is also affected by relative cost, by the method of printing, and by the deadline—factors the client or art director controls. The illustrator is told in advance if he or she should work in line only, in line and tone, or in full continuous tone (halftone).

Illustrators should nevertheless be aware of certain cost and printing considerations. Line art is the most economical to reproduce. Halftones are more expensive, and combination shots can be even more. Silhouette and vignette halftones generally cost more than square halftones. If you intend to do a lot of silhouetting, make sure your client's budget allows for this.

For illustrators, the deadline is more than just a date to be met; in many cases, the technique is determined by the deadline. Certain techniques, such as stippling, are very time-consuming and therefore inappropriate for a rush job. Figure out how much time it generally takes to produce different types of illustrations.

Illustration by Paul McCusker. India ink and pen.

Possibilities for Line and Halftone

As we saw in Chapter 7 all illustration techniques fall into two main categories of printing reproduction: line and halftone. Pen and India ink drawings are a good example of pure black line. Pencil or wash drawings, which produce various grays, are reproduced as halftones. It is possible, however, to convert a predominantly gray illustration or a tonal pencil drawing into line art by photographic techniques, such as using a photostat camera. The artwork is simply shot "hard," so that all dark grays reproduce as black and very light grays disappear.

To gain an appreciation of the range of possibilities, look at the examples of line and halftone techniques in Figures 8–1 through 8–4. You might try a similar exercise on your own, taking the same subject and rendering it in various ways.

Keep in mind that the surface you work on will affect the technique you use. Paper ranges from very smooth (hot-pressed) to extremely rough (handmade papers). A paper with greater roughness is said to have "tooth." If, for example, you want a heavy texture, you might work with Conté crayon on a paper that has a lot of tooth. Experiment with one medium, using different techniques on different paper and board surfaces, to discover what effects can be achieved with it.

ILLUSTRATION **189**

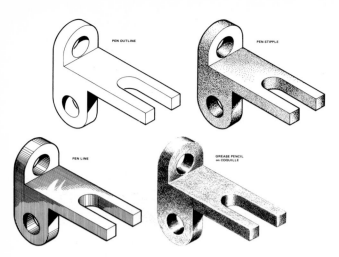

8–1. Line reproduction techniques by Frank Miller: pen outline, pen stipple, pen line, and grease pencil on coquille boards. Reprinted by permission of Mrs. Frank Miller.

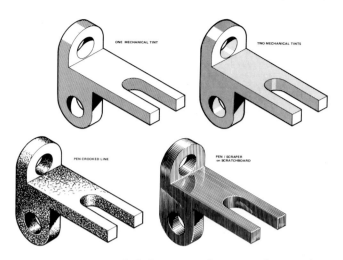

8–2. Line reproduction techniques by Frank Miller: one mechanical tint, two mechanical tints, crooked pen line, and pen/scraper on scratchboard. Reprinted by permission of Mrs. Frank Miller.

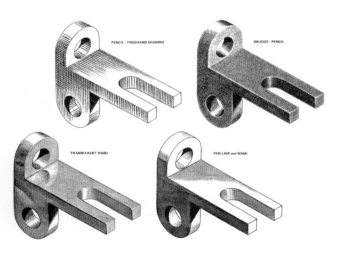

8–3. Line and halftone reproduction techniques by Frank Miller: pencil with freehand shading, smudge pencil, transparent wash, and pen line and wash. Reprinted by permission of Mrs. Frank Miller.

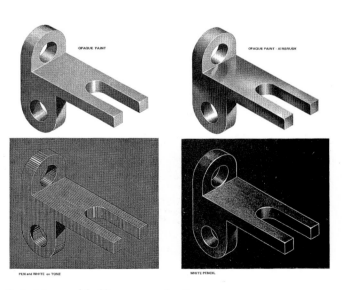

8–4. Line and halftone reproduction techniques by Frank Miller: opaque paint, airbrushed opaque paint, pen and white paint on tone, and white pencil on black paper. Reprinted by permission of Mrs. Frank Miller.

Experimenting with Line Techniques

The key to understanding existing techniques and developing new ones is experimentation. Begin with the basic medium of the illustrator, pen and ink. Explore the variety of expressive lines that you can achieve just by manipulating the pen nib. The way you draw can convey the essence of character of the subject. By twisting, rolling, stabbing, stroking, scratching, and varying the pressure of the nib's tip against the paper surface, you can achieve any number of effects.

Figures 8–5 and 8–6 offer examples of line qualities that express different feelings. Expressive line can be particularly important for editorial and book illustrations, commonly called *story illustrations*. To understand the emotive potential of a line, take the same subject and draw it three or four times, using contrasting kinds of line: peaceful versus agitated, assertive versus vague, and so on.

Now investigate a more controlled kind of line, one more suitable for advertising or product illustration of both objects and figures. Here line may be used on its own as an outline or as tonal shading. Figure 8–7 shows a number of ways tone can be achieved with line. Take care not to make your crosshatching too fine, however, or it may reproduce as solid black.

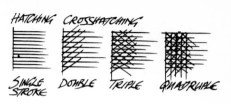

8–7. Achieving different tones through hatching and crosshatching.

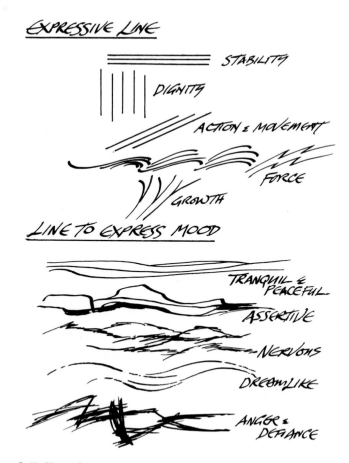

8–5. Using line to express mood. Pen and ink.

8–6. Experimenting with expressive line quality.

ILLUSTRATION **191**

Experimenting with line

Apply all that you have learned about line techniques so far to an illustration of a subject of your choosing. Select a subject that seems appropriate for line techniques only, and restrict yourself to pen and black ink. Tonal shading may be done with line, dots, or spatters of undiluted black ink (Figs. 8–8 through 8–16). Avoid pencil shading or washes.

8–8. Illustration by Ron Fyke. India ink and pen. Loose crosshatching and pen stipple contrast with the bold shapes of the design.

8–9. Illustration by Paul McCusker. India ink and pen. Multidirectional linework used to create tone.

8–10. Illustration by Paul McCusker. India ink and pen. Different line techniques.

8–11. Illustration by Paul McCusker. India ink and pen. Curvilinear and rectilinear lines contrast with stippling technique.

8–12. Illustration by Mark Smith. India ink, pen, and brush. Sensitive, curvilinear lines contrast with bold, black and white shapes.

8–13. Illustration by Paul McCusker. India ink and pen. Tightly rendered crosshatching contrasts with toothbrush splatter and curvilinear linework.

ILLUSTRATION **193**

8–14. Illustration by Ron Fyke. India ink and pen. Sensitive use of stipple technique conveys the delicate nature of the subject.

8–15. Illustration by Gary Alphonso. Black grease pencil. Loose, directional line and texture.

8–16. Illustration by Patrick Sayers. India ink and pen. Variations of vertical lines explore rhythm and texture.

Combining line and tone

Now try combining the pen line techniques with grays or tones and various mixed media. The best way to gain an understanding of both line and halftone techniques is to do both simultaneously for contrasting effects (Fig. 8–17). Do these on two different paper surfaces and make comparisons. Let yourself go, and have fun. Later on, you may be able to use these experiments individually in illustrations.

Figure 8–18 shows various techniques done in both positive and negative ways on heavily textured paper. Try some of the line and tone techniques on smoother layout paper, sometimes laying it over the textured paper. To get a dotted, spattered effect, paint or spray ink or paint over resists such as rubber cement or candle wax. Try using a brush, a spray diffuser, or even a toothbrush to apply the ink or paint.

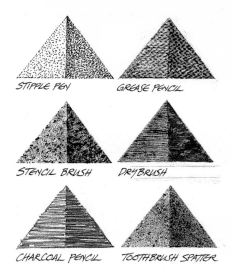

8–17. Lines and tones produced using different media on a variety of surfaces.

8–18. Experiment using different techniques, such as resists (rubber cement, candle wax, etc.).

ILLUSTRATION **195**

Experimenting with line, tone, and resists

Now explore some of the techniques discussed. Select six or nine photo references of people, and arrange them in a square or rectangular format. Try to find portraits that are lit in a dramatic way. Use different paper surfaces, including chemically treated papers such as photostat paper; and in negative and positive ways use line, tone, and resists. Do the experiments individually, and then paste them down to form a square or rectangular shape (Fig. 8–19). After you have finished, identify the techniques and media used on the back of the board, for later reference.

8–19. Finished artwork for Exercise 2 by Henry Van Der Linde. India ink, pen, and brush.

Tint screens

Tint screens on transfer sheets — also known as self-adhesive line tint screens — are available in art-supply stores. Create a few illustrations with these, doing the linework in pen and ink and then applying line or dot shading with tint sheets. Look in a transfer-type catalog to see the varieties of patterns available. You may wish to try combining various textures in one illustration.

Figures 8–20 and 8–21 were produced using adhesive tint screens, while Figure 8–22 shows an imitation of these done by hand with pen and ink. Notice that any line drawing can be overlaid with a screen by the printer to create a different effect; however, you must specify which screen you want used.

8–20. Using adhesive tint screens in a cartoon by David Milne. India ink and pen.

Converting tone into line

Media such as pastel, charcoal, and pencil are usually considered to be tonal, but as noted earlier they can be converted into line with a photostat camera (Fig. 8–23). Pale tones and light lines disappear, leaving only black and white. If you plan to use this effect, draw the original using relatively high contrast. If you lose too much definition in the photostat, have the operator adjust the exposure. If that does not work, add more contrast to the artwork and then reshoot it.

Experimenting with Tonal Techniques

Continuous-tone art containing gradations of gray tones is reproduced by the halftone process. Such art gives illustrators great freedom of expression, since anything drawn or painted, from the lightest to the darkest tones, will reproduce. You can use any medium — graphite pencils, pastels, chalks, watercolors, gouache, tempera, acrylics, dyes, inks, or oils. Collage can also be used, as long as it is fairly flat. Assemblage, which is three-dimensional, is not suitable. Photographs can be combined with drawings or painting in a multi-image illustration.

When working in continuous tone, you should slightly exaggerate the tonal contrast in your renderings, because this type of artwork tends to soften and lose its contrast when shot as a halftone and printed. Of course, in some situations an overall grayness may be exactly what you want.

8–22. Imitation of a tint screen, done by hand, by Stephen Quinlan. India ink and pen.

8–23. Line photostat of a tonal graphite rendering by Normann Roussaint. Pencil.

8–21. Using adhesive tint screens in a stylized composition by Henry Van Der Linde. India ink, pen and brush.

ILLUSTRATION **197**

Experimenting with tone

As in Exercise 1, choose a subject that interests you, but this time make a continuous-tone illustration (Figs. 8–24 through 8–27). Avoid linear shading techniques such as hatching; instead use gradations of gray.

8–25. Continuous-tone still life for Exercise 3 by Mark Hughes. Graphite pencil on heavy, textured Ingrés paper.

8–24. Continuous-tone fashion illustration for Exercise 3. Pen, ink, and grease pencil on vellum tracing paper.

8–26. Continuous-tone composition for Exercise 3 by Henry Van Der Linde. India ink, pne, brush, charcoal pencil, and white paper on gray stock.

8–27. Continuous-tone drawing of a car for Exercise 3 by David Milne.

India ink, glazing medium, acrylics, pen, and brush.

ILLUSTRATION **199**

Simulating Printmaking Techniques

Several interesting printmaking techniques—both line and continuous tone—may be used effectively in illustration. Examples include linocuts, woodcuts, wood engravings, etchings, lithographs, and serigraphs or silkscreen prints. You do not have to learn all these processes; instead, you can simulate them in various ways. This is important to realize, because most people do not have access to printmaking materials and presses. Moreover, in our business, time does not usually allow for the production of one-off original prints. Finally, the inks used in printmaking take a long time to dry. Therefore, producing print effects by hand with a pen, brush, or other device is far more practical commercially.

Linocut

To achieve the rough-cut look of a linocut, use broad brisk brushstrokes of thick white paint on black paper (Fig. 8–28). A no. 7 chisel-point sable is ideal for simulating the cut marks made by linocut tools. Use it in thick-and-thin strokes.

Woodcut

To approximate the look of a woodcut, repeat the same process as for a simulated linocut, but leave more black paper showing between the white brushstrokes (Fig. 8–29). Remember that you are simulating the effects of tools cutting into wood. Apply the paint so that the strokes appear hacked and rough-edged.

Wood engraving

To simulate a wood engraving, again apply white paint to black paper, but use a very fine chisel-point sable (Fig. 8–30). Your brushstrokes should be clean, precise, and regu-

8–28. Simulation of a linocut by Mark Smith. White paint on a small chisel-point sable brush, applied in short and definite strokes to the surface of heavy, black paper stock.

8–29. Woodcut simulation by Mark Smith. White gouache on black paper, using hacked strokes applied to black paper with a chisel-point sable brush.

lar. The main characteristics of wood engraving are the rich tonal effects that can be achieved through fine delicate lines, crosshatching, and decorative textures.

Scratchboard

Scratchboard is a medium that produces effects very similar to wood engraving. Tonal effects are achieved by scratching into the surface of a board with sharp tools. There are two types of scratchboard. One has a white clay surface; the other, a clay-covered surface coated with black ink. Illustrators paint black ink on white scratchboard when a section of the artwork is to remain primarily black. This technique is used to reduce excessive scraping, which would otherwise be unavoidable.

Etching

India ink drawn with a pen and spattered with a toothbrush on white scratchboard is the best method to use to imitate an etching (Fig. 8–31). Brush and ink can also be used with penwork. Scrape back into the illustration with a sharp knife.

8–30. Simulation of a wood engraving by Patrick Sayers. India ink, pen, and brush. Detailed drawing done with pen, using parallel strokes. Large areas painted in a loose and jagged fashion.

8–31. Simulation of an etching by Henry Van Der Linde. India ink and pen, toothbrush-spatter technique and scraper tools on white scratchboard.

8–32. Simulation of a lithograph. Gouache paint transferred from thick paper hinged onto illustration board.

Lithography

Use hard colored pencils or grease pencils on textured paper to impart the look of a lithograph (Fig. 8–32). A monoprint can also be made by painting on a sheet of glass or acetate with printer's ink that has been diluted with turpentine or rubber-cement thinner and then pressing a sheet of paper into it. Work back into this with charcoal pencil, dry-brushed India ink, or a felt-tip pen. Paint can also be applied over a thin coat of rubber cement to create the texture of a lithographic print.

Silkscreen

To simulate a silkscreen print, transfer ink or diluted paint from one paper surface to another. Then fill in some shapes flatly with crisp edges, and fill in others with rougher edges (Fig. 8–33). Use reverse linework on dark shapes. You can also simulate the flat, sharp shapes typical of the silkscreen method by stenciling. Cut the desired shape out of a heavy

8–33. Simulation of a silkscreen by Donna Kwasnicki. Gouache and brush. Edges of shapes painted loosely.

piece of paper and, using a stencil or stipple brush, apply color all over. Be careful not to overload the brush, or the color will creep under the edges of the stencil.

exercise 4

Experimenting with simulated printmaking techniques

Choose two or three very different printmaking techniques to simulate, and use an actual example of each printmaking method as a guide. Study these prints separately, analyzing the marks, accidental effects, and line qualities they possess, in order to understand the medium's unique qualities. In simulating linocuts and woodcuts, it is particularly important to re-create how the tools cut away the surface. The brushwork must be done to show gouges and cut marks, since you are trying to imitate the negative pieces of the surface image left in these prints. That is why working on black paper (in reverse) is preferable to working on a white surface.

ILLUSTRATION **201**

Drawing portraits

Using photo references, do ten portrait studies of various interesting people, male and female, of different ages and races. The majority of these studies should be executed in line, and the remaining ones in line and wash tones. Do each portrait on a separate piece of paper in India ink only, using a pen, a brush, or a combination of both. Dilute the ink for washes. Decide which technique to use in each drawing in order to capture the essence of the character being portrayed. When you have finished, cut each study out and mount all of them together within a rectangular shape on a sheet of black cover-stock paper (Fig. 8–34).

8–34. Finished set of mounted portraits for Exercise 5 by Henry Van Der Linde. India ink, various pens and brushes.

Guidelines for Black-and-White Techniques

The following guidelines should be observed in developing your mastery of black-and-white techniques:

- Experimenting with different media and techniques, and becoming adept at using those that are known to reproduce well

- Becoming fluent in expressive line drawing, especially in pen and ink

- Incorporating a strong sense of design in your work, using contrasts of size, weight, and value

- Specializing in one type of black-and-white illustration, such as scratchboard

- Before beginning, ascertaining whether your client wants line or halftone artwork

- Always using white illustration board or thick white paper stock—for reproduction purposes, do not do line or halftone illustrations on colored paper

Mistakes to Avoid

Here are some tips on what to avoid doing:

- Avoiding an overall grayness of equal value in your work

- Avoiding media that smear or streak when rendering finished art—no one wants to be responsible for artwork that can easily be damaged

- Not working at more than 150 percent of the final size if your work is to be reproduced—otherwise fine detail will fill in or be lost when the artwork is reduced for reproduction

ILLUSTRATION **203**

Illustration Assignments

Illustration is an applied art, incorporating fine-art creativity, design principles, and business skills. It is not solely a vehicle for self-expression. The function of illustration is to inform, to educate, and above all to communicate ideas.

Executing an illustration involves analyzing a given problem and producing a visually stimulating solution in accordance with specific requirements. Illustrators must have excellent skills in both drawing and painting, along with a strong sense of design. And since illustrators work with professionals in many disciplines, they must be able to present ideas verbally.

Illustration can be divided into two main areas: interpretive and technical. Types of interpretive illustration, where the illustrator interprets the meaning of the text, include advertising, book, and editorial magazine and newspaper illustration. Types of technical illustration, which involves preparing extremely accurate drawings or paintings that convey information in an easily understandable manner, include mechanical, architectural, scientific, and medical illustration. Technical illustrations show how things are constructed, how they operate, or how they work. This specialty requires not only accurate draftsmanship, but also a love of research and analysis.

Background Knowledge

Drawing, painting, and design skills are obviously essential for all illustrators, but different areas of specialization typically have different emphases. Advertising, editorial, and book illustration all require figure work, much of it realistic (Fig. 9–1). People, scenes, situations, and products must be rendered in many media and with diverse techniques.

Technical illustration is just the opposite; figure work is rarely required, with the possible exception of medical illustration. In some car advertising illustrations and architectural renderings, a technical illustrator renders the car or building, and an advertising illustrator renders the figures and background.

Other subjects relate to illustration, including photography, three-dimensional studies, computer graphics, and printmaking. If you

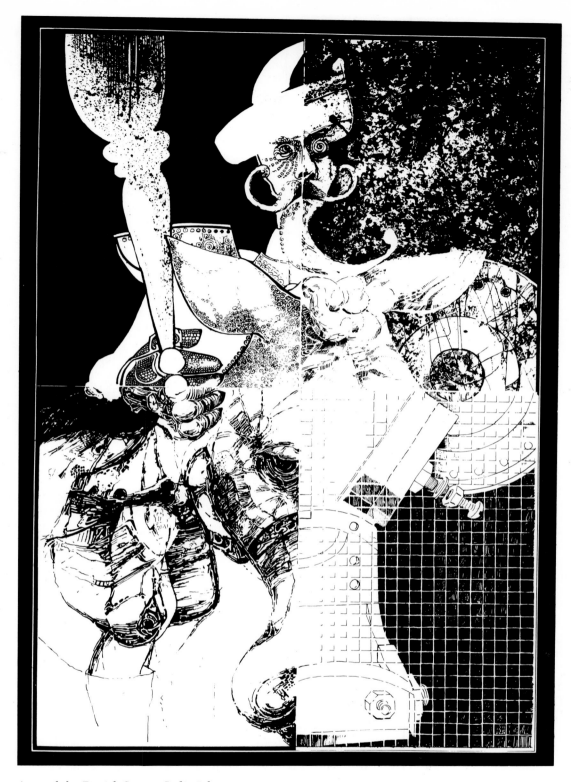

Artwork by Patrick Sayers. India ink,
pen, and brush.

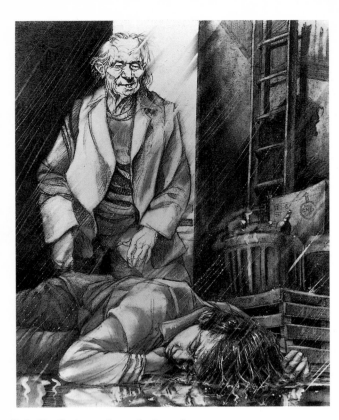

9–1. Realistic wash rendering of figures by Paul McCusker. India ink, pen, and brush.

great benefit to the illustrator to know a lot about graphic design. Since graphic designers and illustrators often work on the same assignments, insight into each other's field can result in more effective solutions to problems.

Strengthening Your Design Skills

To produce effective illustrations, you must first strengthen your two-dimensional design skills. Modeling form or shading to create the illusion of three-dimensional reality comes later. In illustration, realism is in a sense superimposed on an underlying design.

One of the first steps in mastering design is to visualize all of the subjects to be included as simple, flat shapes. If, for example, you are going to use a figure, try to see it as a simple silhouette. In this early design stage, ignore surface details, textures, perspective, and so on. Simply take this figure and any other subjects to be included, and arrange them within the rectangle or square, paying attention to the negative spaces that are created. In design, the negative spaces are as important as the positive ones. Repetitive and boring negative spaces contribute to a dull illustration. Try to use an asymmetrical arrangement of elements, as well as contrasts of light and dark. If your subject matter calls for a symmetrical composition, you must be especially aware of the negative spaces.

The exercises which begin on page 226 apply what you already know about design to a sequence of black-and-white advertising assignments. Some of these resemble real jobs and cover various areas of advertising—mainstream, soft sell, and hard sell. Deadlines or time limits for working are crucial; set these for yourself before starting each exercise.

are interested in advertising, for example, photography and computer graphics are good subjects to know. For editorial illustration, photography is helpful; and in book illustration, printmaking is quite important. For technical illustration, the most rapidly changing area of all, model building and computer graphics skills are virtually indispensable.

Illustrators of all types are now working with computer technology. Many advertisers use computer graphics in their TV commercials, promotional presentations, industrial product designs, and information packages. Computer graphics are supplementing (but not replacing) conventional forms of two-dimensional print media illustration.

The influence of animation and illustration on each other is also no-

table. Animators and illustrators need the same sense of design and composition, the same rendering skills, and especially the same high level of drawing ability. Technical animation is very similar to technical illustration, and both are now working together in computer graphics.

The impact of photography on the visual arts has been tremendous. Still photography is illustration's main competitor, but photographers and illustrators can learn a lot from each other. In particular, camera and darkroom techniques (as well as color effects) can inspire the illustrator.

Another field that has a significant bearing on illustration is graphic design—the overall organization of typography, photographs, and illustrations in print media. It is of

Making a Tracing Sheet

Many people trace a drawing onto the paper or board for their finished art by shading the drawing on the back in pencil and then rubbing the drawing onto the new surface. This approach is extremely slow and messy.

Instead, use a sheet of medium-weight tracing paper, and rub a graphite stick all over one side of it, staying just inside all four edges. Next, rub a ball of cotton batting soaked in rubber-cement thinner over the graphite in circular strokes, spreading the blackness of the graphite evenly over this sheet. It dries instantly. You now have a carbon sheet that is practical and clean to use and will last for years. Put a tab of masking tape on one corner for pinning it to your board.

Advertising Illustration

About 80 percent of commercial illustration is advertising-oriented. This is a creative and highly competitive field. To do well, you must have both ability and drive.

Most advertising work can be classified as product illustration. In contrast to story illustration, which illuminates the text of a story or article, product illustration promotes a product or service, or communicates information. It sells by creating a mood, by making a product appealing, or simply by depicting the product. Product illustration can be found in magazines, newspapers, and posters, as well as on TV. It can be divided into three categories: direct, indirect, and institutional advertising.

Direct advertising uses a strong attention-getting approach to sell a product or service (Fig. 9–2a). The combination of words and pictures used is designed to motivate the consumer to buy. This type of advertising is called *hard* sell. Another version of this is the type of ad-

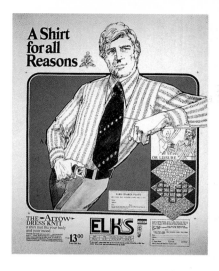

9–2a. Printed news ad using direct, hard-sell advertising.

9–2b. Illustration for an indirect, soft-sell advertisement by Eric Colquhoun. Acrylics.

vertisement that informs the public about topical issues such as ecological problems or the dangers of cigarette smoking.

Indirect advertising is more subtle in its message, but it has the same objective: to sell (Fig. 9–2b). A client who chooses this type of approach is interested in both immediate and long-range effects. Indirect advertising is more subtly persuasive, building a reputation for the company. In the business, this approach is called *soft sell*.

Institutional advertising is the most subtle form of selling. It relies solely on the association of a company or organization with a visual image (Fig. 9–3). The objective is to sell by stressing goodwill, trust, and reliability. The client is not usually mentioned except allusively by a trademark or logo.

9–3. Institutional advertising. Markers and black felt-tip pen.

The role of agencies

Advertising is generally handled by agencies and art studios that retain specialists for every aspect of the finished advertisement. Producing an advertisement is a team effort with various people responsible for concept, design, pictorial content, and production. The main functions of the ad agency are to handle the client's budget, to create verbal and visual concepts, and to buy space or time in the appropriate media—whether newspaper, magazine, or television.

In most cases, the advertising agency's art director formulates the initial concept and the overall design. This is often done in conjunction with a copywriter, who writes the text of the advertisement, including heads, subheads, and body copy. When the concept has been established, the illustrator is called in; the art director then explains the concept, either verbally or in the form of a very rough marker layout, to the illustrator and asks him or her to develop this idea in markers. If the developed idea is approved by both the art director and the client, the illustrator does the finished artwork. Usually twice as much marker rendering as finished art is produced in this end of the business.

Newspaper space advertising

Newspapers sell advertising space in areas of specific shapes. Three systems of measurement are used: module units, columns by inches, and columns by agate lines. As an illustrator, you should be familiar with all three systems. Before starting any newspaper ad illustration, you must confirm the ad size and the system being used.

Module Units A modular system has recently been introduced in North America in an attempt to standardize sizes for advertisements in newspapers. It is based on a module unit of 30 agates deep and 1 column (or $2^1/_{16}$ inches) wide. Each module unit thus represents $2^1/_8 \times 2^1/_{16}$ inches of space. Broadsheets (large daily newspaper sheets) and tabloids (small newspapers) are composed in multiples of this basic unit. A 5-on-3 ad is thus 5 units deep by 3 columns wide and occupies a total of 15 module units of space ($10^3/_4 \times 6^3/_8$ inches).

Columns by Inches Although minor variations exist in newspaper sizes, a typical full-page ad is 8 columns × 21 inches deep, and thus occupies 168 square inches of space. A full page is divided into areas suit-

able for smaller advertisements. For example, as Figure 9–4 illustrates, a half-page ad could be run in the following sizes: 4 columns × 21 inches, 5 columns × $16^3/_4$ inches, 6 columns × 14 inches, 7 columns × 12 inches, or 8 columns × $10^1/_2$ inches. Each of these variations adds up to a half page, or 5 columns × $16^{13}/_{16}$ inches (84 square inches of space). Note that column widths vary, depending on the size of the newspaper. The number of columns also differs in different sections of the newspaper. Calculations are based on the unit width of one column, regardless of how many inches it is wide.

Columns by Agate Lines A full-page newspaper is 8 columns wide by 300 agate lines deep, making a total of 2,400 agate lines of space. (Column width is calculated in inches, whereas agate lines are only used for measuring depth.) If you are designing and illustrating a half-page ad, for example, you have the option of working within the following areas:

4 columns × 300 lines = 1,200 lines
(approximate)

5 columns × 240 lines = 1,200 lines
(approximate)

6 columns × 200 lines = 1,200 lines
(approximate)

7 columns × 171 lines = 1,200 lines
(approximate)

8 columns × 150 lines = 1,200 lines
(approximate)

As you can see, it is simply a matter of dividing the total number of lines by the number of columns. Some of these shapes are square, while others are vertical or horizontal rectangles.

Try working out the ad proportions and variations possible on 1,800, 150, and 800 lines. Remember, the maximum depth of a newspaper page is 300 lines and the maximum width is 8 columns; you cannot exceed these dimensions.

British and European newspapers use the metric system, selling space in columns (measured in millimeters) by centimeters deep. For example, a typical small-space ad (called a "20 double") in the London *Times* is 88 mm x 20 cm deep. In-house research has shown that the most effective ad size is 44 mm x 40 cm (1760 mm units of space). Of course, there are many possibilities and most often the client or art director will determine the ad size.

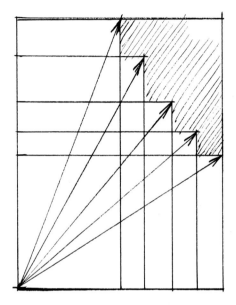

9–4. Half-page ad variations using different combinations of columns (width) and inches, modular lines, or agate lines (depth).

Print media advertising

The term *print media advertising* applies to anything that is two-dimensional and printed on paper by a printing press. Newspapers are the most widely used vehicle for print media advertising. News ads are printed (or run) in black and white, in black plus one color, in two or three colors with or without black, and sometimes in full-color. The last type of ad is usually used to launch a new product.

Magazine Advertising Space Unlike newspapers, magazines (European and American) sell space in fractions of a page (Fig. 9–5). If a full-page ad has a margin around it (usually a white border), all the artwork and type must stay within this type safety area (Fig. 9–6). If an ad contains an illustration, photograph, or background that extends to any of the three cut edges of the paper, it is called a *bleed ad.* The size of the paper to its cut edges is referred to as its *trim size.*

Other Formats Various other formats can be used for print media advertising:

Color Supplement: This is in a newspaper insert printed in full-color or sometimes in two colors. It is usually for one advertiser.

Brochures, Booklets, and Pamphlets: These are small books with a limited number of pages. Booklets of twelve or sixteen pages can be made from one sheet of paper, which is folded, cut, and then stapled or stitched.

Folders: One sheet of paper can be folded in single, double, or multiple accordion folds (Fig. 9–7).

Point-of-purchase (POP): This usually refers to a three-dimensional display unit or other promotional material set up near the cash register.

Direct mail: These are two- or three-dimensional promotional materials that are mailed directly to potential customers by manufacturers or advertisers.

Flyers: These promotional pieces are delivered by hand to potential customers. They are usually hard-sell ads.

Dealer kit: This package of information is sent to retailers or wholesalers to inform them of a new product or an updating of the promotion of a product (Fig. 9–7).

Indoor posters: These are usually printed on a single sheet of paper or board. They may be posted in shopping malls, stores, transit systems, and municipal buildings.

Outdoor posters: Usually in a horizontal format, these are printed in single sheets that, when pasted on a billboard, make up a single image. They are made up in fixed standard sizes, usually of a 2-to-1 ratio (twice as deep as wide).

Outdoor bulletins: These very large billboard posters are printed or painted by hand on separate panels and then assembled in a large, braced frame. These may be placed along highways or at intersections. A superboard or painted bulletin board is a variation of the outdoor bulletin board. It has extensions that project beyond the usual size of a billboard to the top, bottom, or sides. A trivision board is made up of individual three-sided panels. These turn at fixed intervals to show three different images, one at a time. A client may buy a period of time on one, two, or all three sides of a tri-vision board. (Note: If bulletin boards are printed rather than painted by hand, they are considered a print media format. The illustration, whether eventually printed or painted, should be rendered in scale to the final size.)

Tent cards and easel cards: These are small display units printed on one or both sides. They are held up by self-locking devices and stand on store counters, shelves, or tables (Fig. 9–7).

A total media advertising campaign would also involve radio, television, audiovisual material, and possibly computer-animated graphics. Window displays may also be included if the client operates a retail store.

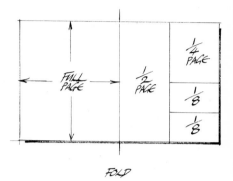

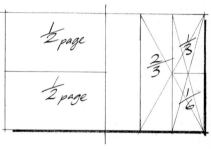

9–5. Magazine advertising space is bought and sold in fractions of a page.

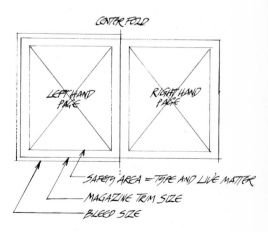

9–6. Terms used by art directors.

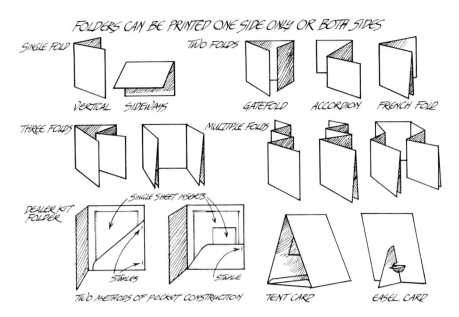

9-7. A single sheet of paper can be folded in a multitude of ways. Folders, dealer kits, and easel/tent cards are vehicles for two-dimensional print media and point-of-sale advertising.

Editorial Illustration for Magazines and Newspaper

In contrast to advertising illustration, editorial or story illustration interprets the written word (usually a manuscript). The possible subjects cover a wide spectrum, encompassing fashion, science, the environment, sports, travel, and entertainment (Fig. 9–8). Other areas include social commentary illustrations on political issues, social policies, religious controversies, personal relationships, and the like. In all such work, virtually total freedom can be enjoyed with regard to imagery and technique; but the illustrator must have keen conceptual ability, facility in design and composition, and excellent drawing and painting skills.

Magazines and periodicals appear on newsstands weekly, biweekly, monthly, or quarterly (four times a year). The quality of the paper varies, but it usually consists of a glossy coated paper stock. Printing a magazine—especially a weekly—is an enormous undertaking, with constant deadlines governing production of both the editorial content and the advertising. Monthly magazines have more time to play with; and they usually work two or three issues ahead of publication.

Magazines are often aimed at a particular audience. This is reflected in the content of their stories and articles and in their artwork. For example, some magazines are aimed at young women (*Seventeen*) and some at older, more sophisticated women (*Elle* and *Bazaar*). *GQ* and *Esquire* are aimed at the sophisticated male, while *Road and Track* and *Sports Illustrated* are aimed primarily at men interested in sports and outdoor activities. Magazines such as *Discover* and *Omni* are aimed at a mixed readership that shares an interest in science.

The editorial content—that is, the illustrated stories and feature sections—is what the public is primarily interested in and why the magazine gets purchased. Although editorial illustration does not sell a product in the same way that advertising illustration does, it does help sell the magazine.

The assignment process

The editor and art director decide which articles require illustrations, what size and how many illustrations are needed, and whether to use color or black and white. Often a piece of fiction or a feature article will start with a two-page spread in color, together with the heading and a minimal amount of text. The story or article is then continued on other pages, called *turn pages*.

In picking an illustrator, the art director is to some extent choosing the look that he or she wants. Sometimes the art director even specifies the kind of illustrations to be produced.

The illustrator's task

Having read the manuscript, the illustrator submits a few roughs, usually in half-size, for the art director's approval. These roughs do not have to be rendered in markers (as is common with advertising clients); they can be done in pencil, colored pencils, colored inks, or paint. Two or

9-8. Editorial illustration by Michael McKeever. Black felt-tip pen and wedge-tip marker.

three different ideas should be shown. Roughs can be loose (Fig. 9–9), but they should be cut out and rubber-cemented onto a clean sheet of paper for presentation. Try to sell your best idea to the art director, so you will enjoy working on it. All of the ideas presented should be equally interesting, however.

The art director is always looking for an exciting solution with visual impact. Composition, color, and rendering technique are all important. They must work together to interpret the article and to express its mood.

The finished art for magazine illustration is done half up or twice up—150 or 200 percent of the printed size. The illustrator is given a credit line, which usually appears somewhere near the illustration. (You are not given credit in either advertising or technical illustration, only in editorial and book work.)

Tips for magazine illustration

In magazine illustration, never place the center of interest within or overlapping the gutter (where the two pages meet in the middle). Because spread illustrations are printed on two separate pages, they may not meet exactly where they are supposed to when the magazine is assembled (Fig. 9–10). In addition, because the open pages curve into the binding, a certain amount of distortion occurs. This happens to a lesser degree on most center spreads. Of course, large and medium shapes can overlap the gutter.

Editorial story illustration usually covers a full page (called a *single page*) or two facing pages (called a *double-page spread*). A center spread is a double-page spread exactly in the middle of a magazine. Upon turning a page to the opening of a story, the reader's eye is likely to move first to the lower right of the right-hand page and then move up and over to the top left of the left-hand page. A single-page illustra-

9–9. Editorial concept roughs can be rendered in any medium for client presentation.

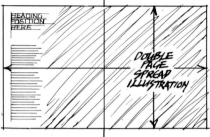

9–10. Important elements and details should be kept out of the gutter area.

tion is thus often placed on the right-hand page, with the heading and story beginning at the top of the left-hand page (Fig. 9–11).

Now look at Figure 9–12, which illustrates the terminology that magazine art directors use when

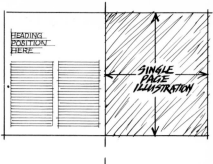

9–11. Single- and double-page spread for editorial magazine.

giving an illustrator a job. It is important to know the following terms so that you can understand the instructions you are given:

Center spread: The exact middle of a publication (1)

Gutter: The areas immediately adjacent to the center seam (2)

DS (double-page spread): Two facing pages (3)

SP (single page): One full page (4)

Heading: The main copy title (5)

Subhead: A secondary heading or title (6)

Blurb: A featured quote (7)

Byline: The author's name, and any related information (8)

Caption: Explanatory copy, usually placed beside an illustration (9)

Cutline: A single line of copy, usually placed under photo or illustration (10)

Cut and copy: A square halftone or illustration with pertinent copy (11)

Credit line: The artist's or photographer's typeset name (12)

Body copy: The text of the story or article (13)

Vignette: A shape with irregular edges (14)

Lead in: Special type that starts off the body copy (15)

Spot illustration: A small illustration (16)

Pic: A picture or photo (17)

Figs: Figures (18)

Bleed: The part of a printed image that extends beyond the trim edge of the page or sheet (19)

9–12. Terminology used in magazine and newspaper editorial design.

Newspaper work

Like magazines with their four F's (fashion, fiction, features, and food), newspapers are divided into specific sections for news, features, business, sports, fashion, food, family, and entertainment. Most newspaper illustration is done in black and white, but sometimes color is used. Generally, newspaper art directors use the same terminology magazine art directors use.

Deadlines

The main difference between work for daily newspapers and work for magazines from the illustrator's point of view, is the time allowed for the production of roughs and finished artwork. A newspaper art director may want rush same-day service or may allow up to a week for certain illustrations. It is therefore imperative to be able to think through and execute high-quality work quickly. Because magazine art directors have longer publishing deadlines, they can allow anywhere from two to six weeks for illustration assignments. When you work on ed-

itorial illustrations, it is important to have a self-imposed deadline that is even shorter than the given one. Try to meet this deadline, in order to avoid last-minute panic.

Exercises

In light of the great diversity of editorial story commissions and the limitless variety of illustrations and techniques used by freelancers doing this type of work, the exercises on pages 248–59 cover a variety of subjects. Typical design formats and subsequent mechanical requirements of magazine and newspaper art will be discussed. Remember that newspaper printing methods require greater tonal contrast in the artwork. Magazine work, which is mainly full-color continuous-tone art, allows for greater subtlety of detail and tone. The upcoming exercises freely intermix the two areas, enabling you to gain experience in one of the illustrator's tasks: to keep in mind throughout an assignment how the illustration will be reproduced.

Book Illustration

The book is the oldest and still the most powerful form of mass-media communication, television notwithstanding. Putting together a book is a collaborative affair involving the author, the editor, the art director, the illustrator, the production manager, and the printer all working together.

For the artist, book illustration offers considerable latitude for creativity. The subject may be educational, technical, fiction, nonfiction, poetry, or children's literature. Often the images called for can be imaginary or abstract rather than realistic. Nonetheless, book illustration is still a business. The book is a marketable product, and the illustrator's work helps sell it.

Some people think that, because the illustrations and text usually complement each other so well, the illustrator works directly with the author. This is not usually the case. Instead, the author works with the editor and the illustrator works with the art director. In most cases, however, the art director and the editor decide jointly who is the best illustrator for the job.

Book illustration tends to fit into three main categories: decorative, interpretive, and informative. Decorative illustration is flat and two-dimensional, emphasizing pattern and various line qualities. Interpretive book illustration interprets and supports the text, either realistically or in a stylized manner (Fig. 9–13 and 9–14). To do this, it relies on perspective and some illusion of dimensionality. Informative illustration is a diagrammatic type of illustration that describes or explains a subject. It is usually quite realistic and sometimes approaches the precision of technical illustration. Examples of informative illustration can be found in textbooks.

Many different parts of a book may involve illustration, including the book cover, the frontispiece, the title page, the contents page, chapter openings, and, of course, the various inside pages, either full, half, or quarter size. An inside illustration may also span a spread, filling either the entire two pages or a portion of them.

Developing preliminary character studies is an essential step in the working process. The characters in a book need to be well established visually in order for the illustrator to portray them consistently in various situations (Figs. 9–15 and 9–16).

Semicomps and comps are produced to establish the look of the book in relation to the overall design and to confirm the unity of the illustrations with the text. Illustrations and text must work together. Finally, the art director may ask for a few sample illustrations to solidify the finished art style and technique.

The bulk of book illustration is done by freelancers, although a few book publishing companies (especially educational ones) have an illustrator or two on staff. If you want to do book illustration, contact the art director and present your portfolio. Book illustrators must know the

market and the type of work suitable for readers of different groups or different age levels.

9–13. Interpretive, stylized illustration by Neil Ballantyne. India ink and pen. Multidirectional lines accentuate texture and pattern, creating interesting tonal areas.

9–14. Book illustration by Adriana Taddeo. India ink and pen. Contour line opposes textural areas. Three-point perspective.

9–15. Artwork by Ron Fyke. Character study for a children's book illustration. India ink and pen.

Figure. 9–16. Artwork by Ron Fyke. Preliminary character study for a children's book illustration. India ink and pen.

Technical Illustration

Today high technology demands greater proficiency and understanding on the part of the technical illustrator than ever before. Very complicated information has to be explained in simple graphic terms.

Technical illustration is quite distinct from advertising and editorial illustration, which stress figure work. The main emphasis in this type of illustration is on precise line drawings of inanimate objects (Fig. 9–17). A technical illustrator must have an interest in the structure and functioning of things. Technical illustrations are visual aids showing how things are constructed, how they work, or how they are operated. The adage that a picture is worth a thousand words is especially meaningful here. Formal training in the use of basic geometry, in the reading and interpreting of blueprints, in the use of mechanical perspective, and in model building is required.

Technical illustration comprises technical-manual (Fig. 9–18), mechanical, architectural (Figs. 9–19 through 9–21), medical, and scientific illustration. Automotive illustration may be technical or interpretive, depending on the message being conveyed and the medium, technique, and type of rendering used.

The great majority of technical illustrators work within industries and institutions. A few freelance. Engineering and high-tech industries, boat-building companies, design departments in automotive plants, aeronautical firms, government offices (such as the departments of defense and agriculture), pharmaceutical companies, architectural offices, hydroelectric companies, atomic energy commissions, natural history or science museums, universities, scientific laboratories, manufacturing firms, and art studios all may employ technical illustrators.

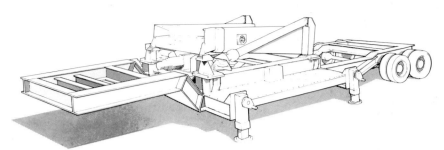

9–17. Technical line illustration by Gary Mundell. The technical illustrator must be able to convey complex data in the simplest way.

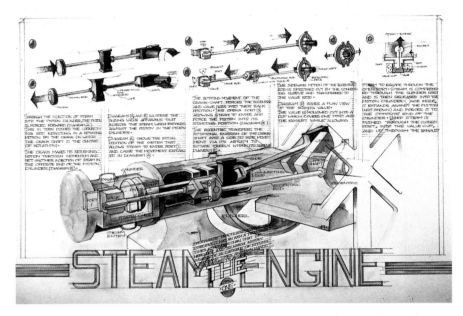

9–18. Conceptual comp layout for a museum display poster by Alex Hawley. Watercolor, India ink, pen, and brush. Phantom view.

Work methods

Three standard work methods are used in technical illustration:

1. *On-site location-recording drawing:* Accurate freehand perspective drawings are done on the spot and refined later in the studio.

2. *Studio assignments, using photo references:* The illustrator uses 35mm or Polaroid photographs that he or she has taken and works with photoprints or photostats in producing the finished art.

3. *Isometric and orthographic projections done in the studio:* The artwork requires the illustrator to project angles and planes mechanically. The ability to visualize three-dimensional forms in the mind's eye is important.

9–19. Exterior view, architectural rendering combined with figurework by Alex Hawley. Gouache.

9–20. Interior rendering from architect's blueprints by Alex Hawley. Felt pen, markers, and India ink. See Figure 9–19.

9–21. Architectural rendering by John Hurley. Gouache and watercolor.

Tools and equipment

Technical illustrators use various high-precision tools, including conventional drafting equipment such as T-squares, dividers, rulers, and triangles. High-quality ruling pens and technical pens are essential. Interchangeable nibs are available for the technical pen so that you can draw lines of different thicknesses. Plastic ellipse guides or templates are indispensable, as are French curves.

The airbrush is another important piece of equipment for many technical illustrators. Not all illustrators use it, however, since the bulk of technical work is done as line drawing only. Further, a technical illustrator should be proficient at perspective drawing and painting before attempting to use an airbrush. High-realism illustration relies heavily on this medium and for this reason, a solid knowledge of light and shade and their relationship to three-dimensional forms is essential. If you are interested in becoming skilled in airbrush illustration, courses and videos covering this complex subject are offered at some visual arts schools, and a wealth of information can also be obtained from the numerous books devoted specifically to this medium. Please refer to the bibliography for further information.

Types of perspective drawing

One-point, two-point, and three-point perspective, which were discussed in Chapter 2, are used in overall views of mechanical objects (Fig. 9–22) and especially in architectural renderings (Fig. 9–23). They are also used in technical manuals and mechanical illustrations (Fig. 9–24).

Mechanical perspective

Two good methods are used for drawing accurately using mechanical perspective: the projected plan method (Fig. 9–25) and the measuring point system (Fig. 9–26). These are primarily used in architectural and technical illustrations that involve two-point and three-point perspective.

The difference between the projected plan system and the measuring point system is as follows: the plan projection system uses a plan and elevation view of an object to establish its exact measurements and dimensions in a drawing, while the measuring point system uses fixed points and scale increments to determine the object's exact measurements, position, and size relative to other objects. The plan system is the easier of the two systems to use, since it does not require elaborate measuring steps.

The measuring point system uses the right measuring point (RMP) and left measuring point (LMP) on the horizon, in conjunction with the scale increments on the ground line, to determine the dimensions and exact measurements of the base of an

9–22. Example of symmetrical, one-point perspective by Michael Cranwell. Watercolor, India ink, pen, and brush.

9–23. Modified two-point perspective rendering of proposed architectural interior by David Milne. Black marker and felt-tip pen. See Figure 9–20.

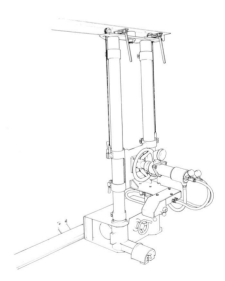

9–24. Two-point perspective illustration of a mechanical device by Gary Mundell. India ink and technical pen.

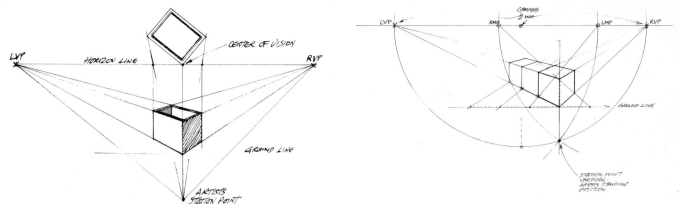

9-25. Projected plan method of mechanical perspective drawing.

9-26. Measuring-point system for using mechanical perspective.

object. The RMP is established by drawing an arc with a compass from the right vanishing point (RVP) through the station point. Similarly, the LMP is plotted from the left vanishing point (LVP) through the station point.

A large, 180-degree semicircular arc is used to determine the LVP and RVP in conjunction with the horizon line. (A 45-degree-angle triangle can be used instead of a compass.) The artist's station point can be centered or placed slightly off-center, as in Figure 9-26.

Isometric and orthographic drawing

An isometric drawing of an object has its base set at two angles of 30 degrees. Shapes and forms are described through variations of thick-and-thin lines. In this type of technical drawing, work is begun at the bottom front corner of the subject, and the angles there remain at a constant 30 degrees (Fig. 9-27). Surface planes do not converge as they do in perspective drawing. Isometric ellipses are not true ellipses, since they are constructed around four points instead of two. To simplify the drawing process, isometric ellipse templates are used.

The other main drawing method—orthographic drawing—is the most basic form of outline drawing. It projects a subject onto the surface by using projection lines. Three views or planes are projected: the front view, the profile or side view, and the plan or horizontal view. As shown in Figures 9-28 and 9-29, the plan view is simply angled to 45 degrees by using a 45-degree-angle triangle, and verticals are drawn up to complete the drawing. The angles of any drawn sides or top and bottom edges are maintained at a constant 45 degrees. Again, surface planes do not converge but remain parallel. This is referred to as an oblique projection view. Notice that in orthographic projection drawing a plan view can be positioned at any angle from the horizontal; however, standard triangles of 30, 40, and 60 degrees are normally used.

Different views

Five different views are used in technical illustration:

1. *Overall view:* This type of view depicts the exterior of an object, which is rendered realistically—usually in line and tones showing light and shade (Figs. 9-30 and 9-31). Retouched photos are often used in this type of view.

2. *Cutaway view:* In this type of view, the illustration shows inter-

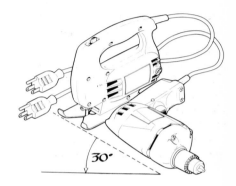

9-27. Isometric drawing of two products by David Milne. Technical pen. Angles remain a constant thirty degrees.

nal details within the overall outer form of an object (Fig. 9-32). Subsurfaces are cut away to create this effect. Isometric and perspective drawing are most commonly used to produce this view, although the orthographic method is used in some cases.

3. *Phantom view:* Like the cutaway view, this view shows internal details. Instead of cutting away the surface, however, the phantom view makes the surface transparent (Figs. 9-33 and 9-34). The surface is rendered in a light or gray tone, which allows the interior areas to be emphasized. Perspective or isometric drawing can be used to produce this view, although perspective drawing seems to be the most effective approach.

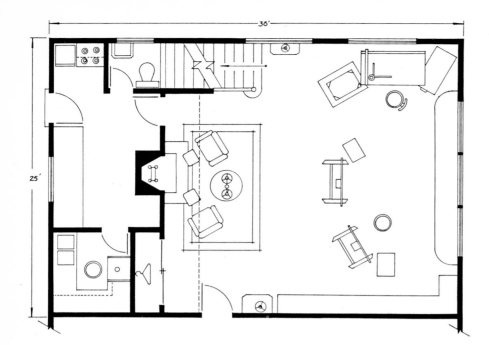

9–28. Floor plan, or horizontal view, of an architectural interior by David Milne. Technical pen.

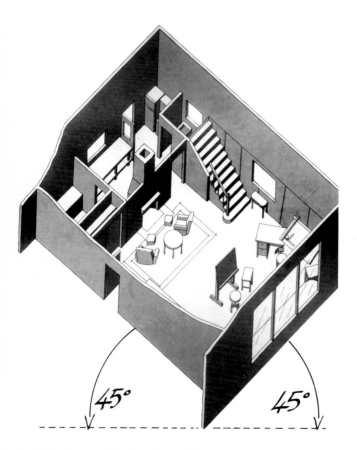

9–29. Orthographic drawing of the same floor plan used in Figure 9–28 by David Milne. Technical pen and adhesive color film. Oblique, 45-degree projection.

9–30. Retouched photo by David Milne. The upper addition of the building was superimposed over a photograph to indicate proposed changes to the existing building.

9–31. Continuous-tone rendering by David Milne. Overall view of a product.

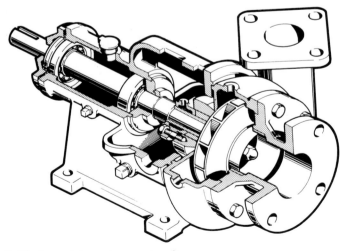

9–32. Isometric, cutaway-view line drawing showing internal details of machinery by David Milne. Technical pen.

4. *Exploded view:* This type of view is used primarily in technical manuals, to show how parts are assembled (or disassembled for maintenance) and to identify parts. It is also used to show how to construct, remove, or install a product. As Figures 9–35 and 9–36 show, the parts are exploded along an axis or centerline, using isometric or perspective drawing methods. The parts or steps are then numbered in sequence.

5. *Action view:* There are two basic types of action view: those showing the function and action of equipment (Figs. 9–37 and 9–38) and those showing the actions that a person must perform in order to operate or maintain equipment (Fig. 9–38). In the latter type, it is important to show the correct body positions, hand and wrist action, and position of tools while in use.

Technical-manual illustration

Technical manuals provide basic information on the operation, maintenance, and identification of parts. They range in size from a single sheet or small folder to a full-size book. Some manuals provide information to consumers about simple home appliances; others focus on complicated industrial equipment. A good example of a technical manual is the literature that comes with a new car, audio system, or copier machine (Fig. 9–39).

Technical manuals vary in size and complexity, depending on the subject and the production budget. They are prepared by a team consisting of at least one technical writer and one technical illustrator. Exploded, views as in Figures 9–35 and 9–36, are used along with other views. These manuals also may contain graphs, charts, and tables.

9–33. Illustration by Michael Cranwell. Graphite pencil. Surface shapes are treated transparently to show phantom view.

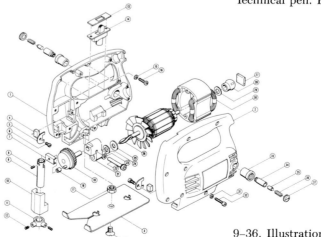

9–34. Illustration by David Milne. Graphite pencil. Phantom view emphasizes internal details. Engine rendered in light and shade using tone.

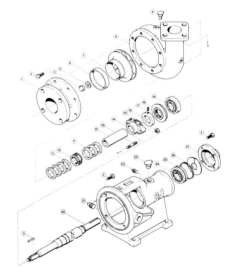

9–35. Illustration by David Milne. Technical pen. Exploded view.

9–36. Illustration by David Milne. Technical pen. Exploded view.

9–37. Action view by David Milne shows the function and action of equipment. Watercolor, India ink, and adhesive film.

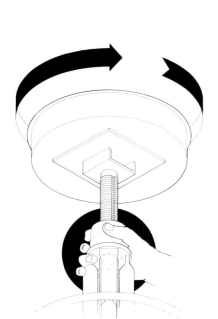

9–38. Action view by Michael Cranwell shows how to perform tasks or operate equipment. India ink and technical pen.

Mechanical illustration

Mechanical illustration deals exclusively with the conceptual, developmental, and final stages of mechanized products. First, these illustrations enable designers and engineers to see how their ideas translate from blueprints into clear visual form. (The ability to read blueprints is obviously essential in this type of work.) The intended product can then be checked for potential problems in design and manufacture. Finally, this type of illustration is used to sell products in full-color and black-and-white print media advertisements in magazines, newspapers, posters, folders, and so on (Fig. 9–40).

All types of drawing and views are used in mechanical illustration, since the products dealt with are quite diverse. Choosing the appropriate medium and rendering treatment is very important here because the materials and their surface textures must be accurately depicted. The airbrush, for example, is indispensable for rendering the high luster of polished metal surfaces (Figs. 9–41 and 9–42).

Architectural illustration

There are two main types of architectural illustration: exterior-view rendering and interior-view rendering. Both are prepared from the architect's working blueprints and are used in presentations and proposals to show clients how a building or development will look when finished. An architectural rendering must indicate design features, construction methods, materials, color, and how the building fits into its environment (Figs. 9–21 and 9–43).

In the case of interior rendering—in addition to conveying the overall design concept, colors, and materials—the work must indicate

9–39. Artwork by David Milne. Comp layout for a technical manual showing the operation of equipment. Markers and felt-tip pen.

9–41. Illustration by David Milne. Using an airbrush to render polished metal surfaces.

9–40. Mechanical illustration by David Milne. Graphite pencils.

9–42. Illustration by David Milne. Airbrushing creates a highly realistic look.

9–43. Exterior architectural rendering in line from blueprint by Gary Mundell. India ink and technical pen.

fixtures, furniture, plants, and other details. People are often included to give a sense of the scale, although the figures are stylized and simplified. A thorough knowledge of two-point and three-point perspective is necessary, even though the renderings may be exaggerated for drama (Figs. 9–20 and 9–23).

Full-color illustrations are typically rendered in paints or markers. Exterior views are usually painted, while interiors are usually done in black or brown felt-tip pen linework and colored markers. Color is used to create a mood and atmosphere. To be a skillful architectural illustrator, you must understand color theory, draw accurately, and have a good command of various media. Good architectural illustration is precise; yet the work should also make interesting use of color, mood, and technique (Figs. 9–19 and 9–20).

Medical illustration

This highly specialized type of illustration combines medical science and art. A medical illustrator must draw realistically and accurately (Figs. 9–44 and 9–45). No errors are permitted. A two- to four-year course in a university medical arts program must be taken to gain a thorough knowledge of the human body as well as the requisite art and design skills.

A medical illustrator produces artwork for both conventional printed literature (textbooks, brochures, and leaflets) and audiovisual media. All types of views are employed, and various media may be used. Acetate overlays are used extensively to show different aspects of one subject.

Scientific illustration

Scientific illustration deals with scientifically oriented subject matter other than that covered in medical illustration. Biology, geophysical sciences, astronomy, and oceanog-

9–44. Medical illustration by David Milne. Watercolor.

9–45. Medical illustration by David Milne. India ink and watercolor.

raphy are among the areas that require scientific technical illustration (Fig. 9–46). Very complicated information must be designed and rendered so as to be clearly understood by the viewer. All techniques and media can be used. As in medical illustration, overlays are common.

Scientific illustration is used in textbooks, museum displays, and teaching aids. It also appears in professional trade publications such as those for botanists or geologists, in scientific journals such as *Scientific American*, and in pictorial maps such as those found in *National Geographic* magazine.

Model building

The building of three-dimensional models is a unique area of technical illustration (Fig. 9–47). Perfectly detailed and colored scale models are used extensively in architectural proposals, industrial product design, and teaching. Model building requires a thorough knowledge of blueprint reading and the ability to construct structures and forms out of many different materials. Because of the work's highly specialized nature, art studios that deal with model building tend to do it exclusively.

Apart from architectural applications, three-dimensional models

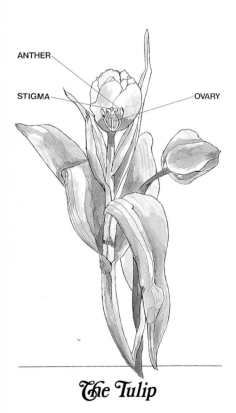

9–46. Botanical illustration using a variety of line by Martha Staigys. India ink and pen.

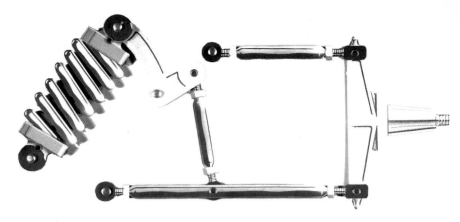

9–47. Rendering by David Milne. Three-dimensional model build as a teaching aid.

are used by institutions such as museums, planetariums, and universities, as well as by high-tech space and engineering industries. Often these companies and institutions have model builders on staff. Trade, business, and manufacturing exhibitions also incorporate models into their displays and presentations. These are usually made by model builders employed by display companies.

Computer graphics

The field of computer graphics is an exciting marriage of traditional creative visual arts and technology. It is an important and innovative new art form, supplementing conventional forms of two-dimensional print media. Because computer graphics is a complex and sophisticated subject, the following only briefly covers the various applications and possibilities of computer-generated imagery today. If you are interested in this field, it is recommended that you enroll in one of the many computer graphics courses now offered, as well as keep abreast of new developments by reading some of the books and magazines devoted to this subject.

Innovative developments within the computer graphics field has allowed more imaginative and expressive use of this medium. The artist

can choose drawing techniques using different media, painting techniques, style variations, and specific types of illustration imagery, ranging from stylized two-dimensional illustration to highly realistic representation.

Computer graphics has developed several specialties, including computer-aided design drafting (CADD), computer-aided manufacturing (CAM), computer animation, and computer-generated graphics for TV commercials, station identification screens, and programming titles.

Technical illustrators, for example, can use the computer to produce many preliminary underlays. Any object or human form can be shown in different perspective views once the initial image has been programmed into the computer (Fig. 9–48). Design modifications can be made instantly. The computer can also store vast quantities of technical information and engineering drawings.

Desktop publishing

Desktop publishing (sometimes referred to as desktop production) is another computer-generated visual arts profession, which has had tremendous impact on all conventional types of print media communications. The contemporary illustrator must be fully aware of their role within the desktop-publishing industry, since all conventional or traditionally rendered illustration can

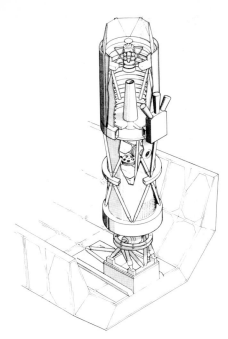

9–48. Computer-generated graphic of a detail of the Starlab space facility by Gary Mundell.

be used and incorporated into this page-making electronic medium. Many art directors and designers now use the computer to generate their preliminary ideas and comp-design visuals for client presentations.

Desktop publishing combines two disciplines of visual communications: graphic design and electronic page assembly. The skilled professional in this field needs a wide-range of knowledge, including graphic design, book design, typesetting, and production, in addition to computer operation.

Many corporations and businesses who used to rely entirely on outside sources, now have their own in-house desktop publishing facilities and are producing their own two-dimensional print media promotional materials; for example, posters, flyers, folders, brochures, newsletters, journals, magazines, financial statements, business forms, data sheets, and catalogs. Consequently, the desktop publishing industry has forced many traditional typesetters and printing houses to

restructure and update their plants in order to compete. Further, the various divisions within the visual arts industry have also dramatically changed.

If you are interested in desktop publishing, as with other computer graphics specialties you should consult some of the literature available, as well as seriously consider taking a course.

Guidelines for Advanced Illustration

Here are some general hints about how to prepare yourself for advanced illustration assignments:

- Striving to be as creative as possible within the limitations of the job

- Meeting all your deadlines

- Paying special attention to production requirements, and confirming sizes before beginning any artwork

- Always working out your ideas in small roughs that are in proportion to the final printed size of the job

- Practicing your drawing and painting skills by producing new samples of work for your portfolio

- Becoming familiar with the work of the best contemporary illustrators

- Keeping up to date with current trends in all art forms

- Taking courses in computer graphics and computer animation

- Experimenting with media and techniques; Specializing in one only to make your work more saleable

- Purchasing a 35mm camera or Polaroid, and using it to shoot your own references

- Changing figure poses, details, and colors when working from magazine photo references

- Keeping a good reference file

- Collecting art-related books (illustration, photography, and so on) and studying the work of earlier illustrators and painters

- Studying the history of illustration

- Specializing in advertising, editorial, book, or technical illustration

- Joining organizations of illustrators and designers

- Developing a good sense of time management, and accurate bookkeeping records

Mistakes to Avoid

Make every effort to avoid the following pitfalls:

- Being late for appointments, and missing deadlines

- Copying directly from magazine photo references or plagiarizing others' work; you could be sued

- Drawing figures without good photo references

- Working in isolation; it is visually unhealthy

- Compromising your integrity when you accept a job

- Forgetting to double-check sizes

- Failing to keep reproduction and printing processes in mind when doing finished art

Black-and-white contrast

The first problem stresses some basic principles of art, such as black-and-white contrast, symmetrical and asymmetrical balance, shape and line, cropping, and counterforms or negative space. To foster your intuitive sense of design, don't do any preliminary sketches for this assignment. Instead, use an X-Acto knife and cut your compositions directly out of a large sheet of black paper.

DIRECTIONS: Use a 20- × 30-inch (51 × 76 cm) sheet of black cover stock. Leaving a border around the edge, divide the sheet into six or eight rectangles of various sizes. These shapes can be ruled in with pencil. Leave a border around each rectangle; and within it, visualize one or two figures (full or partial) and a supporting object such as a bicycle or chair in an indoor or outdoor setting. If you use the outdoors, include the sun or moon, trees, and a small building. Use shadows or reflections if you wish.

Once you have visualized your first composition, start cutting out the black paper to define the subject, and place the shapes on a white cardboard backing sheet. While working on each design, remember to strive for simplicity. Create excitement with the contrast of light and dark shapes, areas, lines, and solids, with form and counterform, and with asymmetrical composition. Figure 9–49 shows a finished black-and-white composition.

This type of illustration, with no tones, is called *high-contrast.* To be effective, each illustration should probably be 10 to 20 percent cut away (leaving 80 to 90 percent black paper) or 80 to 90 percent cut away (leaving 10 to 20 percent black paper). If the whites and blacks are equal in importance, the effect will be a visually dull 50 percent gray.

The silhouette as shape

This exercise explores the power of basic shape, using the figure as a positive form. In any given subject, you will have hundreds of variations to choose from. Select and use *only* the most dynamic shapes and poses of the subject. It is all too easy to get lost in details, color, texture, and pattern so that you fail to see the shape itself.

DIRECTIONS: Use a layout pad, a black chisel-tip marker, and a felt-tip pen or pen and India ink on illustration board. Investigate the basic shapes of people of different ages, with objects that relate to the figures. Render the figure and object shapes in solid black, focusing on their outer edges. Aim for a dynamic composition. The result, with strong black-and-white contrast, should be intriguing (Figs. 9–50 and 9–51).

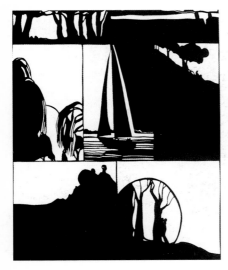

9–49. Finished studies for Exercise 1 by Wendy Losee-Orr. Cut black paper.

9–50. Finished silhouette illustration for Exercise 2 by Stephan Quinlan. India ink and brush. Silhouettes reduce subjects to strong, basic shapes.

Simplified shapes and contrast

This exercise again uses two-dimensional shapes, in negative and positive form, in conjunction with high-contrast black and white. This type of strong contrast is referred to as *notan,* a Japanese design term.

At this point, concentrate on achieving the level of accuracy in figure work required in advertising art. Although they are treated two-dimensionally, the figures must be well proportioned and realistically drawn, using photo references.

DIRECTIONS: Design and illustrate a full-page 15- × 21-inch (38 × 53 cm) black-and-white newspaper ad for fashion swimwear. Feature the garments on five or six figures in action poses that create interesting shapes. Treat the swimsuits very graphically, accentuating shapes, stripes, and patterns.

Because you are using extremely high contrast with no tones, the flesh-tones become either white or black on a black or white background. Hair should be treated as a combination of simple shapes, again either black or white.

Render the layout in black felt-tip pens and markers. To make this exercise more realistic, write a heading and indicate where it and about 150 words of body copy will go in the layout. Render the finished ad on illustration board, using India ink with a pen and a brush (Fig. 9–52).

9–52. Finished illustration for Exercise 3 by Gordon Pronk. India ink and brush. Silhouettes can be reversed: white positive shapes against a dark background.

9–51. Finished silhouette studies for Exercise 2 by Robert Johannsen. Black markers.

Letters and figures

Type letterforms and figurative elements can be used in many creative and practical ways. Notable examples of this from the past include the decorative initials on medieval illuminated manuscripts and alphabets composed entirely of figures in different poses.

DIRECTIONS: Choose any three capital letters, and combine each with a figure in a different pose. Emphasize the linear quality of both the letters and the figures. Use pattern on the clothing of the figures to make the design more interesting.

Do your layouts in line only with a black felt-tip pen, and do the finished art in India ink on illustration board (Figs. 9–53 and 9–54).

9–53. Combining figures and letterforms for Exercise 4 by Stephen Quinlan. India ink, pen, and brush.

9–54. Combining figures and letterforms for Exercise 4 by Gary Alphonso. India ink, pen, and brush.

Collaged silhouettes

Imagine that you have been asked by your city council to create a poster on the urban environment. You may focus on either a positive or a negative aspect of city life. The client wants all the elements collaged into a strong silhouette of a figure. A comprehensive full-color layout is required.

DIRECTIONS: Work on a 20- × 30-inch (51 × 76 cm) surface. Because this is a poster, it must have direct visual impact. Leaf through old magazines, looking for appropriate subject matter, geometric patterns, and textures to clip out. Then use this material, along with colored papers and India ink, to create your image. Keep your drawing to a minimum. Instead, "draw" with the clippings and papers (Fig. 9–55).

Figures 9-55 through 9-58 are on pages 230-31.

Using the silhouette

For this assignment imagine that there are two clients. One owns a hairdressing salon, and the other owns a boutique. Both require business cards, and the boutique owner also needs a poster that bears the same design as the card. The assignment thus incorporates one of the smallest printed commercial jobs with one of the largest. Your illustration must take the size difference into account so that it reproduces equally well in both cases. Keep the designs very simple, and use color in a bold and vibrant manner. Use curvilinear-shaped silhouettes to oppose the rectilinear shapes of the cards and poster. Pay special attention to silhouettes that have interesting or irregular edges. Use the silhouettes to complement the shapes you choose, and emphasize them by repeating strong verticals, horizontals, or curves.

DIRECTIONS: Choose a local hairdresser and design a business card, size 2½ × 4½ inches (6 × 11 cm) in black plus two colors. Leave room for copy at the bottom of the card.

Design a business card of the same size for a local boutique, but this time use only one color on colored paper. At the same time, create a silkscreen poster of the same design for the boutique, 14 × 26 inches (36 × 66 cm) in three colors.

Prepare rough marker layouts before doing the finished artwork. As shown in Figures 9–56 and 9–57, simplify the figure to its most basic shape.

Using a closed composition

A complex illustrative image can be greatly enhanced by being framed with a bold flat border. Such a border complements the subject by offering a contrast to it. The illustration itself should be treated in a decorative or patterned way, with high contrast of black and white.

DIRECTIONS: Design a poster announcing a gallery exhibition of a well-known artist's work (Fig. 9–58). Render a linear or two-color clean rough layout in markers. Complete the comp layout in India ink and the border in colored adhesive sheet film on illustration board.

Using asymmetric design

In this exercise, apply what you know about asymmetrical design, negative space, strong shapes, silhouettes, and value contrast. Choose the history of industry or agriculture for subject matter and integrate type and illustration in a creative yet functional ad. (Fig. 9–59).

9–59. Ad design for Exercise 8 by Mark Grice. India ink, pen, and brush.

9–55. Finished collage for Exercise 5 by Martha Staigys. Contrast of shape, value, and color are stressed. Asymmetrical balance.

9–56. Business cards for Exercise 6. Positive and negative silhouette shapes are stressed.

9–57 Poster for Exercise 6, using closed composition, asymmetrical balance, and repetition of line.

9–58. Poster for Exercise 7 by Andrew Hladkyj. India ink and self-adhesive color film.

Emphasizing line

This four-part exercise is a further refinement of Exercise 7. The assignment is to create a black-and-white poster for an arts festival. Again, reinforce the rectangular shape of the illustration with a wide border. The closed type of composition stresses the edges. In the poster use only linework to render the figures and to create a sense of realism. The underlying shapes will be less obvious, but they should be there. Suggest space, depth, and form through the quality of line you use on each figure. Let the line make the figures slightly three-dimensional.

DIRECTIONS: Using Figure 9–60 as an example, interlock four figurative illustrations on a centrally placed grid. Treat each illustration slightly differently through your choice of the figure, pose, and type of performing art being depicted. Render the finished art in India ink, using a pen and a brush.

9–60. Finished composition for Exercise 9 by Steven Quinlan. India ink and pen.

Depicting change

Metamorphosis (or growth and change) is a good subject to illustrate because it gives you an opportunity to experiment with various line qualities, shapes, and textures as the image evolves. This assignment calls for a four-part black-and-white illustration of "The Changing Woman," beginning with a realistic image on the left that gradually becomes more abstracted as the composition moves toward the right.

DIRECTIONS: Use a photo of one figure or draw a person from life. Use the same pose for all four illustrations. Analyze the negative and positive shapes of your composition, and then begin the first illustration, using a minimal amount of line and shape. Introduce more linework in the second illustration so that the figure presents a stronger shape against the background. In the third illustration, make strong use of line to suggest tone, pattern, or texture in contrast to the figure and background. The negative space and shapes should predominate. In the final illustration, accentuate the negative spaces. Indicate them with India ink. The figure can be left as an almost completely white shape, with very little linework.

Include the heading "The Changing Woman" and a fair amount of body copy, as shown in Figure 9–61. The same exercise can be done with a changing man.

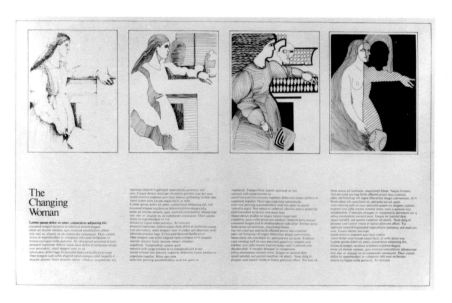

9–61. Finished composition for Exercise 10 by Steven Quinlan. India ink, pen, and brush.

More linework

Linework is the most widely used technique in illustration, and it reproduces well. Line can be used to describe shapes and forms, to indicate solidity through shading, and to simulate textures and patterns. Line weight can be varied from very fine to very heavy.

DIRECTIONS: Using a photo as reference, create a black-and-white poster depicting the people of a foreign country in a typical setting (Fig. 9–62). Use strong shapes, both negative and positive. Contrasting the sizes and shapes of the negative spaces is the key to designing this illustration.

Render the image in various line weights. Use linework to emphasize decorative patterns and textures in clothing and other objects. Draw the garments so as to describe the form of the body beneath. Leave fleshtones as white or black dropout shapes. Choose a type style appropriate for the country you are depicting, and use it for a heading at the bottom of the poster.

9–62. Poster for Exercise 11 by Steven Quinlan. India ink, pen, and brush.

Seeing the basic shapes

Full realism is explored in this exercise involving variations of line, shape, and contrast. Concentrate on seeing the subject matter as a collection of strong basic shapes, regardless of how detailed, decorative, or modeled it is.

DIRECTIONS: Choose a subject such as musicians, athletes, or dancers. As in Figure 9–63, treat the figures as simple shapes and place them in a way that creates exciting background forms. Use high-contrast lighting to get the maximum play of dark and light on the clothing and body. Use a geometric shape in contour line to contrast with the irregular black shapes of the figures, and to connect them. You may include a

9–63. Finished photographic collage for Exercise 12 by Donna Kwasnicki. Note use of symmetry and bold shapes contrasting with line.

heading in type if you wish, but it should not interfere with the pictorial elements. You may choose either an illustration or a photographic collage.

Creating a newspaper ad

The assignment is to create a newspaper ad that announces a new line of cosmetics (Fig. 9–64). The design must attract the reader's attention, but the client wants an indirect (soft-sell) approach. The products should be featured in an interesting illustration; the type should be quiet and of secondary importance.

The client wants to see small roughs and a full-size layout linear before you go on to do a comprehensive layout.

DIRECTIONS: Print the following heading: "Announcing Fashion's New Accent." Leave room for one or two blocks of body copy (approximately 100 words or 12 lines) to describe the featured products.

For the ad size, choose either 6 columns × 12 inches (30 cm) or 7 columns × 10½ inches (27 cm). In agate lines, this comes out to 6 columns × 166 lines or 7 columns × 142 lines. Each option is a strong shape and thus a good basis for a strong design.

The ad is to be printed in black plus one color of your choice. The comps should be rendered in India ink. The second color can be painted, or it can be cut out of colored paper and glued to the illustration board. (For finished art, you would prepare the mechanical as line art.)

Put everything you have learned in Exercises 1–12 to use. In rendering any figures, pay special attention to shape and contrast, using minimal linework to supplement the basic shapes.

9–64. Comp layout for Exercise 13 by Sharon Matthews. Markers and black felt-tip pen.

exercise 14

Selling a political message

The assignment here is to create a strong design and illustration concept that can be used in various rectangular shapes of different proportions—in other words, in various print media formats. To do this, use a single graphic shape underlying a realistic illustration. Make the type an integral part of the design.

The message to be communicated is the diversity and unity of the people of your country. This is a soft-sell political message. The heading should read: "Canadian Unity" or "American Unity" or whatever is applicable (Figs. 9–65 and 9–66).

DIRECTIONS: Working in black and white or color, make comprehensive layouts for five of the following formats:

• Full-page newspaper ad

• Half-page newspaper ad

• Poster for use in a transit system (subway or bus)

• Outdoor poster, 10 × 20 feet (3 × 6 m)

• Poster for a shopping mall

• Ad for *Time* magazine 7 × 10 inches (18 × 25 cm)

• Front cover of a single-fold folder

• Front cover and two inside spreads (pairs of facing pages) of a brochure

You will be using the same piece of artwork, but adapting it to different size formats. Certain minor elements on the outside edges may be eliminated to suit the design.

exercise 15

Promoting a favorable company image

Imagine that the client is a paper manufacturer interested in a soft-sell institutional campaign that projects a favorable image of the company rather than of a particular brand-name product. The client wants the main feature to be the depiction of interesting people (Figs. 9–67 and 9–68). Use many figures from different walks of life. To create a composition full of vitality, use what you learned about silhouettes, shapes, and high contrast.

DIRECTIONS: Choose two of the following formats:

• Full-page news ad

• Poster

• Half-page news ad

• Ad for *Time* magazine, 7 × 10 inches (18 × 25 cm)

9–65. Master piece of artwork for institutional advertising campaign for Exercise 14 by Raffi Anderian.

9–66. Artwork for Exercise 14 by Marie Sequens. India ink, pen, and brush.

9–67. Comp rendering for Exercise 15 by Gordon Pronk. Twelve-page institutional brochure. Sepia markers and felt pen on colored stock. The final images were laminated.

9–68. A poster design for Exercise 15 by Gordon Pronk. Combination of type and illustration. Markers and adhesive rub-down dummy type. The final art was covered with acetate.

- Twelve-page brochure in a square format, using paper stock of different colors

In the twelve-page brochure, each double-page spread can be of a different size as long as each forms a square when folded (Fig. 9–67).

Render everything in line, using black or a dark color such as sepia or dark blue. Use the title "People and Paper" and whatever text seems appropriate.

Rendering a testimonial ad

The client is a home-insulation manufacturer who plans to run a series of ten full-page black-and-white newspaper ads featuring different homeowners and their insulated houses. This is a testimonial campaign, based on unsolicited letters homeowners have written to the manufacturer praising the insulation. The client wants each ad to feature a different couple and to be rendered in a different line technique. The design format should remain constant, however, in order to give the series unity.

DIRECTIONS: Find houses that have interesting features and take photos of them for reference. Choose a view that best suits the house you are drawing. Do a line art rendering that combines the home and its owners (Fig. 9–69).

9–69. Finished design illustration for Exercise 16 by Donna Kwasnicki. India ink on rubber cement. Rubber cement resist used to create textural tone.

Promoting a product

The assignment here is to do a newspaper or magazine ad featuring a camera. The idea to be emphasized is that, wherever people travel in the world, they take this camera with them. You can depict any country, including its people, landmarks, or landscapes, in a multi-image illustration (Fig. 9–70).

As an added challenge, the client wants the perspective view purposely distorted to create the impression of being a wide-angle shot from the camera itself. This is difficult to draw because the telephoto lens is foreshortened and the ellipses are different sizes and shapes. To succeed, you must bring the vanishing points closer together than they actually are when you are viewing the subject. A slight amount of distortion must also be used in rendering the camera.

DIRECTIONS: Do both a marker layout and finished art for a newspaper ad of 6 columns × 16¾ inches (43 cm) or for a full-page magazine ad for the magazine of your choice. You should use plastic ellipse guides for rendering the lens and camera rings in the finished art, but you can draw them freehand in the marker layout.

9–70. Finished multi-image product illustration for Exercise 17 by Richard Long. Markers, India ink, and felt-tip pen.

Advertising the product in an environment

In this variation on Exercise 17, combine a product with figures in a setting that includes either a jet plane or an ocean liner, to convey the idea of worldwide use of the product. The different subjects in this exercise—figures, product, background, and transportation vehicle—will test your versatility, a crucial attribute for an illustrator.

DIRECTIONS: Design a full-color half-page ad for the magazine of your choice. Use markers for the layouts and watercolors or acrylics for the finished art.

Practicing your marker rendering skills

Because marker rendering is so integral a part of the illustration business—especially in advertising work—you should frequently practice drawing and rendering. With print media advertising in mind, you should work boldly and expressively in your layouts. The very nature of newspaper reproduction and other types of print media calls for simple artwork with plenty of contrast. Fine details do not print well in newspapers as a result of the printing process used.

Because of the very constricted time limits governing much print media advertising, concentrate on drawing quickly and accurately, no matter what the subject matter is. It is possible to render figures, faces, and backgrounds by visualization alone, if you spend time practicing this skill.

DIRECTIONS: It may seem odd, but the first stage in improving your visualization skills is to practice tracing. This is the only place in this book where tracing is suggested. The point is that, by tracing over photos, you can learn exactly how much linework is necessary to render a subject.

Take five or six sheets of tracing paper and a black felt-tip pen. Find some dramatically lit photos in a fashion magazine, and trace these onto the tracing paper, concentrating on making the facial features accurate. Try to draw expressively, giving the figures life at the same time. Keep the drawing to a minimum; that is, do not overdraw. You may wish to use a chisel-point pen so that you can work with a thick-and-thin line.

When you have completed a couple of direct tracings, begin to draw slightly different views based on your reference. At this point, rather than tracing, you are using your knowledge of drawing. Mix both methods, tracing and freehand drawing, until you are satisfied that you can draw as accurately as you can trace (Fig. 9–71).

Now use the fluency you have developed in drawing with a felt-tip pen to work with colored markers. Use these just as you used the black and gray markers in Chapter 3, replacing the different gray tones with colors of the correct warmth or coolness. Keep in mind that warm colors advance and cool colors recede, enabling you to create the sensation of form through light and shade. The lighted side of a form has a hint of warm color, and the shaded side has a hint of cool color. For example, a cylindrical kitchen appliance—say, a chrome coffee pot—should be rendered with a warm pale yellow ocher

9–71. Tracing and freehand drawing with markers for Exercise 19 by Carmen McClure. Marker felt-tip pen.

marker stroke next to the highlight and a cool pale blue stroke in the shaded area. These will make the pot appear round and solid.

The same principle applies to all subject matter rendered in markers. The effect is similar to that used by the French Impressionists in their landscapes, still lifes, and portraits. Look at some reproductions of Impressionist paintings, and try to analyze their use of warm and cool color. Another similarity to Impressionism is that color marker rendering should suggest form rather than try to replicate photographic realism.

Using the photo references if you wish, practice rendering the following subjects, emphasizing the warm and cool color factors:

- Cube, prism, cone, cylinder, and sphere

- Kitchen utensils and appliances

- Simple landscapes

- Studies of heads and faces

- Combinations of the above

Use your markers in both positive and negative ways. Let dark colors hold light or white shapes. For example, let a blue sky define the shape of a white building. Very little rendering is then required to make the building appear three-dimensional. You can add a single color to the shaded side and use minimal linework on that side to render details such as windows. This negative use of colored markers is a simple but effective technique. Practice as much as possible to become proficient in line drawing and color marker rendering.

Showing people in action

To continue practicing your marker rendering skills, find action shots of people and do quick, simple renderings, along the lines of those in Figure 9–72. Once you feel confident in your ability to make rapid depictions of people in action, you're ready for this assignment.

A television station wants a multi-image illustration for a poster that features its fast, in-depth reporting of worldwide news events. The station's objective is to increase the size of its viewing audience and in that way attract more advertisers.

Work on a 19- × 24-inch (48 × 60 cm) layout pad, and use a black felt-tip pen to do the drawings. Try to employ a conscious sense of intuitive design when drawing from figure references. By varying figure sizes, weights, and directions, you can achieve a multi-image composition of contrast, rhythm, and movement.

9–72. Marker sketch for Exercise 20 by Michelle Gauthier. Markers and felt-tip pen.

Rendering diverse subjects

To give you practice in rendering the many products and types of figures an illustrator is expected to draw, this assignment focuses on a credit card. The task is to design a poster in which each subject can be rendered separately and then pasted together in a final arrangement. Consequently, if you make mistakes, you can redo the rendering easily. If you feel particularly confident, however, you may do the complete layout on a single sheet of paper.

DIRECTIONS: Practice doing marker sketches of products and activities that a credit card might be used to pay for, such as shoes, cosmetics, perfume, table lamps, glassware, kitchen appliances, furniture, audio equipment, plants, antiques, traveling, and dining out (Fig. 9–73).

For the poster itself, use a grid to arrange various-size squares and rectangles into a composition, as shown in Figure 9–73. Work in color. Carefully consider the choice of color for the backgrounds, as well as the shape of each subject within its frame of reference. When the individual components are assembled, the design should exhibit balance and unity.

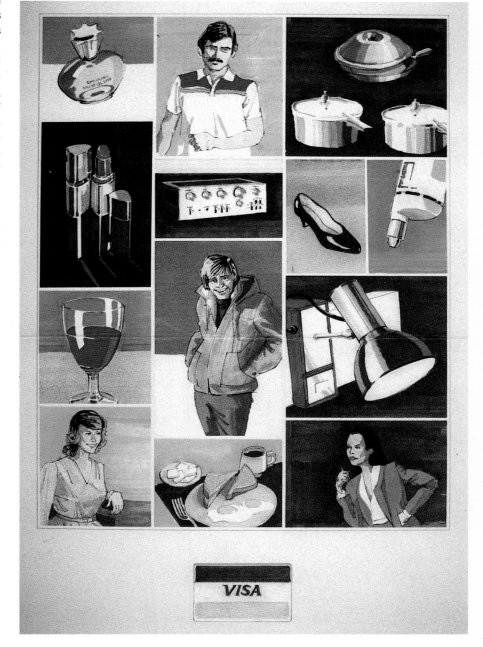

9–73. Finished poster for Exercise 21 by Gary Alphonso. Markers and felt-tip pen.

Advertising multiple products

Another kind of ad that can involve diverse subjects is a department store ad. For this assignment, create an ad featuring different cosmetics and fashion accessories for women. In this situation, you must combine your skills in realistic drawing with an abstract overall design, making the diverse elements work together visually. A grid is one way to organize everything, but try other possibilities as well.

DIRECTIONS: Work in black and white, in a medium and size of your choice. Mix realistic renderings with more stylized drawings, as in Figure 9–74. Include a headline in lettering that fits the rest of the design.

9–74. Comp layout for Exercise 22 by Marie Sequens. India ink, pen, and brush.

Featuring automotive products

For this assignment, your client is a company that manufactures automotive parts and accessories. The client wants you to develop a campaign with related ads that can be run in different sizes in both newspapers and magazines.

DIRECTIONS: Select whichever automobile, parts, or accessories you wish to illustrate from reference photos. Render a three-color single-page magazine ad, a black-and-white full-page ad with tone, a small black-and-white news ad in line only, and a full-color outdoor poster. The main challenge here is to find a concept that can be adapted to all these formats (Fig. 9–75).

9–75. Comp illustration for Exercise 23 by Warren MacDonald. Charcoal pencil, acrylics, and colored adhesive film.

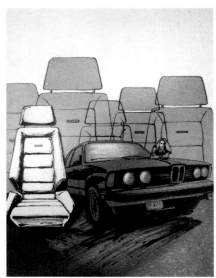

Doing a fashion illustration

When doing a fashion illustration, remember that it is customary to elongate the figure. In normal drawing, the length of the body is about 7½ to 8 times that of the head. In fashion illustration, the body length may be between 9 and 16 times the head length (10 and 12 being standard). The body is usually stretched from the waist to the feet, creating a long-legged look. The arms are also usually stretched slightly in relation to the length of the legs. The face, shoulders, waist, and hips are thinned to give the figure a look of elegance.

DIRECTIONS: You may choose to illustrate spring, summer, fall, or winter fashion merchandise (Figs. 9–76 through 9–79). Decide on a location to serve as a background, creating the mood and concept. Use two or three figures, male or female for the ad. You may also wish to combine figures with fashion accessories. A clever concept can be used to relate all elements of an accessories-only ad. As part of the total job, you may write your own heading and include small blocks of copy keyed to the items in the ad. Alternatively, you may just leave space for these.

The accessories that accompany the figures must be rendered in a size that makes them easy to see. Small items should be enlarged to show detailing. The garments must be very accurately indicated. The fabric patterns, sleeve lengths, cuffs, colors, fastenings, and gathers or pleats are very important from a customer's point of view.

Before you begin the ad itself, practice drawing heads and figures, using fashion magazines for reference. Then render a comprehensive layout for a newspaper ad in gray markers and a black felt-tip pen. For the finished art, use India ink with a pen or a brush.

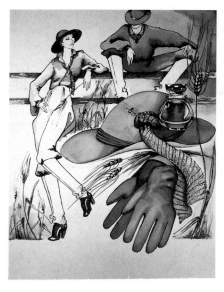

9–77. Spring fashion illustration for Exercise 24 by Lynne Baille. India ink, pen, and brush.

9–78. Fall fashion illustration for Exercise 24 by Warren MacDonald. India ink, pen, and brush.

9–76. Summer fashion illustration for Exercise 24 by Mark Grice. India ink, pen, and brush.

9–79. Winter fashion illustration for Exercise 24 by Michelle Gauthier. India ink, pen, and brush.

Rendering rush layouts

A critical aspect of illustration is speed. For this assignment choose any product or subject that appeals to you, to use in a media campaign. Imagine that your client wants a major campaign, including all of the following formats:

- Full-page newspaper ad

- Half-page newspaper ad

- Front cover of an 8½- × 11-inch (22 × 28 cm) folder

- Front cover of a twelve-page brochure

- Ad for a news magazine, 7 × 10 inches (18 × 25 cm)

- Outdoor poster

- Outdoor painted billboard

- In-store poster

- Direct-mail single-fold piece

- Point-of-purchase promotional piece

- Single-page bleed ad for a popular magazine

- Transit pass (bus or subway)

- Shopping mall poster

- Displays for store windows

Most of these pieces should be done in black and white, but you can add two or three colors to the posters and brochure.

DIRECTIONS: Take a layout pad and draw in all the ad sizes, each on a

9–80. Artwork by Gary Alphonso. Master art must be adaptable for various ad sizes. Placement and cropping are crucial.

9–81. Adaptation of master art by Gary Alphonso. Markers and felt-tip pen.

9–82. Artwork by Gary Alphonso. Marker and felt-tip pen. Master art can also be adapted for point-of-sale material.

9–83. Another adaptation of master art by Gary Alphonso.

separate sheet, using a ruler, T-square, and black felt-tip pen. Then compare the sizes. If any of the formats have similar proportions, write these down on the bottom left-hand corner of the commonly shaped rectangles. For example, you may find that the full-page newspaper ad, the half-page newspaper ad, the news magazine ad, and the in-store poster are similar.

A size similarity may be determined by drawing a diagonal line in pencil through the largest of the ads and then using this method to determine whether any of the other ads scale down in the same ratio. A ½- to 1-inch (1.3 to 2.5 cm) difference in any dimension is close enough. (Remember that this is a rush job. By using this method, you will only have to do one master piece of art; and by adapting it to the basic common proportions of the four-

teen assignments, you will only have to render approximately four layouts.)

Allowing yourself ten or fifteen minutes, quickly work out some ideas and choose one to develop. Pin it up in front of you and, using separate sheets of paper and the sheets listing the ad sizes underneath as a guide, quickly transfer the composition as a rough sketch. Work with a black felt-tip pen, one sheet at a time. Remember to keep everything simple. Don't overdraw. After the main lines are down, lay in gray or colored markers, one tone or color at a time. Do this for all the layouts at the same time. This method is much faster than working at random or on one piece at a time. Remember that a sixteen-hour job like this is worth far more financially than sixteen hours spent on another type of illustration. See Figures 9–80 to 9–83.

Attracting attention from a distance

Your client wants a full-color poster announcing the coming performance of a national folk dance troupe (Figs. 9–84 and 9–85). The most important task here is to make the poster attract attention from a great distance. It should arouse the curiosity of viewers and make them want to come closer to read the information. Strong design and color are important in achieving this effect.

DIRECTIONS: The size of the poster is optional, but 16 × 22 inches (41 × 56 cm) in a vertical format is suggested. Explore as many ideas as possible in marker layouts before settling on one that seems to work best. You have complete freedom with regard to the medium and technique of the finished art, so be experimental and free in your approach.

9–85. Painting for Exercise 26 by Ian Beveridge. Gouache and big, 2 1/2-inch brush was used to capture the motion of this dancing figure.

VARIATIONS: After doing this poster, you might want to create some related advertising pieces, such as movie posters, theater posters, record album covers, and book jackets. All of these must have strong visual impact from a distance, to attract attention.

Producing a rush poster

A client asks you to create a large, painterly full-color poster within three hours. The subject is "Parks Are for People." The size is not specified, although 16 × 22 inches (41 × 56 cm) is suggested. You also have a choice of medium and technique, but designers' colors on colored paper are recommended because of the time limit.

This assignment is an excellent test of your decision-making skills because of the freedom of choice and the tight deadline (which should prevent you from overworking the illustration). Look at the excitement and freedom expressed in Figures 9–86 and 9–87. All too often illustrators' roughs are more creative and effective than their finished illustrations. You must recognize when to stop working on an illustration. In doing this exercise, you can discover how little work is required to produce dynamic results.

9–84. Artwork by Kevin Breen.

9–86. Illustration for Exercise 27 by Colin Gillies. Gouache on colored paper. Complementary colors and asymmetrical balance.

9–87. Illustration for Exercise 27 by Ritta Malm. Gouache on colored paper. Symmetrical balance.

Creating an institutional illustration

This is a two-part soft-sell institutional advertisement: you are not selling a product or service, but an image. The client wants a black-and-white full-page newspaper ad (Figs. 9–88 and 9–89) and a full-color continuous-tone poster (Figs. 9–90 and 9–91) to promote a particular town. Your illustration should show various interesting aspects of the town — historical buildings, statuary, parks, waterways, sports, civic events, or any other special attractions.

DIRECTIONS: Use your own hometown or another place you know well. Visit local museums and libraries to obtain the necessary reference materials.

Your choice of medium and technique is open, but for the four-color poster, watercolors, acrylics, gouache, or colored pencils are recommended. The only firm requirement is that approximately one-third of the space be left for a type heading and body copy. The illustrations may break up the copy in places. Do a semicomp marker layout before rendering the finished art.

9–90. Multi-image institutional poster for Exercise 28 by Les Marubashi. Watercolor and India ink, pen and brush.

9–89. Variation on multi-image institutional ad for Exercise 28 by Brenda Clark. Black and white mixed media, pen, and brush.

9–88. Multi-image illustration for Exercise 28 by Les Marubashi. Black and white mixed media, pen, and brush.

9–91. Multi-image color institutional advertisement for Exercise 28 by Brenda Clark. Watercolor.

Constructing a three-dimensional illustration

Not all illustration has to be rendered two-dimensionally. Three-dimensional illustration can be both exciting to produce and effective as finished art. Many materials can be used, including paper, board, wood, fabric, papier-mache, wire, and metal. The resulting composition is then shot by a professional photographer.

DIRECTIONS: Using materials that are easy to work with, such as foamcore, plywood, and balsa wood, design and render one of the following illustrations: a fashion illustration for a poster and print media campaign; an editorial magazine story illustration; or a poster on one of the five senses for a soft-sell anti-drug campaign (Figs. 9–92 and 9–93).

Developing a magazine ad

Now tackle a four-color double-page-spread magazine ad for a breakfast cereal. The client wants a series of ads that feature well-known sports personalities. Each ad will be rendered by a different illustrator in acrylics or gouache mixed with glazing medium. The medium will help maintain continuity in the series, as will the design format, which has been determined by the art director.

DIRECTIONS: A large portrait and action poses of the sports figure, enclosed by a colored border, are to occupy the left page. The person's name should be part of the border design (Fig. 9–94). The right page should show four or five spot illustrations, together with the product. The cereal package must be realistically rendered as part of a breakfast table arrangement (Fig. 9–95).

Using the split-fountain technique

This exercise introduces you to a relatively little known printing process: the split-fountain or rainbow process, which presents the effect of a full-color printing even though the paper only goes through the printing press once. The ink tray or fountain on a printing press normally holds one color of ink at a time. Consequently, in a one-color illustration the paper goes through the printing press only once; in a two-color illustration the paper goes through twice; and so on. For a typical split-fountain printing job, however, the printer uses two cardboard dividers to separate the ink tray into three sections, each holding a different color. The illustrator specifies the three colors to be used. When printed, the colors blend together where they meet. The three bands of color can be printed either vertically or horizontally, depending on the position of the artwork relative to the direction of the paper going through the printing press.

Since this process costs about the same as a one-color job, it is a good way to get more color while staying within a client's budget. Make sure ahead of time that the printer is willing to use this special process.

When doing the finished art for split-fountain work, use linework only and render tonal variations through line shading, adhesive dots, or prepared adhesive screens. To render a layout for the split-fountain process, use pastel sticks or colored pencils, blending the colors where they meet. All linework must be indicated entirely in the three selected colors. White shapes, areas, or type can simply be cut out of the layout at the end. Then the final piece can be rubber-cemented onto a fresh sheet of paper.

Figures 9–96 and 9–97 were done with this process. Note that the widths of the bands of color can be varied by having the printer adjust the location of the cardboard walls in the ink tray.

9–92. Three-dimensional illustration for Exercise 29 by Michael McKeever. Acrylics on plywood.

9–93. Three-dimensional illustration for Exercise 29. Acrylics, plywood, and balsa wood.

9–94. Four-color magazine advertisement for food product for Exercise 30 by Raffi Anderian. Gouache and acrylic glazing medium.

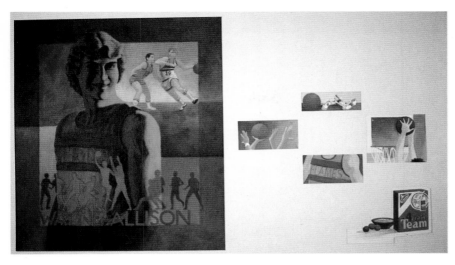

9–95. Multi-image illustration for
Exercise 30 by Cindy Holmes.
Gouache. Note use of transparency,
change of scale, and spatial divisions.

9–96. An invitational poster using the
split-fountain, or rainbow, technique.
Split-fountain printing produces the
effects of a full-color piece, but for
about the same price as a one-color
job.

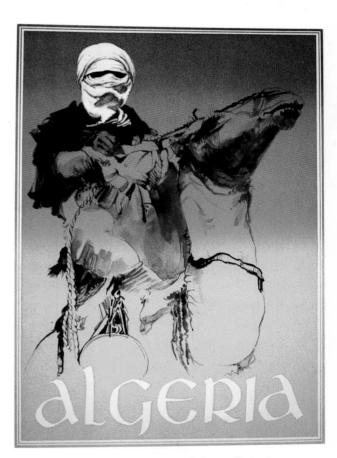

9–97. Artwork by Raffi Anderian.
Experimental finished rendering for a
poster investigating the split-fountain
process. Gouache, pen, and brush.

Varying your approach

Now create various one-page illustrations or double-page spreads for different kinds of articles. Begin by finding several magazine articles that interest you; then decide on the concept to be emphasized in each case. Next do linear or color roughs to work out your ideas.

Vary your style in accordance with the subject. In some cases, you may want a free, painterly approach; in others, a tightly rendered realistic image; in still others, a more abstracted design (Figs. 9–98 through 9–103). Remember that your illustration can help set the tone for the reader.

9–98. Artwork for Exercise 32 by Kevin Breen. Single-page stipple illustration for article featuring well-known personality. India ink and pen. High contrast and texture.

Doing a single-page portrait

Your first assignment is to do a single-page illustration depicting a famous person for a small-format magazine of about the same size as *Time* magazine. The left page will contain the beginning of the article, with a heading and typeset body copy (all in black and white); your illustration will appear on the right page in full color. The objective is to capture an accurate likeness of the person who is the subject of the article, as if you were doing a portrait.

DIRECTIONS: After choosing your subject, use photo references and complete a layout linear with markers. Then go on to the finished art. Choose a specific medium and technique, using as much or as little as seems appropriate. The objective is to produce an illustration that simultaneously captures the reader's attention and conveys a likeness (Figs. 9–104 through 9–106).

9–99. Artwork for Exercise 32 by Patrick Sayers. Double-page illustration for a psychological article. Gouache and acrylics. Cubist-style imagery.

Making a romantic illustration

Clinch is a term often used by art directors and editors to describe a romantic story, whether historical or contemporary. The most important criterion for this type of illustration is that the details of the artwork correspond to the written descriptions of the characters, settings, and objects in the story. The physical characteristics of the characters—including height, weight, color of hair and eyes, facial structure, and clothing—all must match the one written about.

In this type of work, you are usually expected to establish a strong mood to capture the attention of the reader. The background location can be especially important in creating a romantic setting. This kind of illustration also calls for idealized yet realistic figure work (Figs. 9–107 and 9–108).

DIRECTIONS: Start with a romantic story or novel that has not been illustrated. Read it carefully and then choose an interesting portion to depict. Aim to capture the mood, the correct attributes of the characters, and the look of the setting (Figs. 9–109 through 9–111).

In a real assignment the art director would specify the number of colors to work in and the trim size of the magazine. You would then choose to work either half up (one and one-half times reproduction size) or twice up (double reproduction size). Remember as you work, that, when the illustration is reduced for reproduction, small details and fine work will be smaller and may become difficult to see.

9–107. Experimental mixed-media romantic illustration accentuating curvilinear shapes and contrast using asymmetrical balance. Gouache, colored inks, and India ink. Producing new samples for your portfolio is important.

9–108. Finished romantic illustration for Exercise 34. Charcoal pencil, acrylic glazing medium, gouache, and gesso. Use of three-point perspective makes this composition dramatic.

9–109. Double-page romantic illustration for Exercise 34. Charcoal pencil, acrylic glazing medium, gouache, and gesso. High contrast, positive and negative shapes.

9–110. Figurework for a romantic illustration by Paul McCusker. Black oil paint. Painting method #4.

9–111. Finished double-page, romantic illustration for Exercise 34. Gouache, acrylic glazing medium, and gesso.

exercise 35

Preparing a TV storyboard

Television is so important as an advertising and communication vehicle that you must know how to render a TV storyboard for a commercial in markers and felt-tip pen. A storyboard is a visual and copy guide for both the video and the audio components of an ad. Once approved by the client, it is passed on to a production house as a guide for shooting the actual commercial. Storyboard work requires fast, accurate drawing and marker rendering. The ability to indicate facial expressions and hand gestures is particularly important. You also need to have an appreciation of camera angles and techniques.

There are three types of storyboard format. The first uses a conventional TV storyboard layout pad, which may vary in size and in number of frames per sheet. The video picture action is indicated inside the rounded-corner rectangles, and the copy is handwritten or typed and then pasted into the thin rectangular audio shapes below the video frames.

The second type of storyboard, called a *New York board,* is done on a very large sheet of layout paper or on two sheets taped together. The general concept of the commercial is indicated in the frames along the bottom row. One or two large figures at the top create the mood and impact that the commercial should have. The copy or script for this type of board is typewritten and accompanies the board when sent to the client for approval.

The third type of TV storyboard involves drawing your own rectangles on a sheet of bond layout paper, rather than working on a preprinted storyboard pad. The individual rectangular frames should be either 3 × 4 inches (8 × 10 cm) or 5 × 7 inches (13 × 18 cm). As usual, the storyboards are rendered with black felt-tip pen and markers. Then, however, they are shot on video film and synched to a soundtrack containing narration and music. When this is shown on a TV set, it simulates the effect of the intended commercial. This approach, called *animatic storyboard rendering,* simulates the sensation of motion for TV clients' presentations. Figures, backgrounds, and products can be shot with a video camera and spliced together.

Television advertising spots are sold in time blocks of 10, 20, 30, and 60 seconds. For a 30-second commercial you should render separate illustrations on the storyboard to suggest the action that is taking place every 2 or 3 seconds. Thus, for a 30-second ad board, fifteen frames might be required to do the job effectively.

In preparing a storyboard, the illustrator always works from a scripted

Illustrating books

This assignment is similar to Exercise 32, where you varied your approach to magazine illustration, except that this time you are doing book illustration.

Start out with a children's fairy tale or fable, so the story will be relatively short. Plan eight or ten illustrations. Do roughs of each before doing finished

9–113. Realistic, interpretive style of book illustration by Mark Smith. India ink, pen, and brush. Curvilinear lines oppose bold shapes.

art. The size and technique are open — as is the style.

Now go on to other kinds of books, both fiction and nonfiction. Do several book cover illustrations, as well as some frontispieces. Experiment with different kinds of inside illustrations, using both black and white and full color. Study Figures 9–113 through 9–125 for ideas.

---

copy sheet and illustrates what has been indicated there. This copy also provides the instructions to be followed by the TV production crew.

Here are some terms you may encounter on a TV copy sheet:

Pan: The camera moves across the set following the action.

Dissolve: The image fades out or away.

Truck in or out: The camera moves in toward or away from the action in a rather exaggerated way.

Zoom: the camera lens moves in on a subject, from a distance to very close.

CU: The camera shows a closeup shot of the subject.

ECU: The camera shows an extra-closeup shot of the subject.

Super: A name or title is superimposed over the visual image.

Voiceover: The narrator's voice is heard reading from the script.

DIRECTIONS: Try your own storyboard rendering. First, choose a client who manufactures or sells a product. Take a sheet from a TV layout pad, and write the audio/instruction portion of a commercial. For example: (1) Zoom to beach scene. . . . CU on figure action. (2) Voiceover: "It's your health that counts. . . ." (3) ECU to product, and dissolve.

Now, rough out compositions in the video frames, using a black felt-tip marker pen. Strengthen the lines of the drawing, slip this sheet under a fresh one, and redraw the sketches very quickly and accurately in black felt-tip pen. Next, using one colored marker at a time, render everything on the entire sheet where that color appears. Do this with every color. Finally, add little

touches of detail, more modeling, or extra colors (see Fig. 9-112 on p. 254).

RELATED WORK: Illustrators are also used in TV programs for TV titles — the graphics used at the beginning and end of a program, during newscasts and sportscasts, and even during technical difficulties. Although these are usually done by an illustrator in the TV station's art department, freelance illustrators are sometimes used.

In addition to creating TV storyboards, you can also make storyboards for audiovisual presentations. These storyboards should be rendered in much the same way as TV ones, but the artwork will ultimately be shot as 35mm slides or as filmstrip. The finished art should be done to fixed size in constant proportions on separate boards, and then it should be photographed.

9–114. Decorative book illustration by Adriana Taddeo. India ink, pen, and brush. Flat shapes and pattern.

9–115. Another variation of decorative book illustration by Adriana Taddeo. India ink, pen, and brush.

9–112. New York-style TV storyboard rendering for Exercise 35 by Gary Alphonso. Black felt-tip pen and color wedge-tip markers.

9–116. Comp by Ron Fyke. Gouache and watercolors, India ink, pen, and brush. Color illustration for a double-page spread in a children's book.

9–117. Children's book illustration by Paul McCusker. Watercolor, India ink, pen, and brush. Action and focal point are reinforced through color, value, and detail.

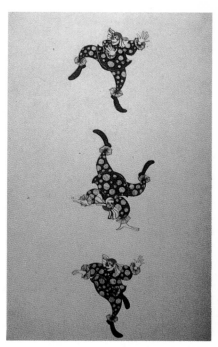

9–118. Book illustration adapted for use on a menu in a family restaurant by Ron Fyke. Watercolors, India ink, and pen.

9–119. Book illustration adapted for use on a menu in a family restaurant by Ron Fyke. Gouache, India ink, pen, and brush.

9–120. Artwork by Martha Staigys. Decorative illustration for a double-page spread for a book on fairy tales. India ink, colored inks and various pens.

9–121. Artwork by Martha Staigys. Interpretive and decorative illustration for O. Henry's *The Gift of the Magi*. Pen and ink. Pattern and texture emphasized.

9–123. Inside-page illustration by Adriana Taddeo. India ink and pen. Contour line contrasts with texture. One-point perspective.

9–122. Artwork by Martha Staigys. Decorative double-page book illustration for O. Henry's *The Gift of the Magi*. India ink and various pens.

9–124. Artwork by Ron Fyke. Double-page illustration for Edgar Allan Poe's *The Raven*. India ink and pen. Combination of stipple, line, and crosshatching.

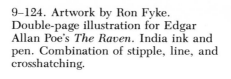

Back into the chamber turning, all my soul within me burning,
Soon again I heard a tapping somewhat louder than before.
'Surely,' said I, 'surely that is something at my window lattice;
Let me see, then, what thereat is, and this mystery explore—
Let my heart be still a moment and this mystery explore;—
'Tis the wind and nothing more.'

Open here I flung the shutter, when, with many a flirt and flutter,
In there stepped a stately raven of the saintly days of yore;
Not the least obeisance made he; not a minute stopped or stayed he;
But, with mien of lord or lady, perched above my chamber door—
Perched upon a bust of Pallas just above my chamber door—
Perched, and sat, and nothing more.

Then this ebony bird beguiling my sad fancy into smiling,
By the grave and stern decorum of the countenance it wore,
'Though thy crest be shorn and shaven, thou,' I said, 'art sure no craven,
Ghastly grim and ancient raven wandering from the Nightly shore—
Tell me what thy lordly name is on the Night's Plutonian shore!'
Quoth the Raven, 'Nevermore.'

Much I marvelled this ungainly fowl to hear discourse so plainly,
Though its answer little meaning—little relevancy bore;
For we cannot help agreeing that no living human being
Ever yet was blest with seeing bird above his chamber door—
Bird or beast upon the sculptured bust above his chamber door,
With such name as 'Nevermore.'

But the raven, sitting lonely on the placid bust, spoke only
That one word, as if his soul in that one word he did outpour.
Nothing further then he uttered—not a feather then he fluttered—
Till I scarcely more than muttered, 'other friends have flown before—
On the morrow he will leave me, as my hopes have flown before.'
Then the bird said, 'Nevermore.'

9–125. Conceptual science-fiction illustration by Paul McCusker. Acrylics.

Illustrating newspaper articles

As was noted earlier, the vast majority of newspaper editorial illustration is done in black and white. In special cases, a second color may be run with the black. (This color may need to be preseparated by the illustrator on an overlay sheet.)

Most newspaper artwork either is square or rectangular or is done as an irregular vignette. The art director will tell you the type of shape required, as this is determined by the design of the page. The size, dimensions, and placement of the illustration are all dictated by the number of columns of copy in the feature article.

Because of the great variety of newspaper articles that may require illustrations, this exercise is presented as a multiple-choice assignment. You may follow the suggestions given for illustrations or choose your own articles to illustrate from an actual newspaper.

FAMILY SECTION: Use photos of your own family as references for an article dealing with ethnic origins or roots. Render the illustration in black and white within a rectangular shape. Use a multi-image, nostalgic approach (Fig. 9–126).

LIFESTYLE SECTION: Depict the psychological pressures of living in a contemporary urban environment. Use either line only or line and halftone combined, and make the illustration a vignette shape. Choose one person, male or female, to act as the focal point for this illustration, and make your treatment of the person express the mood of the article (Fig. 9–127).

SPORTS SECTION: Illustrate any sports or martial arts article. Vignette one figure, using a line technique (Fig. 9–128).

POLITICAL SECTION: Depict a controversial topic of the day. Emphasize the potential dangers of the situation. Use line only in a rectangular shape (Fig. 9–129).

BUSINESS SECTION: Choose a topic such as the stock market, international trade, labor relations, or health hazards in industry. You may choose either a negative or positive approach. Use line art in a rectangular shape (Fig. 9–130).

9–127. Lifestyle section illustration for Exercise 37. Vignette line illustration using a broad-tip marker pen on a textured surface.

BOOK REVIEW OR ENTERTAINMENT SECTION: Find an article that has a historical slant. Then choose any two letters of the alphabet, and combine these with depictions of historical characters. The people should tie in with the letters as shown in Figures 9–131 and 9–132. Use line art techniques in a rectangular shape. This type of illustration is very suitable for both magazine and book work.

FOOD SECTION: Illustrate a specific food recipe or dining-out article. Use a vignette shape occupying the full length of the newspaper page by 3 columns wide. Use line and halftone combined or continuous-tone techniques. (See Figure 9–133.)

9–126. Family section illustration for Exercise 37 by Martha Staigys. Graphite pencils. This rendering emphasizes placement and contrast. It was converted to line art using a stat camera.

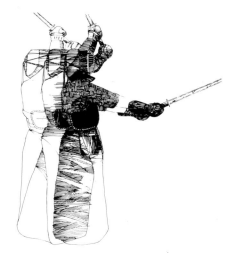

9–128. Sports section illustration for Exercise 37 by Les Marubashi. India ink and pen. Progressive repetition and multidirectional line.

9–129. Political section illustration for Exercise 37 by Henry Van Der Linde. India ink and pen. Multidirectional lines create texture and tone.

9–130. Business section illustration for Exercise 37 by Henry Van Der Linde. India ink, pen, and scraper on scratchboard. Multidirectional black linework and stipple contrast with white linework scraped with scratchboard tool.

9–132. Book review illustration for Exercise 37 by Henry van der Linde. India ink and pen. Dramatic use of light and shade is achieved through multidirectional line techniques.

9–131. Book review section illustration for Exercise 37 by Henry Van Der Linde. India ink and pen.

9–133. Food section illustration for Exercise 37. Dr. Martin's dyes and India ink. Line and wash techniques.

Designing a double-page spread

This exercise deals with a double-page spread for a magazine feature article. The subject is weight loss through dance exercise. The heading is "Dance Your Inches Away." The art director wants you to illustrate this article in a stylized but light-hearted manner.

DIRECTIONS: After first making some sketches, do a layout linear, rendering your ideas in black felt-tip pen. Pay careful attention to the production requirements; for example, keep type within the safety area, and place important details of the illustration away from the gutter (Fig. 9–134).

For the finished art, choose whatever medium you wish, since the artwork will be printed in full color. You may also use an overall background color that extends to the trim edges. Your artwork must allow for this by extending the background color 1/8 inch (3 mm) beyond the trim size on all four sides.

9–134. Double-page layout for Exercise 38 by Colin Gillies. Black marker felt-tip pen.

The Business of Illustration

by now you have realized that good illustration is not only creative, it is also functional. This is not art for its own sake, but art intended to communicate something—the qualities of a product, a story, or an image. Moreover, illustration can provide a livelihood, so long as you understand the business side of it. You must, for example, know how to promote yourself, present your portfolio, price your artwork, and manage the necessary paperwork.

There are several different ways of working as an illustrator. You may work as a self-employed artist, an agency artist, an art-studio illustrator, a staff artist at either a printing or engraving house, or a member of a design team. Among the possible areas of specialization are advertising, book publishing, magazine publishing, newspaper publishing, television storyboarding, production of audiovisual instructional materials, fashion illustration, technical manuals and catalogs, architectural and interior rendering, mechanical illustration, scientific or medical illustration, and computer graphics.

Whatever area you go into, however, remember that illustration—especially freelance illustration—is not guaranteed steady work. There's a built-in element of insecurity. The illustrator is constantly looking for new clients and constantly trying to improve his or her art. It is not easy, and no professional will tell you that it is. But when everything goes right, it is one of the most creative and exciting jobs in the world.

Types of Employment

Look at Figure 10–1, which indicates possible sources of work for the freelancer and (in most cases) for the full-time or part-time employee. Notice that in many instances the art director does the employing.

As the title implies, an art director directs the visual content of a book, magazine, or advertisement. He or she decides which type of art is best for a particular job and then chooses the most appropriate illustrator or photographer to do the job.

Airbrushed art by David Milne.

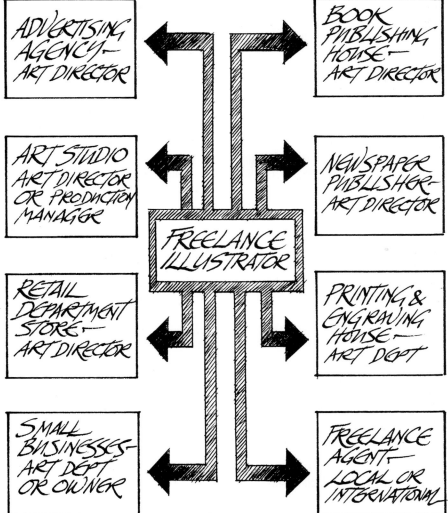

10–1. Sources of work for the freelance illustrator.

Full-time work

It is possible to work full time, on salary, as an illustrator for an ad agency, art studio, or art department in a large company. When you apply for a job, you may be asked how much money you would like to earn. Do some research first to determine how much you would like to earn weekly and yearly.

Beginners do not earn as much as experienced personnel. Be prepared to start at a lower rate and learn on the job. On the other hand, find out when you can expect a salary review, and make sure that this is clearly spelled out.

Part-time employment

If you would like the security of some steady income along with the freedom of freelancing, you might be able to work on a retainer. In this case the employer pays you to work a certain number of hours per week, usually fifteen or twenty. Generally, the choice of which days and which hours to work is left to you. If you have more work to do in a given week, you are paid for the additional hours on top of the agreed weekly minimum.

The advantages of this system for the company are that they do not have to provide the benefits associated with a full-time salary and, when there is no work, they don't have to pay you more than the agreed minimum to sit and do nothing. In your favor, this system allows time for you to go around with your portfolio and look for freelance work. Be careful, however, not to do work that conflicts with your retainer work, since this would be unethical. If, for example, you do fashion illustration on retainer for a retail department store, you might look for freelance work in editorial magazine illustration. Another advantage of retainer work is that you have a chance to work in the studio with other artists, from whom you can learn a great deal. Besides illustrators, the studio may employ graphic designers, calligraphers, mechanical artists, and photostat operators.

Freelancing

Self-employment or freelancing means that you have no guaranteed income. You must constantly take your portfolio out, make contacts, and try to pick up work from clients and art directors. Doing this takes some skill in presentation and selling. Once you get a job, you must be completely professional with your clients: meet all the deadlines, work within the restrictions of the job, and never let the client down. Even if you get a job you do not like, you must do your best because every assignment is a potential source of more work. Your reputation will quickly deteriorate if you don't maintain a high professional standard.

Obviously, once you gain a steady clientele, your earnings will improve; you may even earn more than you would on staff. The volume of work always fluctuates, however. When you first start, you may want the security of a salaried job, at least until you feel ready to work on your own. You can prepare for this by doing freelance work on your own time and thereby gain some steady clients.

Look again at the possible sources of work in Figure 10–1. In most cases, the illustrator deals only with the art director. And in this regard there are basically three types of agencies, studios, or art departments you will encounter. The first type is the very large, reputable firm, which has a big budget. Such a firm can therefore afford to use the very best illustrators, designers, and photographers. Large clients pay well, and you should expect them to pay you well, too.

Medium-size firms generally have medium-size accounts along with a few large ones. When they can afford to, they will use top illustrators. Generally, though, they use medium-priced illustrators and pay a medium price.

Small companies may give interesting assignments, but they usually can not afford the best illustrators. Often they use beginners, or anyone else willing to take low pay. If you get steady work from a small company, however, you can make a fair amount of money over a period of time.

Beyond the studios and agencies, some small companies handle their own advertising or promotion and do not place accounts with advertising agencies or art studios, usually owing to their small budgets. In this case you may deal directly with the company's owner or managing executive. Unfortunately, these clients may be difficult to deal with because they often do not know anything about art. It is then up to you to persuade them to choose a creative solution to their advertising problem. In addition, small businesses often haggle over money. Be prepared for this.

Some clients give illustrators good work but do not want to pay much. If you go along with this the first time, you may find that, if you ever do comparable work for this client again, you will not get a fair price: they know how little they paid you before.

Another danger to watch out for is work on speculation. Small companies sometimes ask beginners to do work for which they will be paid only if the idea and artwork are accepted by a client. This way, the company has nothing to lose. But the illustrator does—time, money, and reputation. A large company can afford to absorb the costs of doing a free job for presentation to a client; but as a self-employed individual, you cannot.

After you have freelanced for a period of time, you may want to expand your business. This usually means that you will not have time to do your own selling. At this point you might think about hiring an agent to represent you. The agent makes the contacts and shows your portfolio, picks up any work, and brings it to you. In return, he or she receives a commission, a percentage of the fee.

Preparing a Portfolio

Your portfolio should be neat and clean, both inside and outside. Its condition represents your attitude about your artwork. An art director who sees you carrying a dirty portfolio will be reluctant to give you work, fearing that the job may come back dirty. To clean your portfolio well, you should vacuum it. This prevents the buildup of static electricity, which can cause dust to stick to your artwork and to the plastic sleeves in some portfolios.

When you have cleaned your case, place your samples in it in a book format—that is, with all the pieces turned the same way around and the bottoms to one side of the case. Use about twenty good pieces that show the range of your work (Fig. 10–2). Be objective about your own work, and try to evaluate it as if you were the interviewer. Be tough with yourself.

10–2. Artwork by Raffi Anderian. Select samples for a portfolio that demonstrate your best work.

When showing your portfolio, do not criticize your own work. If you are unsure about any piece, do not include it. One bad piece can negate all the good work you have, by giving the interviewer the impression that you do not know the difference between good illustration and bad illustration.

Once you get past the beginner stage, your portfolio should change to include less student work and more professional work. You can also include some creative and stimulating samples as discussion pieces.

At this point you may be interested in expanding the range of work you get. If your portfolio consists entirely of safe mainstream work, that is the type of work you will continue to get. If you want to go beyond this, you must try some experimental work and show it to potential clients.

The Interview

Before you can begin to make appointments to show your portfolio, you must become aware of all the places where you might be able to get work. The *Yellow Pages* lists companies under various categories, including Advertising Agencies, Artists (for art studios), and Publishers (for editorial magazine and book illustration). Look up newspapers by name. If you are interested in technical illustration, contact the appropriate manufacturing, engineering, scientific, or industrial companies and government agencies. You can also learn about potential work sources by speaking to associates who work in the business.

Whether you are interested in freelance work or a salaried job, you must contact the art director or the head of the art department of the company you are interested in. Call the receptionist and ask for the name of the person you should talk to. Then speak to that person and arrange a time for an interview.

Most people are nervous when being interviewed for a job. You can prepare for the interview by learning as much as you can about the company, the type of work it handles, and even about the interviewer. Most interviewers are favorably impressed by a person who has done some homework.

Try to relax as much as possible. Smile and be pleasant. Don't be aggressive and try to sell yourself too hard. Let your work speak for you. Answer any questions in a positive and informative way. When the interview is over, thank the art director for his or her time and for the opportunity to show your work.

Pricing a Job

Imagine that a client has called and wants you to pick up a job that involves layout and finished art. At the office you discuss the job, and the client asks for a quote of how much it will cost to do this job. There are a number of ways to handle this:

1. If you are asked to give a price on the spot, try to quickly calculate the costs in your mind. Think of the materials that will be involved, how long the assignment will take, and how much you wish to be paid.

2. The art director may have a set price and tell you what it is. Again, calculate all the costs, including the time required to complete the job. If the set price seems too low, see if you can negotiate with the art director to find a price that is mutually agreeable.

3. You may be asked for a formal quote—that is, an accurate breakdown of the costs of each aspect of the job. Sometimes this can be telephoned in, but sometimes it is requested in writing so that the art director can compare your price to that of other illustrators.

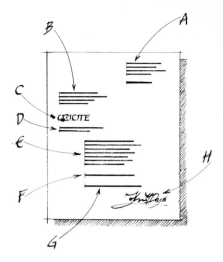

10–3. Sample quote format.

Figure 10–3 presents a suggested format for submitting a quote. At the top right, put your name and address and the date (A), with the client's name and address at lower left (B). Use the heading QUOTE (C), and then include the name of the art director or other person you are dealing with and the title of the job (D). Next give a brief description of the job and your price (E). It's a good idea to include the line CLIENT CHANGES EXTRA to let the client know that you will charge extra for work not included in the original discussion (F). Then add a closing line (G) and your signature (H).

In figuring out your price, you should be aware of what the going rate is. Especially when you are just starting out, ask others in the business for advice. Don't forget to count your art supplies and overhead; such as rent and telephone. These expenses should not be broken down and itemized, but computed as part of your overall wages. You should, however, indicate any special charges you will incur, such as typesetting and photostats. Many illustrators add a 15 percent surcharge to these expenses for time spent contracting these services. The important point is to tell the client about these charges in advance.

Contracts

The art director is purchasing services and artwork from you, the supplier. When you are given a job, ask for a purchase order. This serves as a contract.

Some small business clients do not have purchase orders for illustrators, so you must make up your own. You can buy a pad of standard purchase-order forms from an office-supply store or type your own form. Complete the form in triplicate and have the client sign it. Now you have a binding agreement, which you can use if you encounter problems in getting paid. Fortunately, this rarely happens.

For editorial illustration there is usually no purchase order. The agreement may be verbal.

Deadlines

Professional illustrators not only have to be able to do the work, they must have it completed by the promised date. Their reputations depend to a great extent on their reliability. For example, if an advertisement is going to appear in a magazine on a certain date, there are set deadlines for production, printing, and distribution. Every person working on this ad—including the illustrator—has a deadline.

When you are offered a job, make sure that you have all the information you need to complete the illustration on time. Ask the art director the following questions:

1. When is the job due?

2. Does the job require a layout, finished art, or both?

3. What is the size of the artwork?

4. How many colors will it be printed in?

5. How do you want this artwork prepared—as line, line and tone, halftone, or full-color?

6. Is there a rough sketch to follow, or can the concept be modified?

With this information, you can judge whether it is possible to complete the artwork within the allotted time. Be realistic; if the time seems too short, voice your reservations at the start. Later, if you run into problems with the deadline, get in touch with the client and see if an extension is possible.

Bookkeeping

The very word *bookkeeping* may seem intimidating, but keeping good records is important for a freelancer. When you set up your business, find an accountant who has other clients in the visual arts. You may even find an accountant who deals mainly with illustrators and other commercial artists. This is important because not all accountants are fully informed about the types of deductions illustrators are allowed. A specialist will know the appropriate deductions for rent, telephone, transportation, art supplies, photo supplies, and other items. Be sure to keep accurate records of all these expenses, as well as of the income you receive. Consult your accountant to determine what taxes you are required to charge your clients, if any.

Purchase orders

As was noted earlier, the purchase order serves as a contract, setting out the agreed-upon price. Figure 10–4 shows a sample purchase order. Different firms may use different formats, but the information is essentially the same.

At the top right is the date (A), and beneath it is the client's purchase order number (B). On the left is the client's name and address (C), and somewhere below this the name and address of you, the supplier (D). Other information that usually appears—although its positioning varies—includes the deadline or due date (E), the specific client who ordered the artwork (F), a docket number (G) for the client's bookkeeping records, and a job title (H). The main body of the form is devoted to the job description (I)—sometimes called the *confirmation*—which describes what you have been asked to do. A line usually appears at the bottom (J), with the notice, "Submit invoice in triplicate and cite client's name, P.O. number, and docket number." Finally, space is reserved for the purchaser's authorizing signature (K).

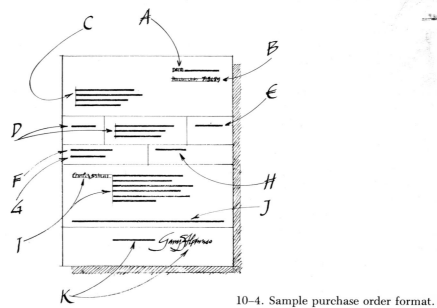

10–4. Sample purchase order format.

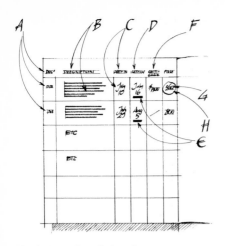

10–5. Sample job log format.

Job log

Enter each job into a log book, which should resemble the one in Figure 10–5. First list the job or docket number (A). Then describe the job, and enter the purchase order number (B). Next list the date in—that is, when you picked up or received the work (C)—followed by the deadline or date out (D). Below this, leave a space for recording the date on which you bill the client (E). The next column (F) is for any outside costs such as special art supplies, photostats, or typesetting. And the last column (G) is for the agreed amount, which you should circle or check off when you have been paid in full (H).

Invoicing

Invoicing refers to the process of billing the client after the job has been completed. The work may have been a layout, a layout and finished art, or finished art only. Usually, if you have done both the layout and the finished art, these are itemized separately and then totaled.

Any outside costs, such as typesetting and photostats, are added to the cost of the job. If the client asked for additional work or made changes, charge for these, too.

Figure 10–6 provides a guideline for your invoice. At the top right is your name, address, and telephone number, social security number, and the invoicing date (A). On the left is the client's company name and address (B), followed by the name of the art director you worked with (C). Next enter the client's purchase order number and the docket number (D).

The main part of the purchase order is a brief but itemized description of the services you provided (E). Close with the words "as discussed with [art director's name]" or "as agreed upon" (F). Some illustrators also include payment terms (G), offering the client a discount if payment is made within 30 days. Finally, sign the invoice (H). Always submit an invoice in duplicate or triplicate, as specified on the purchase order.

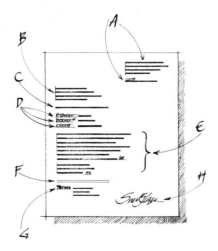

10–6. Sample invoice format.

For editorial illustration for magazines, newspapers and books, there may be no purchase order. In this case your invoice, or bill, should simply include your name and address, the date, the name of the art director, the publishing house and address, a description of the work, followed by the price, and your signature.

In general, the editorial illustrations you do will be returned to you after use, while advertising illustrations become the property of the client.

Self-Promotion

For freelancers, self-promotion is very important. The publicity you generate for yourself can influence the type of work you get. Self-promotional material is usually tax-deductible as a business expense.

Beyond showing your portfolio, you can advertise yourself by using well-designed business stationery, by mailing pieces such as flyers and posters that show examples of your work, and by circulating a visually exciting résumé. Another way of expanding your contacts is by joining a professional association for illustrators and designers.

Your stationery—letterhead, envelope, and business card—represents you and should create a good impression. Some illustrators design their own stationery, while others hire graphic designers. Figure 10–7 shows a letterhead (also used as an invoice) that has worked well for many years. It is a tongue-in-cheek rendition of the line "Please, Sir, may I have a little more?" from Charles Dickens's *Oliver Twist*.

If you change address frequently, leave your address and phone number off your stationery and type them in as needed. Too often, artists spend money printing new stationery, only to move—leaving them with a stack of unusable material.

Self-promotional mailers are used by many illustrators. These can be a single sheet of 8½ × 11 (22 × 28 cm) or 8½ × 14 (22 × 36 cm) inches, with a single or accordion fold. A mailer can be a striking reminder of your work (Fig. 10–8), or

10–7. Letterhead for a freelance illustrator.

*New residence

10–8. Self-promotional mailer focusing on the illustrator by Steven Quinlan.

it can show the variety of work you are capable of doing (Fig. 10–9). You can update it two to four times a year, bringing your latest work to your clients' attention. When you send out these pieces, be sure to keep a list of the people you mailed them to. You can then follow up with telephone calls.

Although résumés are not used very often by illustrators, they are a good vehicle for making contact with long-distance clients. Technical illustrators need résumés more than advertising or editorial illustrators do since they are more likely to be employed by companies than to do freelancing. Again, since your résumé represents you and your work, you must make it visually interesting. You might include your photograph and examples of your work on one side of a sheet and a list of your work experience on the other. It is a good idea to have this information typeset, to give it a professional look. The recommended order in which the information should appear is: your name, address, and telephone number, followed by your work experience in chronological order (with the latest information first), exhibitions and/or awards, and education.

Another form of self-promotion involves buying space in a graphic arts publication that art directors and clients subscribe to, such as *American Illustration Showcase* or *The Black Book*. This may be costly, but a full-color page can do wonders and often is worth the investment.

Exhibitions and award shows are another important part of self-promotion, and you should try to enter your work in these. Such shows are usually juried, and having your work accepted can be a boost to your career.

10–9. Self-promotional mailer focusing on the illustrator's range of work by Henry Van Der Linde.

Bibliography

Barratt, Krome. 1989. *Logic and Design in Art, Science, and Mathematics.* New York: Design Press and London: Herbert Press.

Berstein, Saul, and McGarry, Leo. 1986. *Making Art on Your Computer.* New York: Watson-Guptill.

Birren, Faber. 1969. *The Principles of Color.* New York: Van Nostrand Reinhold and London: Schiffer Publications.

Bloomer, Carolyn M. 1990. *Principles of Visual Perception.* 2nd ed. New York: Design Press and London: Herbert Press.

Chwast, Seymour. 1985. *The Left-handed Designer.* New York: Harry N. Abrams and London: Booth-Clibborn Editions.

Cook, Theodore Andrea. 1979. *The Curves of Life.* New York: Dover.

Craig, James. 1980. *Designing with Type: A Basic Course in Typography.* Rev. ed. New York: Watson-Guptill.

————. 1983. *Graphic Design Career Guide.* Watson-Guptill.

————. 1990. *Production for the Graphic Designer.* 2nd ed. New York: Watson-Guptill.

Crawford, Tad. 1989. *Legal Guide for the Visual Artist.* New York: Allworth Press.

Deken, Joseph. 1983. *Computer Images.* New York: Stewart, Tabori & Chang.

de Sausmarez, Maurice. 1990. *Basic Design.* Rev. ed. New York: Design Press and London: Herbert Press.

Doczi, György. 1981. *The Power of Limits: Proportional Harmonies in Nature, Art, and Architecture.* Boulder, CO: Shambala.

Donahue, Bud. 1978. *The Language of Layout.* Englewood Cliffs, NJ: Prentice-Hall.

Eckstein, Arthur, and Stone, Bernard. 1983. *Preparing Art for Printing.* Rev. ed. New York: Van Nostrand Reinhold.

Edwards, Betty. 1989. *Drawing on the Right Side of the Brain.* Rev. ed. Los Angeles: J. P. Tarcher and London: Fontana.

Fogle, James, and Forsell, Mary E. 1989. *Comps, Storyboards, and Animatics.* New York: Watson-Guptill.

Gerken, J. Ellen. 1990. *Click: The Brightest in Computer-Generated Design and Illustration.*

Cincinnati, OH: North Light Books.

Gikow, Jacqueline. 1991. *Graphic Illustration in Black and White.* New York: Design Press.

Glaser, Milton. 1973. *Milton Glaser Graphic Design.* New York: Overlook Press and London: Penguin.

Goldstein, Nathan. 1973. *The Art of Responsive Drawing.* Englewood Cliffs, NJ: Prentice-Hall.

Gorringe, Roger, and Gould, Edward. 1989. *The Complete Airbrush Course.* New York: Van Nostrand Reinhold and London: Trefoil Publications.

Gray, Bill. 1976. *Studio Tips for Artists and Graphic Designers.* Englewood Cliffs, NJ: Prentice-Hall and London: Lund Humphries.

Heller, Steven, ed. 1986. *Innovators of American Illustration.* New York: Van Nostrand Reinhold.

Herring, Jerry, and Fulton, Mark. 1987. *The Art and Business of Creative Self-Promotion.* New York: Watson-Guptill and Bromley: Columbus Books.

Huntley, H. E. 1970. *The Divine Proportion.* New York: Dover.

Hurlburt, Allen. 1977. *Layout.* New York: Watson-Guptill.

Itten, Johannes. 1970. *The Elements of Color.* New York: Van Nostrand Reinhold.

Johnson, Cathy. 1989. *Drawing and Painting from Nature.* New York: Design Press.

Kaupelis, Robert. 1980. *Experimental Drawing Techniques.* New York: Watson-Guptill.

Kemnitzer, Ronald. 1987. *Rendering with Markers.* New York: Watson-Guptill.

Kerlow, Issac Victor, and Rosebush, Judson. 1986. *Computer Graphics for Designers and Artists.* New York: Van Nostrand Reinhold.

Kleper, Michael L. 1987. *The Illustrated Handbook of Desktop Publishing and Typesetting.* Blue Ridge Summit, PA: TAB Professional and Reference Books.

Lambert, Patricia. 1991. *Controlling Color: A Practical Introduction for Designers and Artists.* New York: Design Press.

Lauer, David. 1979. *Design Basics.* 3rd ed. New York: Holt, Rinehart, & Winston.

Lewell, John. 1985. *A-Z Guide to Computer Graphics.* New York: McGraw-Hill.

Lewis, John. 1984. *The Twentieth-Century Book.* 2nd ed. New York: Van Nostrand Reinhold and London: Herbert Press.

Lozner, Ruth. 1990. *Scratchboard for Illustration.* New York: Watson-Guptill.

Martin, Judy. 1989. *Technical Illustration.* Cincinnati, OH: North Light Books and London: Macdonald Orbis.

Mayer, Ralph. 1981. *The Artist's Handbook.* 4th ed. New York: Viking.

Meyer, Franz Sales. 1974. *Meyer's Ornament: A Handbook of Ornament.* Rev. ed. London: Duckworth.

Miller, David, and Effler, James M. 1987. *Dynamic Airbrush.* Cincinnati, OH: North Light Books.

Miller, Lauri, ed. 1990. *1991 Artist's Market.* Cincinnati, OH: Writer's Digest.

Morgan, Jacqui. 1986. *Watercolor for Illustration.* New York: Watson-Guptill.

Olsen, Gary. 1989. *Getting Started in Computer Graphics.* Cincinnati, OH: North Light Books.

Owen, Peter, and Rollason, Jane. 1988. *The Complete Manual of Airbrushing.* New York: Alfred A. Knopf and London: Dorling Kindersley.

Parramón, José, and Ferrón, Miquel. 1990. *The Big Book of Airbrush: Basic Techniques and Materials.* New York: Watson-Guptill.

1983. *Pocket Pal.* 13th Edition. New York: International Paper Company.

Rossol, Morona. 1990. *The Artist's Complete Health and Safety Guide.* New York: Allworth Press.

Shulevitz, Uri. 1985. *Writing with Pictures: How to Write and Illustrate Children's Books.* New York: Watson-Guptill.

Shushan, Ronnie, and Wright, Don. 1989. *Desktop Publishing by Design.* Redmond, WA: Microsoft Press.

Snyder, John. 1986. *The New Commercial Artist's Handbook.* New York: Watson-Guptill.

Waite Group, Inc., The. 1987. *Desktop Publishing Bible.* Ed. by James Stockford. Indianapolis, IN: W. Sams and Company.

Ward, Dick. 1988. *Creative Ad Design and Illustration.* Cincinnati, OH: North Light Books.

———. 1988. *Illustration for Advertising.* London: Macdonald Orbis.

White, Alex. 1987. *How to Spec Type.* New York: Watson-Guptill.

White, Tony. 1986. *The Animator's Workbook.* New York: Watson-Guptill and Oxford: Phaidon Press.

Wilde, Richard. 1986. *Problems/Solutions: Visual Thinking for the Graphic Communicator.* New York: Van Nostrand Reinhold.

Zeier, Franz. 1990. *Books, Boxes, and Portfolios.* New York: Design Press.

Note: In case of difficulty in obtaining books not published in the UK, inquiries can be made via:

Internos Books
18 Colville Road
London W3 8BL
tel: 081 992 0008

Cast shadows, *see* Shadows

Chair, freehand drawing from memory, 35

Chambered nautilus, freehand drawing, 54, 55

Change, depiction of, black and white illustration, 232

Character, expression of, line drawing, 191

Chisel-point paint brushes, making of, 136, 137

Chroma, defined, 122

Chrome metal, rendering: airbrush technique, 221, 222; painting, 158, 159

Church, book illustration, 248

Circle: composition, 23, 25; in square, freehand drawing, 44, 45; two-dimensional, change to three-dimensional, 24

Clarity, methods of achieving, 16, 17

Clean layout, defined, 176

Clippings, reference file, 274

Closed composition: defined, 15, 16; exercises, 229, 231

Clouds, freehand drawing, 65

Cober, Alan E., 13

Collage: painting and other material, 152; varnish, use on, 144

Color: achromatic, artwork, 125, 137, 153; adjacent colors, 125; analogous colors, 126, 129; backgrounds, effect on, 126; basic guidelines, 129; characteristics of, 122; chroma, defined, 122; complementary colors, 125, 153; cool colors, 126, 153–154; depth, creation with, 126, 127; dominant tint, defined, 125, 128, 131; errors to avoid, 129; exercises in theory, 128, 153–154; hue, defined, 122; intensity of, 122; intermediate colors,

124; marker rendering, addition to, 109–110; monochromatic, artwork, 125, 137, 153; primary colors, 124; secondary colors, 124; shades, 124, 127; shadows, effect on, 127; space, creation with, 126, 127; split complementaries, 125; sunlight, effect on, 126, 130; temperature of, 126, 153–154; time of day, effect on, 126, 127, 130; tint, *see* Tint; tone, 124, 217; triadic colors, 125, 153; value of, 122, 124, 126, 164; warm colors, 126, 153–154

Color harmony, 122

Color notebook, described, 129

Color reproduction processes, 184, 185–187, 245, 247

Color supplement, newspaper advertising, 209

Color wheel, described, 124, 125

Comp, layout, 173–174

Company image, expression, formats, 234, 235

Complementary colors: defined, 125; exercises, 153

Composition: creation of, 18–23; described, 13–14; elements of, 14–18; errors to avoid, 30; guidelines, 31; painting, 154; sketchbook and studies, 28, 29; skills, improvement, method, 31; unity, achievement, methods, 18, 19, 23

Computer graphics, illustration and, 102, 206, 224, 225

Concrete, rendering in paint, 158, 159

Cone of vision, freehand drawing, 42, 43, 46, 47

Conic forms: freehand drawing, 49, 50; sketchbook studies, 28

Continuous-tone reproduction (*see also* Reproduction of artwork);

described, 182; illustrations for, techniques, 197, 198–199

Contour, element of drawing, 34

Contour drawing: defined, 15, 16; figures, reportage, 99

Convergence (*see also* Perspective); defined, 17, 18, 23; freehand drawing, 34, 36, 37, 38; planes, inclined and declined, 80–82

Cropping, composition, 15, 16, 28, 31

Crosshatching, line drawing, 191, 192, 193

Cubic shapes: freehand drawing, 34, 35, 36, 38, 42, 43; inner structure, freehand drawing, 72, 73; mechanical drawing, 44, 45; positive and negative forms, freehand drawing, 72, 73; rotation in space, drawing from memory, 67, 68; sketchbook studies, 28

Cup and saucer, perspective, freehand drawing, 51, 68

Curvilinear lines and shapes: defined, 15, 16; sketchbook studies, 28, 29

Cutaway view, technical illustration, 217, 219

Cylindrical shapes: freehand drawing, 49, 50; marker rendering, 108; perspective, foreshortening, 51, 52

D

da Vinci, Leonardo, 32, 84, 89, 90

Dealer kit, advertising, 209, 210

Decagon, freehand drawing, 60

Decorative illustration, books, 213, 254, 255, 256

Depth, creation of, 23, 126, 127

Design (*see also* Composition); skills, strengthening of, 206

Designers' colors, *see* Gouache; Tempera

Desktop publishing, illustration and, 224–225

Diminution: cylinder, perspective, drawing, 51; defined, 16, 17, 23

Direct advertising, 207

Direct-mail advertising, 209

Display type, 170

Distortion: freehand drawing, 36, 37; human figure, purposeful distortion, 97, 98

Dr. Martin's watercolor dyes, 152, 155

Drawing, *see* Freehand drawing; Line drawing; Mechanical drawing

Drawing table, specifications for, 105, 270–271

Dropout halftone, reproduction, 184

Drybrush technique, painting, 140, 141

Dummying type, layout, 170–171, 173, 175

Duotone, reproduction, 184

Dyes: errors with, correction method, 159; types of, 152, 155

E

Easel cards, advertising, 209

Editorial illustration: deadlines, 212; described, 204; exercises, 212, 248–259; knowledge and skills required, 204, 206; magazines, 210–212, 259; newspapers, 212, 257–259; terminology, 211, 212

Ellipse, horizontal: freehand drawing, 44, 45; marker rendering, 108

Ellipse, isometric, 217

Ellipse, vertical, freehand drawing, 52, 53

Emphasis, composition, 14, 18, 26

Engraving, wood, simulation, 200

Etching, simulation, 200, 201